D1636292

KEANU REEVES: MOST TRIUMPHANT

Keanu Reeves: Most Triumphant

The Movies & Meaning of an Irrepressible Icon

Alex Pappademas

Illustrations by Eoin Coveney

ABRAMS IMAGE, NEW YORK

Published in 2022 by Abrams Image, an imprint of ABRAMS.

Library of Congress Control Number: 2021946831
ISBN: 978-1-4197-5226-1
eISBN: 978-1-64700-199-5

Printed and bound in the United States
10 9 8 7 6 5 4 3 2 1

Abrams Image books are available at special discounts when purchased in quantity for premiums and promotions as well as fundraising or educational use. Special editions can also be created to specification. For details, contact specialsales@abramsbooks.com or the address below.

Abrams Image® is a registered trademark of Harry N. Abrams, Inc.

"There is four helicopter running after person
and destroy his car. The truth, too, is fourfold:
1) *life sucks;* 2) *for good reason;*
3) *you can sit under a tree;*
4) *the movie never ends, it goes on and on"*

MICHAEL ROBBINS, "DOWNWARD-FACING DOG"

"I need this poor boy! This poor boy is the only one
who knows the frequencies!"

MORGAN FREEMAN AS DR. PAUL SHANNON IN
***CHAIN REACTION*, 1996**

CONTENTS

PROLOGUE
RADIO FREE ALBUMEN

1. Fake Keanu

The fake Keanu wore a surgical mask and a squint. The fake Keanu was pretty obviously not the real Keanu, but until this was confirmed it was exciting to live in a reality where the alternative could be true.

It was the last weekend of May 2020, five days after the police killing of George Floyd in Minneapolis, and millions of people across the country and around the world had taken to the streets, despite a global pandemic, to stand in solidarity with the Black Lives Matter movement and the victims of police violence.

Some of them were famous. John Boyega and a maskless Madonna appeared at protests in London. Ariana Grande and Fiona Apple marched in Los Angeles. In Santa Monica, Timothée Chalamet carried a sign with Kalief Browder's name scrawled on it, and Halsey was struck by a rubber bullet.

And for a short while, between 2:54 P.M. and 4:47 P.M. Eastern time on May 30, many people on social media became convinced that the participants in a car-caravan protest in Baltimore had included Keanu Charles Reeves, a fifty-five-year-old bass player, art book publisher, motorcycle-accident survivor and non-college-graduate from Los Angeles who makes his living as an actor.

The tweet that started it all read "My boy protesting in Baltimore today," with a picture of a masked man with spiky dark hair, standing up through his sunroof, holding a NO JUSTICE, NO PEACE sign.

It wasn't Keanu. It was *so* not Keanu. In May 2020, Keanu had long hair and a full beard, and he still had both in photos taken later that summer. This was some guy with a vaguely Keanuesque widow's peak and a haircut Keanu hadn't had since *Constantine*. The image quickly accumulated tens of thousands of likes and retweets anyway, with enthusiastic captions like "KEANU REEVES IS PROTESTING IN BALTIMORE!!!!!! LETS GOOOOOOOOO" and "now y'all got John Wick fed up."

In his long public life, Keanu has taken few political positions, not even in a Rock the Vote kind of way. But that spring's protests felt like a moment of extraordinary possibility, a statement of collective belief that the world could be changed, the unprecedented made real. Nothing was unimaginable, not even Keanu choosing that moment to stand up for a cause by joining a car caravan in Baltimore, a city where he does not live.

Finally, the person who'd posted the original tweet added a clarification.

"Y'all, this is MY BOY, like my SON. He lives in Baltimore. It's not Keanu. Sorry to disappoint you!"

This story tells us something about the world's relationship to Keanu. A bubble of Keanoid mystery still surrounds him even after thirty-five years of public hyperscrutiny. That mystery makes him into a projection screen for our ideas. What we see is not Keanu but Keanu as constructed by our imaginations.

We think of Keanu as being better than us, more Zen, more ethical, more brave. We assume Keanu shares our political affinities. (Further down in the replies, the original poster of the car-protest Keanu image mused, "I think Keanu owes me something for unintentionally making everyone think he's Antifa lol.") We picture him out there doing the right thing, no matter what he might actually be doing. We conceive of a whole existence for Keanu that may have little to do with who he really is.

"I cannot imagine his inner life at all," my friend Molly once said of him, "which is why he is God's perfect actor."

2. Real Keanu

This is not a book about the real Keanu Reeves, but I have met the real Keanu Reeves. I interviewed him for two hours and then met him again the next day and interviewed him for another two hours, and later I wrote a cover story for *GQ* magazine about what that experience was like.

It rained in my bedroom the day I met him for the first time. That part wasn't in the story.

I live with my family in a rented house that is slowly sliding down a hill on the east side of Los Angeles. The upstairs part of the house is at street level; the master bedroom is downstairs, on the garden level. The night before my first meeting with Keanu Reeves, it rained, and wet leaves blocked a drain outside the laundry-room door. By morning the water outside had risen above the door's bottom edge and a flood began to seep into the laundry room. The laundry room is directly above the master bedroom.

We woke up to rainwater dripping from the seams in the ceiling, the heating vents, the light. The paint on the ceiling buckled and bubbled. There were at least four discrete leaks pinging into buckets and bowls in our room when I left the house to go meet Keanu Reeves.

The fluid dynamics of this event seem pretty straightforward to me as I type this, but later that day I found myself sitting on a damp couch outside the Chateau Marmont hotel in West Hollywood, trying and failing to explain the flood to Keanu Reeves, whom I'd known at that point for five minutes.

I showed up to the Chateau nervously early and interrupted Keanu trying to smoke a quick private cigarette in the otherwise unpopulated waiting area by the valet station at the top of the driveway. So we sat for a minute. He brought up the weather and I told him about the rain in my house.

The story seemed to make him confused and a little frustrated. He seemed puzzled by how the street-level floor and the garden-level floor could both in their own way be the "first floor" but also the "second floor," and he also seemed a little unsure as to why I'd started telling him this story in the first place, which was a feeling we shared.

This was in February 2019. Keanu was promoting *John Wick: Chapter 3—Parabellum*, the one where John Wick kills nearly everyone in a Moroccan souk with the help of Halle Berry and a couple of extremely well-trained Belgian Malinois dogs. Doing the first interview at the Chateau Marmont was his idea. Normally when a famous person or their team suggests the Chateau as a location for the famous person's celebrity-profile interview, it's important to ask if they're open to doing it literally anywhere else. The Chateau is the most cliché celebrity-profile setting on the planet. Interviewing a famous person there is like interviewing a regular person at the Starbucks inside a Barnes & Noble because all it reveals about them is that they don't want to let a stranger see inside their house.

But when Keanu's people proposed the Chateau, I said, "Sure."

I said "Sure" because I knew the Chateau had actual, biographical significance for Keanu. In the early nineties, when he was spending so much time on location that homeownership didn't make sense, he'd basically lived there. He'd go off to shoot and the hotel would put his books and his bass guitar in storage until he got back.

When interviewers asked him about living in a hotel—and few could resist bringing it up—he'd talk about being away all the time, and needing an easy place to come back to, and he'd joke about being unable to give up amenities like room service and the cool stationery the Chateau gave him, which said IN RESIDENCE—KEANU REEVES across the top.

Also, though, the Chateau is basically a castle, built in the 1920s in loose imitation of the Château d'Amboise in France's Loire Valley, set high above Sunset Boulevard at the end of a long, narrow driveway. Although Keanu came up in what now seems like a more genteel and less invasive era, paparazzi-wise, staying in a garrison above the Strip had to have appealed.

For years, the Chateau was part of how Keanu protected himself and also part of how he sold himself in the stories people wrote about him. Like the motorcycle accidents he kept getting into, some of which were close calls with death, his deluxe unhousedness was a data point that fed into a broader notion of Keanu as a man of unextinguishable bohemian predilections, clinging to some essential wildness even as he became increasingly integral to the production of big studio movies.

Keanu has since purchased at least one house. It's in the part of the Hollywood Hills they call the "Bird Streets." It's about eight minutes from where George Harrison lived when he wrote "Blue Jay Way," a song about George Harrison's friends trying to find his house in the hills and getting lost in the fog, which in the days before smartphones gave George Harrison enough time to sit down at the organ and compose a pretty good Beatles deep cut. Supposedly Keanu's next-door neighbor is Leonardo DiCaprio, and supposedly DiCaprio lives in Madonna's old house; I hope both these things are true. Keanu's house reportedly cost over $8 million, but it's unusual by lavish-celebrity-home standards in that it (again, reportedly) has only two bedrooms, in which I assume it never rains.

I talked to Keanu that day and people seemed to like the story I wrote for *GQ* about that experience, and the pictures that ran alongside it, of Keanu wearing a long overcoat over his shoulders like a mob boss who writes poetry on the side. But what I remember about meeting Keanu that first day is that it went badly. It didn't go badly because it took place at the Chateau, or because I chose to open with a confusing indoor-rain anecdote. Nor did it go badly for the reasons some interviews with Keanu have historically gone badly. Especially back in the day, the role Keanu seemed to find most challenging—other than "Man with a British accent," at least—was the part of Guy Who's Comfortable and Easy to Talk To in an Interview Setting. Something about the artificial intimacy of the interaction seemed to thoroughly unnerve him.

My favorite Keanu interviews are the ones where he vents this discomfort by acting out in some chaotic, self-flagellating way. This invariably turns the interview into a little piece of absurdist theater, but you never got the impression Keanu was doing this on purpose. It always seemed like he acted weird in interviews because he genuinely *felt* weird in interviews.

In 1991, Keanu starred in three major films: *Point Break*, *Bill & Ted's Bogus Journey*, and *My Own Private Idaho*. He'd filmed *Point Break* and *Idaho* back-to-back in 1990—*Point Break* from July through October and *Idaho* in November and December—and started on *Bogus Journey* in January of 1991.

The fact that he'd wrapped his first big-time action movie and reported directly to the set of a surreal queer art film said a lot about the range of possibilities he wanted to explore; *Bogus Journey*, however, was just work. It was the sequel to the surprise hit movie *Bill & Ted's*

Excellent Adventure, but there'd been issues with the budget, and the finished movie wasn't what he'd signed up to make. When he went out to promote it, many of his interactions with the media had a punkish, booger-flicking quality to them.

A few years down the road, a reporter will encounter a "more serious, more reflective Reeves" promoting *Speed* while dressed in "a beautifully-tailored black suit," and will reminisce about a *Bogus Journey* junket appearance where Keanu "showed up grimy and unshaven—hair greasy and uncombed, jeans matted with dirt, fingernails sprouting filth—and greeted a table full of reporters by belching into their microphones." When he's reminded of this, the more serious, more reflective Keanu will admit, "I had a certain dissatisfaction with that particular film, and I was fairly immature, I think, in dealing with that feeling."

On another occasion during the *Bogus Journey* press cycle in 1991, Keanu met with Chris Willman of the *Los Angeles Times* in a suite at the Four Seasons hotel in Beverly Hills. At first in Willman's story, he's the fun, goofy Keanu. He mentions "Hades," as in Hell, but pronounces it as a one-syllable word, like "fades." But after about forty-five minutes, Willman writes, things take a turn:

> Reeves—who has answered a lot of questions about acting by slamming his fists on his thighs and swearing at himself, unable or unwilling to articulate what he wants to say—has suddenly exited the room in a mysterious panic. Now he is out on the tiny balcony of his 10th-floor suite, waving his arms agitatedly and vocalizing loud, frustrated profanities over the presumably curious heads of whatever Beverly Hillsians might be lingering below.
>
> Seen in silhouette through the room's billowing white curtain, he's a dramatically framed and lit soliloquist of inner-directed epithets. Eventually he calms down and comes back into the room, picking up the reporter's tape recorder in order to rewind and record over the previous five minutes or so of conversation, none of which has been very revealing.

He explains to Willman that he doesn't feel comfortable talking about his craft: "I think that my journey or anything I have to say about it in the public is . . . I don't have anything to say."

Later, another question about acting touches the same nerve, and sets him off bellowing "Sam Kinison–style" again. He tells Willman he's having a bad day: "Look at me, man. I'm a basket case." But he is never a jerk in this story; at no point does he seem to blame Willman for his distress. The hotel has laid out a spread of Evian and chips for Keanu and his interlocutors, and at the end of their conversation Keanu suggests that he and Willman should split up the refreshments and each take some home. No hard feelings.

A few years later, in another magazine interview, he starts talking about how spontaneous human combustion is real. Sometimes people's bodies just burn up for no reason, he says. He says he heard this from a friend who discovered it while "researching fire." He brings this up apropos of nothing, unless it's to communicate that being interviewed makes him want to immolate from within. Sometimes, he says, "they'll be in a wooden chair, and the chair won't burn, but there'll be nothing left of the person. Except sometimes the teeth. Or the heart. No one speaks about this—but it's for real."

Keanu did not freak out in front of me, nor did he combust. We sat and ate sandwiches. He was friendly and slyly self-effacing. I asked him questions about his movies and the arc of his career, and he answered them as if determined to add as little new information as possible to the shallow pool of known facts about Keanu Reeves.

At one point we left the semisecluded corner table we'd been seated at and crossed the patio to a little curtained-off space behind the bar area so that Keanu could violate state laws and Chateau policy by smoking another cigarette. As Keanu took a seat on a dry chair and I sat down on the dry part of a chair that was otherwise pretty damp from the rain, Keanu asked if this was okay, and I said that it was, and then added that my motto is "I deserve worse." This is not actually my motto. I once heard someone say it was their motto, and sometimes I throw it out in conversation and say it's my motto, like when I'm interviewing Keanu Reeves and can't figure out what the fuck to say next.

I figured he'd laugh at this or ignore it. Instead when I said that "I deserve worse" was my motto, Keanu latched on to it. He seemed genuinely concerned and sad for me, and wanted to know *why* that was my motto, why anyone would go around thinking of themselves that way, and because it wasn't actually my motto I didn't know what to say in response, so I stammered something along the lines of "I don't know, Keanu—don't you feel like you've hurt people in your life?" and of course, because it was Keanu Reeves I was saying this to, his answer was a puzzled "No."

This was as close as we came to connecting. He could not explain to me what it was like to be Keanu Reeves, or what it had been like to be Keanu Reeves in the past, any more than I could explain to him how the water in my house had entered on the ground floor and dripped down to the first floor. If there was rain in his house it was not like the rain in mine.

If I had it to do again I would not have asked him any questions about his movies. There was a moment when he mentioned a point in his life when he began to think more about death, and if I had it to do again I would have asked him only questions about death from that point on—what he imagined it would feel like, if it would be like falling forever through endless blackness the way he and Alex Winter do in *Bogus Journey*, falling for long enough that they have time for a few rounds of Twenty Questions.

I remember very little of what he said that day. I remember even less from our second meeting for this story, when he showed me around the Hawthorne, California, headquarters of ARCH, a company he cofounded in 2011 that makes and sells extremely high-end custom motorcycles. It was a tour he'd previously given to writers from British *Esquire* and *Vanity Fair*, but the bikes were very beautiful, and now if I ever need to blow $85,000 on something that will probably kill me I know where to go.

We talked a little bit about the sci-fi novelist Philip K. Dick, who wrote the book that Keanu's movie *A Scanner Darkly* is based on; I remember mentioning Dick's late-period novel *Radio Free Albemuth* and Keanu pulling out his phone and trying to Google the definition of "albemuth"—a word of Dick's invention, a name he made up for a star he believed was sending him messages—and finding only "albumen," which means "egg white."

3. Keanu as Keanu

I came away from this whole process having learned the same thing countless other reporters seem to have learned from interviewing Keanu Reeves—namely, that interviewing Keanu Reeves is not a particularly good way to get to know him, and might actually be an *impediment* to understanding him. I still don't think I really know anything about Keanu, but this is what I think about Keanu.

I think if Keanu has anything to say about himself and his specific experience as both a professional actor and a person in the world, he's said those things in his work.

I think that all of Keanu's movies are to some degree autobiographical, whether or not he knows this or intends it.

"The thing that matters," the director Robert Bresson wrote about the actors in his films, "is not what they show me but what they hide from me and, above all, *what they do not suspect is in them.*" He wrote this in *Notes on the Cinematograph*, a book that was published in 1975 and never mentions Keanu but seems to say something about him on nearly every page.

I think Keanu is always present in his work, even when he doesn't mean to be.

I think the reason he's so compelling to watch—in good films and bad ones, in movies he doesn't belong in and movies that are only interesting because he's in them—is that he always seems to be looking out at us despite being ostensibly in character, and when he looks at us he's looking at us *as Keanu Reeves*, conscious that we can all see him and that he can't see us, wondering if we've caught on yet that this character is just Keanu Reeves again, negotiating some new set of pretend circumstances.

One of the main criticisms leveled against him by people who don't *get* Keanu is that he just plays Keanu Reeves in every movie. For one thing, there are more facets to that baseline Keanu persona than this criticism gives him credit for, capacities beyond stoicism and air guitar—for vulnerability, cold cruelty, irony, tenderness. I think that these people are not wrong but that they are wrong about this being a problem. In every movie, Keanu both is and is not Keanu Reeves the way David Bowie is always David Bowie even when he's supposed to be singing as someone else. He is and is not Keanu Reeves in movies the way David Bowie is and is not the guy in the space capsule.

This is almost certainly a side effect of watching Keanu's entire filmography while locked down at home for months due to a global pandemic, but I now see each of Keanu's movies as part of one long movie about a perpetually reincarnated Keanu protagonist moving through a series of disconnected and wildly divergent realities.

I think Keanu Reeves might actually be one of the most believable actors working today, because while I rarely forget that I'm looking at Keanu Reeves when I'm watching Keanu in a movie, I almost always believe absolutely that the way Keanu is reacting from moment to moment in a given fictional situation is the exact way that Keanu Reeves would handle that situation were he to encounter it in real life.

"He's always trying to reach out to truth," John Coltrane once said of his bandmate, saxophonist Pharoah Sanders. "He's trying to allow his spiritual self to be his guide." I see that reach for truth in everything Keanu does, even in the movies that—in a broader way, as movies—don't work at all. There's always this secondary drama unfolding in the work—Keanu's own struggle to access something heartfelt and real amid a set of beyond-his-control circumstances that can range from the basic artificiality of moviemaking to a specific movie's outright badness. I see in Keanu's individual performances bum notes and choices that are occasionally laughable but his body of work as a whole has the sweep of a singular, ambitious, and sometimes confounding project by an artist determined to make meaning despite forces arrayed against him.

This book is about watching Keanu Reeves movies and how Keanu Reeves moves through them, and what else we can see in those films and in our broader culture through the keyhole of Keanu as a performer and a star and a human being. I'm pretty sure it is not a book that Keanu Reeves will like, but I can't imagine a book about Keanu Reeves that Keanu Reeves would like. I assume he will never speak to me again, but I doubt we would ever have spoken again anyway.

I deserve worse.

PART ONE

LIKE A YOUNG ROBERT URICH

1 | KEANU REEVES CREATES, THROUGH HIS MERE PRESENCE ON-SCREEN, THE SENSE THAT SOMETHING CINEMATIC IS HAPPENING, EVEN WHEN THAT'S NOT ACTUALLY THE CASE

In 2012, at a time in his career when he has nothing much going on, Keanu Reeves stars in a film called *Generation Um...*, directed by Mark L. Mann. Keanu is close to fifty when he makes the movie but in the movie it's his character's fortieth birthday. His character's name is John Wall, which is the kind of Keanu Reeves character name you might come up with if all you had for inspiration was an empty room. The movie is an empty room that Keanu somehow fills with life.

John shares a grimy apartment in New York with a tech-bro roommate who is grinningly stupid and young enough to be his son. For work, John chauffeurs and chaperones two escorts, Mia and Violet, played by Bojana Novakovic and Adelaide Clemens. They are insufferable and they're also his only friends. One day John gets his hands on a video camera, and that night he interviews Mia and Violet about their lives, and suddenly the movie is aiming for things it can't quite reach—maybe the simmering tension of *Sex, Lies, and Videotape* or the confrontational volatility of *Two Girls and a Guy*.

Most of *Generation Um...* falls away even as you're watching it. It's not one of Keanu's best movies. It's not even one of his best bad movies. And yet I have seen it more than once, because two parts of it are perfect. One of those parts comes at the very end of the movie—after the end, actually. You rarely see a drama with deleted scenes during the credits, but if you had footage of Keanu being cajoled into singing "The Luckiest Guy on the Lower East Side" by the Magnetic Fields in a monotone that somehow makes Magnetic Fields singer Stephin Merritt's actual monotone seem wildly expressive, you wold also bend the rules in order to get that footage into your movie.

Of the sixty-nine love songs on the Magnetic Fields's album *69 Love Songs*, "Luckiest Guy" was the "hit," in the sense that you'd hear it at least four times a night in any Brooklyn indie-rock bar with a jukebox during George W. Bush's presidency. But Keanu sings it like he's never heard it before, like he almost can't believe it's a real song. You never know what Keanu is going to know or not know.

The other perfect passage of the film is like another movie, smuggled inside the one Mann is trying to make. It's a mostly wordless early sequence that follows Keanu—unshaven, hungover, very clearly nowhere near even the middle of the list of the Lower East Side's luckiest guys—walking around Manhattan on what looks like a nice spring day. As if in homage to "Sad Keanu," the widely memed image of Keanu eating a sandwich while seemingly thinking about his entire life, Mann films Keanu sitting in front of a bakery, eating a cupcake he's bought with his last two wrinkled dollars.

Keanu's entire cupcake-eating process unfolds before our eyes, from the first bite, to the moment he wipes crumbs away from his mouth with his hand instead of using a napkin, to the look of relatable self-disgust that darkens his face even before he's finished eating the cupcake.

Then he keeps walking. He looks into pawnshop windows, watches matzoh revolve on a motorized bakery rack. The streets he walks down have not been cleared of non-movie pedestrians, and you can see people reacting as he passes, doing *Was that fuckin' Keanu Reeves?* double takes.

For as long as these scenes last the movie stops trying to be anything except a documentary about Keanu. The bet Mann is making with this sequence is that some people are inherently cinematic and that Keanu is one of those people, and if you point a camera at him, what happens will seem like a movie, even if it's just Keanu dispensing himself a cup of gas-station coffee from a push-button urn or shaking ketchup onto a plate of diner breakfast. Mann turns out to be right about this.

The parts of *Generation Um...* where Keanu does nothing feel more movielike than the parts that advance the plot. Jean-Luc Godard is often quoted as having said that all you need for a movie is a girl and a gun; in this equation Keanu is both the girl and the gun.

Keanu goes back to his shitty apartment and putters around. He feeds his cat and sings his cat a little cat-feeding song. *Super cat, super cat*. He opens a Corona and the mail. He listens to the radio—Barack Obama talking about the economy, a report on the subprime mortgage crisis. Mann films Keanu opening the mail and feeding the cat the way Andy Warhol filmed the Empire State Building, and for the same basic reason: an icon is never not interesting, even if that icon is just standing there.

Before it's over, the movie inside *Generation Um...* that is about Keanu's morning in the city becomes a movie about the experience of being watched and looked at all the time, and a fantasy about taking control and freeing yourself from the camera's gaze. Somewhere on the Lower East Side Keanu sees a woman in a cowboy hat, carrying a bunch of balloons. He follows her to an outdoor basketball court where a guy with a video camera is filming a large group of people hula-hooping in cowboy clothes. Keanu stands there for a minute, watching them hoop. But when the guy filming sets his camera down, Keanu sees an opportunity. He grabs the camera and runs. The cowboys give chase, but Keanu jumps the turnstiles and escapes on the subway.

While he's filming this scene somebody takes a picture of him running, and it makes the rounds as a picture of Keanu having stolen a camera from the paparazzi, even though this isn't what's happening in the picture.

Now, in the movie, Keanu is a man with a camera. He films a squirrel climbing a tree in the park. He films reflections in puddles, water gushing from a fountain, the nose of a golden Labrador through a dog-run fence. Keanu actually shot this footage himself, so in this sequence the director and cinematographer of *Generation Um*...is Keanu Reeves. We are looking at the world through Keanu's eyes.

Keanu lets a birthday call from his mother go to voicemail. Keanu looks into the camera lens and says "Hi" to the camera, as if the camera is in some way his mother, as if the camera and the audience on the other side of it are the forces he's actually accountable to, as if these are the relationships that really matter. The script gives him nothing further to say to the camera. This is preferable. It's cleaner this way.

Later at Mia and Violet's apartment, Keanu will film the legs of chairs, pictures on the wall, and Mia and Violet. It's as if he's making the case—to us, to Mark Mann, to cinema as a medium—that there are more beautiful and consequential things to look at than Keanu that there is nothing so special or interesting about him. No one who's made it this far into a movie like this one would agree, of course. Keanu is the only reason to watch this movie. But Keanu has stolen this camera, and so he controls the camera, and he keeps pointing it at anything that is not Keanu, at the tops of buildings and the sky getting dark and the moon.

2 | KEANU REEVES FIRES A SHOTGUN INTO THE FRESHLY DUG GRAVE OF HIS FATHER, ANDY GRIFFITH

In a Coke commercial he makes in 1984, Keanu sweats through a bicycle race while a rugged-voiced jingle singer belts out lyrics about "reaching for the finish line." He breaks from the pack, then falls short. Some guy in a yellow shirt snaps the tape instead. But after the race an actor playing Keanu's dad finds him in the crowd and says, "Hey, I'm proud of you—really proud."

His commercial-dad hands him a cold bottle and Keanu says, gratefully, "A Coke," like that's exactly the thing he's been craving this whole race, a soda pop.

Yellow Shirt Guy, the winner, asks Keanu, "Who's your coach?" and Keanu says, "My dad," pulling his fake dad close.

***

Keanu's real father, Samuel Reeves, was from Hawaii. He was of Chinese and native Hawaiian descent. Keanu is supposedly named after Samuel's great-uncle Henry Keanu Reeves. In Hawaiian *keanu* means "cool breeze over the mountains," a string of words that recurs throughout Keanu's early press clippings the way references to dawn's rosy fingers do in *The Odyssey*.

Keanu's mother, Patricia Taylor, is originally from England. Keanu is born in Beirut, Lebanon, because that's where his father meets his mother. Beginning in 1975, the country will be torn apart by years of sectarian civil war, but in 1964, a few months before Keanu's birth, the *International Herald Tribune* describes Beirut in a travel story as "the seething communication hub of the Middle East, where planes from every point on the globe touch down, linking four continents."

"In the old quarter," the story continues,

> men sit all day long in obscure cafes, playing cards and puffing at their water-pipes, and the bazaar teems with colors, smells, cries and milling throngs, as it has for centuries.
>
> In the new quarter, wealthy tourists and international businessmen lounge on the terraces and swim in the pools of luxury hotels and shop for Paris fashions hot off the plane.
>
> For fun and games in an elegant setting, there is the casino, a handsome complex situated ten miles from the city overlooking the Bay of Jounieh, where one may dine, attend a movie or a concert, stay on for dancing at the nightclub, and finish the evening with a turn in the gaming rooms until the sun comes up over the Lebanon mountains.

The casino is Lebanon's only gaming venue, the Casino Liban, where the floor show includes elephants and dancing stallions.

Patricia Taylor is either a dancer when she meets Keanu's father or she's a student, depending which accounts you believe. Keanu's father is usually described as a geologist.

In their wedding pictures Samuel Reeves wears a black suit and a skinny black tie and Patricia has a chic bob and stands a few inches taller than her new husband.

Samuel will later say the sixties were "a hard time to be married." They split up sometime after the birth of their second child—Kim, a daughter. After that Samuel Reeves moves back to Hawaii, but sometimes Keanu goes to visit him. He's a teenager the last time they see each other, on the island of Kauai. Later Keanu will remember looking up at the night sky with his father and his father trying to tell him something about the stars, the planets, the shape of the universe.

"Something," Keanu says, "about how the world is a box. And I looked up, and I had no clue what he was talking about. No, Dad. The earth is round. It's not a rectangle, man."

***

The dad who sticks around just long enough to leave unanswered questions, then splits. It has the ring of an origin story, although Keanu's never told it like that's what it is.

He does say, "I think a lot of who I am is a reaction against his actions," in a 1995 interview.

In his movies, he is in conflict with fathers and father figures over and over. It starts in some of the earliest films he makes, before anybody knows anything about his history—as if that history is something casting directors can see in him, just by watching him walk through a door with script sides in his hand.

In 1986, Keanu is in a CBS movie of the week called *Under the Influence*, as the youngest son of an alcoholic hardware-store manager played by Andy Griffith. Griffith's family enables his drinking by ignoring it, until one Sunday morning at church when he coughs up a mouthful of blood and collapses while helping with the offertory. At the hospital the doctors tell Andy Griffith's wife and family that he'll die unless he quits drinking, which as it turns out is not something Andy Griffith is able to do.

For its time, *Under the Influence* is a groundbreaking portrayal of codependency and substance abuse in families. Keanu is angry at his father and desperate for his approval and becomes more like him every day. We see him early on at a bar in the afternoon, hollering along to Bruce Springsteen's "Hungry Heart" like it's an incantation that can summon a better time than the one he's having, buying drinks for girls who roll their eyes. He comes home from the bar and mouths off to Griffith. He tells Griffith to get him another beer, and Griffith gets up, and goes to the fridge and starts whipping cans at Keanu's head.

Later, after the mouth-blood thing, Griffith slips out of the hospital. It's Keanu who finds him at the hardware store, dead at his desk amid a little Stonehenge of empties. Keanu plays his big scene with Griffith playing dead.

Keanu yells, "YOU JUST HADDA DO IT! YOU BASTARD!"

He pounds on Griffith's back, steps away, hits him again. The director cuts the scene right when he seems to be getting somewhere, emotionally.

Keanu will tell stories like this one over and over in movie after movie, playing men in conflict with feckless fathers or defined by absent ones. In *River's Edge* he will grab a bat to fight his stepfather. In *The Prince of Pennsylvania* he'll kidnap his Vietnam-vet dad, played by Fred Ward, and hold him in a coal mine, hoping to collect as ransom an inheritance that Fred Ward turns out to have pissed away. In *Bill & Ted's Excellent Adventure* he'll butt heads with a father who wants to send him to military school and in *Bill & Ted's Bogus Journey* he'll become a ghost who briefly takes control of his father's body. In *My Own Private Idaho* he'll break his real father's heart by acting gay and then break his surrogate father's heart by acting straight. And in *Parenthood* he'll say to Dianne Wiest that while you need a license to drive a car or catch a fish, "they'll let any butt-reamin' asshole be a father," and after he says the words you can see him shake them off, slipping back into character, suddenly very focused on the work of putting away a prop milk carton.

There's also something palpably raised-by-stepdads-ish about the way Keanu plays off older male costars, especially actors with big, passionate, sometimes disorderly presences, like Peter Falk as the rapscallion scriptwriter who advises him on love in *Tune in Tomorrow* or Dennis Hopper in *Speed*—who calls himself "Daddy" when he sets off his bombs—or Al Pacino in *The Devil's Advocate*. An older guy brings out the disciple in him, the student who just wants to sit at the older guy's feet and watch him work but also wants to fight the older guy, a little.

When he gambles his career momentum after *Speed* to go do Shakespeare in Winnipeg, he plays Hamlet, who does everything he does because his father's ghost wants revenge. And in the *Matrix* movies his only real parent is a machine that according to prophecy he's destined to destroy. Instead, by the end of the trilogy, he comes to a truce with the Matrix that is kind of like a reconciliation, and maybe this is a coincidence but—from that point on in his movies, minus the distant dads responsible for Keanu's manly damage in both *The Lake House* and *Sweet November*, the openly contentious father-son relationship recedes as a theme in the work.

***

In *A Walk in the Clouds*, from 1995, Keanu plays Paul Sutton, an orphan, a veteran of the war in the Pacific, and a traveling chocolate salesman. On a train he meets Victoria, a college student played by Aitana Sánchez-Gijón. She's unmarried and pregnant with her professor's child. Keanu agrees to go home with her and pretend to be her husband, so that she won't have to explain this situation to her family, who turn out to be aristocratic Napa Valley vintners of Mexican extraction.

Eventually he and Victoria begin to fall for each other for real, but Keanu has a wife back home, so he holds himself back. "I'm not free," he tells her, "and I don't want to hurt you that way."

The family's elderly patriarch, Don Pedro, is played by Anthony Quinn. Victoria's uptight father isn't crazy about the idea of his daughter having gone off and married some chocolate salesmans, but Don Pedro takes a shine to Keanu.

Don Pedro convinces Keanu to stick around for the grape harvest. Keanu and Victoria work out the feelings they're repressing by really going to town on a vat of freshly harvested grapes. Her family is starting to accept Keanu. Director Alfonso Arau cuts repeatedly to shots of people smiling and making *I'll be darned* faces at each other after Keanu does another thing to win them over.

Keanu knows this is unsustainable, that he's living a lie. At night the house on the vineyard is a Thomas Kinkade house whose lights promise a solace and familial warmth that Keanu knows he has to turn his back on.

When he leaves to go home to his wife he gives Victoria his Bronze Star as a baby present. She says to him, "Paul Sutton, you are the most honorable man I have ever known."

How do you begin to play the most honorable man someone has ever known? Why would you even want to?

Part of it, for Keanu, must have to do with Anthony Quinn. Quinn will be eighty by the time *A Walk in the Clouds* comes out, but he's still busy, playing Greek gods and mob bosses. Later Keanu will remember him checking his messages, waiting to hear if he booked this or that job.

It's Quinn's character Don Pedro who takes Keanu on the actual walk in the clouds. They walk through the family's fog-shrouded grapevines at dawn. Don Pedro takes him to a little hill and shows him two sacred things: the family burial plot and the root of the first vine, from which the rest of the vineyard was cultivated. In this space of death and rebirth Don Pedro tells Keanu, "You are an orphan no longer."

Their walk in the clouds is really a tour of the levels of augmented reality available to filmmakers at the midpoint of the 1990s. Nobody thinks of *A Walk in the Clouds* as a special-effects movie, but it foreshadows Keanu's future on-screen as a human avatar moving in and out of increasingly virtual spaces. In parts of this sequence Keanu and Anthony Quinn are walking in the kind of smoky early-morning mist that occurs naturally in a place like this vineyard. It takes a lot of preparation to shoot in mist like this before it dissipates. But there are also clouds in the walk-in-the-clouds sequence that are pretty clearly matte paintings and clouds that appear computer-generated and clouds that might be dry-ice vapor pumped in from off camera.

Many of the clouds are fake and the story of Keanu and his fake wife's grandfather taking a walk is fake but Anthony Quinn and Keanu are real to each other, and they are really walking in mist that is itself real, sometimes, and that's what there is to see in this part of the movie: Keanu himself having the experience of walking through a vineyard full of fake clouds with Anthony Quinn.

Sometimes a Keanu movie can engage us in spite of great faults, and when that happens it's often because even in a bad Keanu movie we can occupy ourselves with assumptions about Keanu's own inner life. We imagine what it feels like for Keanu to be in Anthony Quinn's presence, soaking up that energy. We imagine some father-thing Keanu feels he's been robbed of and we imagine Keanu going his whole life looking for that thing in other men's faces, without quite knowing what he's looking for. The movie becomes a documentary of Keanu Reeves and Anthony Quinn spanning time together on a movie set. It becomes about the way Keanu Reeves smiles at Anthony Quinn, as if he can't help it.

***

In September 1992, police on the Big Island of Hawaii arrest Samuel Reeves at Hilo International Airport. He's carrying what the police describe to the press as "large quantities of cocaine and heroin." When he goes to trial two years later prosecutors characterize him as a "facilitator" for heroin traffickers. The elder Reeves pleads guilty and a judge sentences him to ten years in prison.

He will serve two years before he's paroled. In 2001, he'll sit in a park that is close to his mother's house in Waikiki Beach and the local methadone clinic and talk to a newspaper reporter about a day when he stood on a lava cliff with his son.

"Occasionally, the spray would wash over the shelf, and the water would rush around our legs, and I would lift him up and hold him really tight," he says. "Then this big old wave really almost swept us right out. I caught my boy just as he was being sucked away by knee-deep water."

Samuel Reeves dies in 2018, at seventy-five, in the town of Ewa Beach on the island of Oahu, and when his niece and his daughter—Keanu's half sister—announce his memorial luncheon on social media, the announcement ends with one terse, paparazzi-deterring line: "Sam's other children will not be attending."

***

After they walk together, Don Pedro makes Keanu sample the first bottle of the harvest. They get drunk together in a wine cave.

In the space of a dissolve, a still life materializes on the table in front of them—melon and *jamón*, some bread and cheese, a little brandy, an oil lamp.

A four-piece band appears from somewhere—two guitars, an accordion, a violin.

Don Pedro starts to sing some old song in Spanish and Keanu tries to sing the old Spanish song with him and Don Pedro says, "That's all right, that's all right" and hugs Keanu's head. Their characters are supposed to be drunk by now and Anthony Quinn and Keanu both seem to bave forgotten the presence of the cameras in a way that makes them seem drunk too.

For at least this minute it doesn't matter if the film they're making is any good, or whether it moves us that Paul Sutton is getting to have these last moments with Don Pedro before he goes back to his old life. We're happy to see this happen *to Keanu*—to see him get the chance to sit here, singing these old songs with Anthony Quinn.

3| KEANU REEVES, AS A CHILD, PLAYS ON THE LOT THAT WILL ONE DAY BE A FOUR SEASONS HOTEL, IN WHAT WILL BECOME THE FIFTH-MOST-EXPENSIVE RETAIL CORRIDOR IN NORTH AMERICA

After breaking up with Keanu's father, Patricia Taylor and her children move to New York. In 1970, Patricia marries Paul Aaron, who at the time is an up-and-coming theater director on and off Broadway. The marriage doesn't last but he and Keanu will stay close, and when Keanu's a teenager and Paul Aaron starts directing feature films Keanu works as a production assistant on a few of them. Aaron starts a production company with a management division. One of his colleagues there is Erwin Stoff, who becomes Keanu's manager when Keanu starts acting professionally.

Keanu's mother then moves with her children to Toronto. The part of Toronto they settle in is called Yorkville, and up until not long before they arrive it has been the hub of Canada's counterculture—home to Gandalf's, Canada's first head shop, and to migrant hippies from all over Canada as well as a draft-swelled population of US expats, a part of town where in the late sixties you could see Neil Young or Rick James or Joni Mitchell or Buffy Sainte-Marie or Gordon Lightfoot at clubs such as the Riverboat, the Penny Farthing, the Purple Onion, or the Mynah Bird.

Read up on what Keanu's neighborhood was like in its sixties heyday and you'll eventually come across the CBC's 1967 documentary about the Yorkville scene. It's a nature show about the habitat and behaviors of the North American stoner, with bemusedly condescending narration by the straight-laced reporter Knowlton Nash: "About noon the hippies start moving—slowly at first, because they flower better at night." Nash submits for our approval a "professional hippie" named Bill, who's filmed gangling down the street smoking cigarettes and eating a Popsicle and saying things like "A nonconformist doesn't necessarily have to be a hippie. A hippie has to be at odds with the Establishment, but he might be conforming to the other hippies."

Decades later, writing as William Gibson, Bill becomes a famous novelist, and from his first book, *Neuromancer*, the English language will get the word "cyberspace" to describe the vibrant and seething imaginary country formed by the planet's networked computers. When Gibson meets Keanu for the first time, Keanu will tell him about growing up in Yorkville and playing in construction-site dirt in the future footprint of the Four Seasons Hotel on Yorkville Avenue. Later Gibson will write about "the truly remarkable ferocity with which the ambient zone I remembered had been malled over. In retrospect this had everything to do with Yorkville 'Village' having been, in the first place, a developers' simulacrum of the West Village, briefly invaded, in my day, by a social simulacrum of the East Village."

By the time Keanu gets to Yorkville, that process of mallification is already underway. In Keanu's first great movie, 1987's *River's Edge*, the memory of the sixties will hang in the air like stale smoke. Aside from the hollowed-out ghost of Dennis Hopper and a few teachers who won't shut up about Vietnam, Keanu and his crew of nihilist punks are what remains, in the film's dead-end eighties, of the hippie dream. When Keanu describes his own life as a child of bohemians seeking his own experience of bohemia in a rapidly gentrifying post-sixties Toronto it doesn't sound that dissimilar.

"We didn't even do graffiti, you know? We'd build go-carts called Fireball 500," he told the novelist Dennis Cooper in a 1990 interview.

"I mean we did sling chestnuts at teachers' heads, and in grade eight hash started to come around, and LSD kinda. But Toronto's become like a shopping center now."

Patricia Taylor works as a costume designer. She makes custom clothes for musicians such as David Bowie and Dolly Parton. She makes the cantilevered black bunny outfit that Dolly Parton wears on the cover of *Playboy* magazine in 1978. In 1983, as an iconoclastic performing-arts high school student, Keanu wears that same bunny outfit as a Halloween costume.

One tabloid describes Patricia wearing her hair in a peach-colored buzz cut and smoking Gitanes. She has music-industry friends and Keanu grows up around them. Their house is down the street from a studio called Nimbus 9, where Alice Cooper does a lot of recording with the producer Bob Ezrin. Keanu's mom knows Alice Cooper and sometimes Keanu hangs out at Nimbus 9 drinking Coke and eating candy. At least once, Alice Cooper comes over to babysit Keanu, bearing the gifts of fake vomit and plastic dog poop. Keanu and his childhood friend Evan Williams wrestle Alice Cooper on the rug and Alice Cooper wins. "He tied us up like a human knot," Williams will later tell *People* magazine.

Patricia Taylor marries a rock promoter. Patricia Taylor breaks up with the rock promoter and marries the owner of a hair salon. Keanu goes to a lot of movies. In 2013, he lists some of the films that changed his life: *Harold & Maude. Monty Python and the Holy Grail* and *Star Wars* and particularly the limb-severing scenes in both. *Eraserhead* ("I did not come out the same kid"), and *Taxi Driver*, and the films of Peter O'Toole, specifically *The Ruling Class*, *Becket*, and *Lawrence of Arabia*. Keanu says he likes O'Toole because he, "played unique individuals with a voice, often tragically trapped."

In a Reddit AMA he will add to this list *Apocalypse Now* and Werner Herzog's *Stroszek*. Herzog's film is one of two movies the director made with Bruno Schleinstein, or "Bruno S.," an eccentric Berlin street performer who had never acted before Herzog cast him. "His performances were riveting," Michael Kimmelman wrote in 2008, "but he was obviously not well mentally, and even as he came across in his own way as knowing, he was at the same time simply being himself, and the question hovered: How much was fiction, how much reality?" *Stroszek* is every actor's favorite Herzog movie.

Keanu knows he wants to be an actor by the time he's fifteen years old. But for money he sharpens ice skates, trims trees, and makes pasta at an Italian restaurant. He works his way up to being manager at that last job but quits to do a play. He's dyslexic. He struggles at regular school and at the handful of theater schools he slips in and out of.

But in 1984, he's cast in his first professional theater role, at the Passe Muraille theater in Toronto, in a play called *Wolfboy*. The play is about the bond between two teenagers who meet in a psychiatric ward. Keanu plays a hockey-team captain who's survived a suicide attempt and Keanu's friend Carl Marotte plays a kid who believes he's a werewolf.

The photographer who shoots the pictures for the *Wolfboy* poster sprays down Keanu and Marotte with water and has them smush their faces together like they're about to kiss. In the outtakes, they're just two guys in wet T-shirts striking an awkward pose. But there's at least one shot where they look like they're into it, and that's the picture they use on the poster.

The play becomes a cult hit in Toronto's gay community, or at least the posters do. People keep stealing them. It's the beginning of people picking up a vibe from Keanu that he is not necessarily deliberately putting down. Over a decade later *People* magazine will refer to speculation about Keanu's sexuality as "the legacy of *Wolfboy*."

In a 1984 episode of *Hangin' In*, a Canadian sitcom about a drop-in youth center, Keanu plays one of the youths who drops in. This may mark the first time a mass audience hears Keanu speak words on a screen. The words are "Hey, where do you keep the towels? Pete said we could use his shower." They let him pick out his own wardrobe for the episode and he picks out a sleeveless leather vest.

On an episode of the Canadian cop show *Night Heat* from January 1985, he's a burglar who gets chased from the scene of the crime by an old lady with a hedge trimmer, and then on another *Night Heat* that airs in February he's "Thug #1," a would-be rapist who gets shot by one of the leads, who's mistaken Keanu's flashlight for a gun and feels bad about it for the rest of the episode. Meanwhile Keanu's also bringing a goofball camp-counselor energy to regular appearances on *Going Great*, a CBC news-magazine show for kids, as a correspondent who goes out and, for example, puts on a beekeeper's mask and meets some bees.

In a cereal commercial he's a bow-tied waiter moved to ecstatic dancing by a bowl of cornflakes. Years later a Leo Burnett Canada creative director will say that Keanu's part was originally supposed to be one scene of many in a cornflake commercial of broader scope, but that when they looked at the footage of Keanu's cornflake dance they saw something undeniable in Keanu and cut the ad around just him instead.

In *Letting Go*—which airs on ABC on May 11, 1985, at 9:00 P.M. EST, displacing from its usual time slot a season-eight rerun of *The Love Boat*—John Ritter is a stereo-store proprietor who warns two obnoxious teens not to mess around with his stereo equipment and Keanu is the teen who messes around with the equipment anyway.

In *One Step Away*, also from 1985, Keanu wears a John Bender–ish trench coat and an earring as a budding juvenile delinquent being peer-pressured into purse-snatching and burglary. *One Step Away* was produced by the National Film Board of Canada and marketed to schools, church groups, and social-services agencies as part of the NFB's Family Crisis Series—movies designed to provide "gripping entertainment as half-hour dramas, and also serve as powerful discussion-starters for programs that deal with the family."

In the various Family Crisis films a young man struggles to cope with his mother's mental illness; a middle-aged man works up the courage to tell his wife and daughters he has an illegitimate son; and a college graduate loses his job and is forced to move back home. There is one film about a man who is jealous, which seems like a very Canadian thing to address as a social problem, and then there is *One Step Away*, where at one point Keanu meets a vampiric-looking junkie type who wants him to help steal car stereos and Keanu won't do it.

"You don't boost?" the guy asks, incredulous. "What do you do?"

Keanu says, "That's a good question."

***

"I read for a Disney Movie of the Week called *Young Again*," Keanu Reeves will explain in a 1988 book, *The New Breed: Actors Coming of Age*, which contains interviews with Patrick Swayze, Johnny Depp, and Robert Downey Jr. but features Lisa Marie (*Mars Attacks!*) and a pouting Stephen Baldwin on the cover, because nobody is one hundred percent right all the time about the long term prospects of actors when they are coming of age. "No one liked me but the director. He hooked me up with Hildy Gottlieb at ICM. I flew out to meet her and eventually got my green card. I got into my dumpy 1969 Volvo and drove here with $3,000. I stayed at my stepfather's"—Paul Aaron, that is—"and proceeded to go into the darkness—the darkness that is L.A." This last part, the part about the darkness, is the kind of knowing joke you make about Los Angeles if you've come from somewhere else, even if you know you'll probably never leave.

When he first arrives in LA, Keanu barely has time to park and shut his car door before his agents tell him he needs to change his name to something less ethnic. In 2017, he'll explain to Jimmy Fallon that when his agents told him this, about his name, he drove to the ocean and asked the ocean what to call himself, and that the ocean had whispered "Chuck Spadina"—presumably a shout-out to Spadina Avenue, a major thoroughfare in downtown Toronto, pronounced with a long *i*, like in "China" or "rhino"—and that when his agents recoiled from that one, he'd suggested "Templeton Page-Taylor" instead, which is presumably how he ends up billed as "K.C. Reeves" in the credits of the 1986 Disney Sunday Movie presentation *Young Again*, although at no point does he stop introducing himself at auditions as "Keanu."

By the end of 1986, the year he moves from Canada to Los Angeles, Keanu has appeared in six made-for-TV movies and two theatrically released feature films. He never seems quite right for any of the parts he plays around this time except for *River's Edge*, which feels like it's tapping into his lived experience as a teenage Toronto headbanger who wants to be sedated. In *The New Breed* he's the only Young Actor Coming of Age who name-checks his favorite punk bands: "I was a lucky kid who heard the Ramones, Violent Femmes, the Clash, Exploited, Joy Division. . . . My worlds got a lot better."

This is who he actually was; that music is the type of expression that fires him up. He grows up in Canada in the sunset of the counterculture, experiencing just enough of it to know what he's missed, and as he grows up he'll go looking for bohemia into books and films and records, and then he'll find something like it—a community of night bloomers—in theater companies and on movie sets, and when his popularity narrows his options to the point that it becomes impossible to pretend the moviemaking life is a bohemian pursuit he'll run off and start a band and ride around on a tour bus for a while avoiding this truth.

He'll be one of the first performers to navigate major mainstream celebrity with a mindset shaped by punk, which will make him one of the emblematic actors of the early nineties, an era that makes stars out of a number of people who tend to writhe and recoil when a spotlight hits them. In the eighties, though, he's cast repeatedly as a more regular teenager than he actually was, and therefore seems not wholly present on-screen. Movies have not yet figured out how to make use of the part of Keanu that's punkish and unruly.

In *Young Again* you can still hear some Canada in his speech pattern, mostly around the *l*'s: "I'm not gonna be happy without you, *Lll-laura*! That's what I've *llllearned* from all this!"

In *Young Again* some seventeen-year-old intern from Robert Urich's office mops up the racquetball court with Robert Urich on what turns out to be the morning of Robert Urich's fortieth birthday, and this humiliation sends Robert Urich into a maudlin spiral about everything age has taken from him. That night, after suffering through his birthday party, Robert Urich walks the streets alone and follows some laughing teens onto a bus, and on the bus he meets an old man in a white suit who seems to know everything about him, including the high school girlfriend Robert Urich let slip away and can't forget about, whose name was Laura.

"I just want a chance to be like that again," Robert Urich says to the old man, looking at the laughing kids. "Is that so much to ask?" Perhaps not, says the old man, who of course is a magical old man because when the bus empties out at the last stop and the driver turns to look at Robert Urich and tells him to move it, Robert Urich has disappeared and there in his seat, wearing Robert Urich's suit and tie, is Keanu Reeves.

Young Again airs on *The Magical World of Disney* on May 11, 1986, with an on-camera introduction by Michael Eisner, who is at the time the chairman of the Walt Disney Company and has a voice like sand and glue and is flanked during his introduction by his associates Donald and Daisy Duck, who seem to be quaking inside their duck suits about sharing the screen with the boss. He doesn't say anything about Keanu or much about the movie, which is one of the earliest and dullest of a wave of mideighties comedies about child-adult body swapping. That wave arguably peaks and breaks when Tom Hanks gets an Academy Award nomination for Penny Marshall's *Big*, a movie about a twelve-year-old boy unleashed in the adult world. *Young Again* is a sour fantasy by comparison—it's about a forty-year-old businessman with a forty-year-old businessman's ego using his calculating adult mind to outthink and occasionally literally dunk on high school kids. Keanu does what he can to bring this conceit to life, imbuing his young Urich with the arrogance of someone who's played the game through to the end already, a swagger that says *I've had sex and paid taxes.*

If there's one moment in *Young Again* where Keanu really seems like a movie star in the making it's after the first bus scene, when he goes home to Robert Urich's building and talks his way past Robert Urich's doorman and begins to dance around Robert Urich's apartment to a cover version of the Isley Brothers' "Shout." The obvious reference point is Tom Cruise's iconic underwear dance in *Risky Business*, except this being a Disney Sunday Movie, it's a G-rated *Risky Business* dance, in which Keanu not only keeps his pants on but puts on an *additional* coat over his clothes at some points, while occasionally popping out of the coat closet as if to surprise someone, even though he is alone. He sings into the mirror a lot, too, pointing at himself and mouthing the song's admonitions—*Don't forget to say you will.* You can practically hear the director calling for more takes, for greater enthusiasm, which Keanu keeps on bringing. It's a ridiculous and derivative moment in a ridiculous and derivative movie, but Keanu is utterly believable as someone thanking the universe for this body and what it can do, someone who's happy just to look in the mirror and see life and light reflected there—to be a face shouting, and telling itself to shout.

4 THE ASSASSINATION OF CHARLES BRONSON BY A SAVAGE, YOUNG KEANU REEVES

In the 1986 HBO film *Act of Vengeance* Charles Bronson is an agitator from the Pennsylvania coal mines who's made too much trouble for the president of the miners' union, and finally on New Year's Eve three men drive to Clarksville to kill him in his sleep. One of the men is Keanu Reeves.

The only part of this movie that I have seen is the part that's on YouTube, which is the part with Keanu Reeves in it. Keanu is the new guy joining two thugs we've already met, to help them close the book on Charles Bronson. The two thugs represent the venality and cynicism of the forces arrayed against Charles Bronson but Keanu is supposed to represent something worse, something more remorseless and amoral and troubled even less by anything like a conscience. On the way to Clarksville he sits in the back seat of the car, drinking a beer. Robert Schenkkan plays the goon at the wheel and Maury Chaykin is the goon in the passenger seat.

Schenkkan is in charge of this operation and knows the most about why they're going to Bronson's place, and what he knows is making him tense. But Keanu's in good spirits. He hasn't been told exactly what they're driving to Clarksville to do, but when he talks about what he's going to do with the money they're going to make from whatever they're driving to Clarksville to do, he asks the other two guys, "Did you ever put your hand—like, your whole fuckin' hand—inside a lady?" so you get the feeling he'll be up for anything.

They park outside Bronson's house and wait for his bedroom light to go out. It's freezing outside and Chaykin wants to turn the heat on and Keanu wants to go in the house and get on with it but Schenkkan yells at them both to quiet down. They're going to wait for the light because this thing they're doing will be easier when Charles Bronson is asleep, but also because they're not here to steal a TV set, Schenkkan says.

"This is big, what we're doin'," he tells them. "It'll be in history."

Finally the light goes out and three shadows make their way up the side of the house and in through an open window and up the stairs to the landing outside the two bedrooms. Keanu, having now realized what they're there to do, stops and says to the other two guys that he doesn't want to kill anybody. The other two guys say fine, then you don't get none of the money. Keanu says okay, then, he'll do it, but they have to do it right—they can't leave any witnesses. And they have to do it at the same time, Keanu says, now really taking ownership of this murder he was about to refuse to do.

So the plan is Keanu Reeves will go into one of the two upstairs bedrooms and Chaykin and Schenkkan will go into the other bedroom and they'll each count to ten and shoot whoever's in there. Keanu looks into the bedroom on the right and sees a woman, Charles Bronson's daughter, asleep in bed and signals the other two guys that he's got this. She's facing the camera, away from Keanu. Keanu points his gun. Has he been counting this whole time? Has he maybe forgotten he's supposed to be counting this whole time? He hesitates, looking freaked out.

In the master bedroom the other two guys stand in the doorway facing the bed where Charles Bronson and his wife, played by Ellen Burstyn, are asleep. Chaykin has a machine gun trained on them. They're also counting. There's a sick, tense pause. Schenkkan, who's still nominally in charge of this whole operation but isn't the one holding the machine gun, whispers to Chaykin, "*Shoot the goddamn thing!*"

But now it's clear what's happening, which is they're waiting for Keanu to shoot and he's waiting for them. Keanu is standing in Bronson's daughter's room, looking at the door and waiting for the sound of gunfire from the other bedroom. He looks back at Bronson's daughter's sleeping body with newfound resolve on his face and shoots her in the back of the head, once and then again. In the master bedroom Ellen Burstyn hears the shots and wakes up screaming. Now Chaykin starts firing but his machine gun jams and in the meantime Ellen Burstyn's screams have woken up Charles Bronson.

Keanu runs into the room still holding the pistol he shot Bronson's daughter with, sees his partner struggling with his jammed machine gun, and shoots Ellen Burstyn twice, efficiently—*one, two*—and she falls back, shuddering, dead. Bronson tries to roll out of bed and Keanu keeps firing and Chaykin finally gets his gun working and sprays Bronson and the bed with machine-gun fire and Bronson falls off the bed and onto the floor. His executioners stand there, breathing hard. The looks on their faces say that this wasn't as easy as they thought it was going to be.

And then up comes Bronson's arm, grabbing at the bedspread. He may be an old man in blue pajamas but he is still Charles motherfucking Bronson. Now we're looking up from Bronson's position and Keanu comes into frame, towering over the camera, a contemptuous look on his face. *This stubborn bastard—*

—and in this moment, whether he's conscious of it or not, Keanu—the actor, I mean, not the kid he's playing—is about to be the last person to join the elite fraternity of actors who've managed to kill Charles Bronson on-screen.

It's only happened a few times. In *4 For Texas* Charles Bronson tumbles into a riverboat's paddle wheel after being shot by Frank Sinatra. In *Guns for San Sebastian* he is stabbed to death by Anthony Quinn. He's shot by the police in *Citta Violenta* and poisoned by Jan-Michael Vincent in *The Mechanic*. And now Keanu Reeves is drawing down on him.

This is a moment of communion, a passing of the torch between two stars who have more than a little bit in common. In *Act of Vengeance* they don't exchange a single line of dialogue in their only scene together. They connect through violence, which is appropriate. Like Keanu, Bronson was often called "wooden" by his detractors. Like Keanu, many of his best performances were the ones that required him to say the least. Like Keanu, Bronson becomes famous anew in his fifties for playing a man who kills a lot of people as revenge for a personal tragedy no amount of collateral murder can reverse. His *John Wick* was *Death Wish*, in which Bronson plays a lily-livered liberal architect who takes up arms against the criminal underworld after home invaders murder his wife and rape his daughter. He's in between his third *Death Wish* movie and his fourth when he does *Act of Vengeance*, an atypical Bronson film in that his character—based on Joseph "Jock" Yablonski, a United Mine Workers labor leader who really was assassinated on orders from the corrupt head of his local, and was, like Bronson himself, a son of Pennsylvania coal country—never once resorts to violence.

"It's a complete departure," Charles Bronson will say to the *Washington Post* before the movie premieres. "I'm not wearing a mustache and I'm not wearing a gun."

I like to think this is Charles Bronson making a joke, but even if he was serious—I assume he *looked* very serious when he said it—I also think he was acknowledging something important about himself as an actor, and maybe about acting in general, which is that you have to know your range and find a way to explore inside it. Charles Bronson did a lot within what he undoubtedly knew to be his limits. He'd worked his way up, from black-and-white television to Italian Westerns ("He's whittling on a piece of wood," Jason Robards says of Bronson's character in Sergio Leone's *Once Upon a Time in the West*, speaking of wood. "I got a feeling that when he stops whittling, something's gonna happen.") and Franco-Italian crime thrillers in the sixties, finally becoming a star in American movies in the seventies, when he was pushing fifty.

One way in which Keanu is unlike Charles Bronson is that it doesn't take him anywhere near as long to work his way up. "I cast him as soon as I saw him," *Act of Vengeance* director John Mackenzie says of Keanu, years later. "The instant you put him on film, he burns up the celluloid. He's not consistent; I don't think he's a very good actor. But when he hits the moment, he's just got a God-given thing."

Mackenzie made one of the great British gangster films, *The Long Good Friday*; he knew a thing or two. In *Act of Vengeance* he pulls something out of Keanu—a capacity for coldness of heart, a bright wickedness—that Keanu won't display in any of his other work for years afterward, and you come away from *Act of Vengeance* wondering where it could have come from, and where it went—

—and then Keanu shoots Charles Bronson.

Bronson goes down again, but rises up, like Dracula from a crypt almost, a supernatural kind of movement, pure will pulling him up by a wire, the fire in his eyes now identifiable as the wrath of a Charles Bronson protagonist who's been pushed too far—and then Keanu shoots him again, this time in the head.

Keanu looks smug, then swallows like he's swallowing puke. He has murdered Charles Bronson in cold blood and now he's left with the consequences of what he's just done. He's made a world with a Charles Bronson–shaped hole in it and someone is going to have to fill it.

Nobody says anything for a while, and then Keanu says, "Let's go."

5 | "YOU RUN THIS ROTTEN, EVIL FOREST, AND YOU STOLE THOSE COOKIES TO DISCREDIT ME"

In her 1990 autobiography, *Little Girl Lost*, in a chapter called "More, More, More," Drew Barrymore writes about the four months she spent in Munich with Keanu, shooting *Babes in Toyland*, a made-for-TV movie that would air on December 19, 1986, the last of the six Keanu movies released in 1986.

The back cover of *Little Girl Lost* reads: "I Had My First Drink at Age Nine, Began Smoking Marijuana at Ten, and at Twelve Took up Cocaine." Barrymore will go to rehab for the first time at thirteen. She is eleven and has already started drinking and smoking cigarettes and getting stoned when she goes to Germany to make *Babes in Toyland*. But it's in Germany, she writes, "that I decided being loaded was a new life for me."

Just before principal photography begins, Barrymore meets up with Rod Stewart, "one of my favorite rockers," who's passing through the area on tour. "He offered me to ride to the stadium on his tour bus and hang out backstage," Barrymore writes. "I was in heaven. Afterward we rode back to the hotel on the bus, and Rod and his girlfriend, Kelly Emberg, a gorgeous fashion model, said good-night and went to their room. But I remained with the band, drinking all night long in one of their suites. We got crazy drunk, the whole lot of us, and someone took a video of everyone stumbling around the room, falling off the beds, downing the tiny bottles of liquor from the minibar."

Around four in the morning, still "obnoxiously, recklessly drunk," they march into the streets with drums and trumpets and make noise until hotel management intervenes. The next day, Rod invites her to ride with them to Vienna for the weekend. Drew's mother vetoes the plan.

By the midnineties Drew Barrymore, then in recovery, will reinvent herself in roles that leverage her fallen-child-star reputation. She'll play a teenager who seduces her best friend's father in the high school erotic thriller *Poison Ivy*, and so-called "Long Island Lolita" Amy Fisher in ABC's *The Amy Fisher Story*. She flaunts tattoos and poses nude for Bruce Weber. That hypersexualized image doesn't last. In adulthood, an upbeat, quirky positivity becomes her brand on-screen and off, a kind of reclaimed innocence. When she tells the Munich story in her second memoir, *Wildflower*—a sunny, boring corrective to the exploitatively juicy *Little Girl Lost*—she confesses to throwing other guests' laundry bags off a balcony into the river and frets about the karmic consequences; ever since that drunken German hotel night she keeps misplacing articles of clothing she likes.

All of this adds a layer of retroactive irony to Drew's role in *Babes in Toyland*, which is one of those Christmas movies where a kid who's been forced to grow up too fast by the modern world must rediscover their sense of wonder. Drew plays Lisa, from Cincinnati, the youngest daughter of a harried single mom. We can tell that some special childlike light has gone out inside Drew Barrymore because she watches the news and tells her older sister to put her shoes away and has to put on a brave face when her Christmas present turns out to be a sled instead of a new blender.

The first time we see Keanu he's wearing a Santa hat and carrying a child-size inner tube shaped like a swan. He works with Drew's sister at a toy store whose sneering money-hungry manager is played by Richard Mulligan. Drew shows up to warn her sister about an impending snowstorm and Keanu ends up driving them both home.

"Welcome to glorious Cincinnati," Keanu says, "queen of Ohio's Alpine ski resorts!"

They sing a song about Cincinnati and then there's an accident. Drew is thrown from the car and into a dream. She finds herself in a village of candy-colored houses. The extras strolling among them are in nursery-rhyme outfits or the kind of big-headed animal costumes you see on amusement-park characters—frogs, squirrels, monkeys, pigs, teddy bears. Many expenses have clearly been spared in its creation, but Munich-as-Toyland has a dusty, deadpan daylight creepiness that renders it more otherworldly than a less visibly cheap otherworld might be. The desired effect has not been achieved, but the specific way in which the production falls short of its intentions elevates it into the mystic. There is a kind of art that resources and competence would only flatten and this *Babes in Toyland* is that kind of art.

Toyland mirrors Drew's Cincinnati the way Oz did Kansas. Richard Mulligan is Jack's evil uncle Barnaby Barnacle. Barnaby is a hissing Gargamelian troll who lives in the haunted forest on the edge of town in a house shaped like a giant bowling ball. He intends to ruin Toyland's joy by any means necessary, especially after Drew's arrival disrupts and prevents his wedding to Mary Contrary, Drew's sister, who really loves Keanu's Jack B. Nimble, of candlestick-jumping fame, the rightful heir to the local cookie factory. As Barnaby, Mulligan goes for it like a camp counselor with a flashlight under his chin. He has alarmingly long fingernails and yellow teeth, and both his manner and his stubble suggest a man who rolled off a metal bunk in the drunk tank to be here today.

Keanu's Jack B. Nimble costume consists of short pants, a white puffy-sleeved shirt, a vest with peaked shoulders, and a pair of buckled shoes. He looks like a Paul Revere who rides around a Revolutionary War theme park shouting about deals on curly fries. He's called upon to simulate a range of emotional states in the course of the movie, including "happy," "determined," and "upset about being restrained by teddy-bear policemen." Keanu's performance brings to mind a big floppy-eared dog; it's like he's playing every line to the back row of a children's theater, and *Toyland* may be the only Keanu Reeves movie that would be no worse if it had been Scott Baio speaking strings of words like "You run this rotten, evil forest, and you stole those cookies to discredit me," instead of Keanu. And yet Keanu doesn't goof around with this text. He seems to have grasped another fundamental principle of movies and life, namely, *Don't act like you're too cool to be there if you're there.*

Eventually, long story, Richard Mulligan gets his hands on a flask full of pure evil distilled in liquid form. He traps Drew and Mary Contrary and Keanu in an underground cell and uncorks the flask. Tendrils of green smoke begin to reach for them.

"Don't breathe it," shouts Keanu. Everyone starts to cough and wheeze—everyone except Drew Barrymore.

"Don't give in to it! Fight it," Drew shouts.

The smoke fills the frame, clouding our view of the actors. Everyone except Drew begins to succumb to this conscious and deliberate pollution of their childlike spirit, snarling and contorting their bodies. Drew watches, unaffected but horrified. *Maybe Drew Barrymore is immune because she's from Cincinnati,* I said, out loud, to an empty room, while watching this movie for the first time, and at that moment Drew, on-screen, said, "It must be because I'm from Cincinnati!"

She starts singing the Cincinnati song, the one from before. She urges Keanu to sing along and he does, and everyone else in the cell joins in. At first they're singing the Cincinnati song in weird, choked troll voices, and then they're singing it in their own voices, and then they are themselves again, redeemed and restored by their love of Cincinnati.

Because this is a story about innocence it feels like a prophetic dream about the off-screen travails of Drew Barrymore, who in real life breathed the green smoke and became emblematic of early stardom's corrupting effects and then lived to tell about it. But the movie—or at least the scene with the cell and the vapor—seems like an eerie metaphor for Keanu's life, too. His incorruptibility despite long-term exposure to the vapors of money and fame will be crucial to his public persona in years to come. It's another thing directors see in him. Kathryn Bigelow will speak admiringly of his innocence when she talks about casting him in *Point Break*; Bernardo Bertolucci supposedly tells him he has an "impossible innocence" when he hires Keanu to play Siddhartha in *Little Buddha*. "From one side, he's very childlike and innocent like Cary Grant, and from the other side, he's so strong," *Speed* director Jan de Bont says in 1994.

By the time he enters middle age he will have weathered loss and disappointment, some if not all the evils of the world, but if it makes him more cynical he'll keep that to himself; instead, in the popular imagination, he'll become Sad Keanu, a public figure defined by his kindness despite great personal hardship and his sandwich-eating martyrdom to unnameable pain, whose refusal to put up a brave front is itself a kind of innocence. So what you're seeing in some inchoate way in *Babes in Toyland* is the beginning of our sense that Keanu is too good for this world, an impossible celebrity for an age of disappointment—although nobody really sees that at the time, because *Babes in Toyland* is a terrible movie.

"The missing ingredient is charm," the critic John J. O'Connor writes in the *New York Times*, the morning of the day *Toyland* airs on NBC. His review also marks the first time Keanu Reeves's name is mentioned in the paper of record: "Mr. Reeves, who in earlier television appearances this year was impressive as a young alcoholic ('Under the Influence') and a psychotic killer ('Act of Violence'[*sic*]), looks understandably embarrassed each time he is required to join in another dreary song." The experience of making it isn't a total wash, though—on the set in Munich, Keanu meets a woman who gets around on a Kawasaki Enduro motorcycle, and she teaches him how to ride.

6| YOUTH OF AMERICA

"My agents tell me this movie is going to do wonderful things for me," Keanu jokes to *USA Today* in May 1987, a week or so after *River's Edge* opens. "But I don't know. I did a very kicked-back performance. Some people think it's just boring. 'You didn't do anything, Keanu, you just stood around and smoked pot.'"

This is actually not a bad description of what Keanu does in *River's Edge*, a grim study of how the Visine-before-homeroom crowd at a rural California high school reacts when one of their friends murders another and the first movie to discover how cinematically rewarding it can be to watch Keanu stand around and smoke pot.

In *River's Edge* Keanu also drinks beer, and watches TV, and makes love under the stars with Ione Skye. Their sex scene unites two actors who'll go on to be crucial players in nineties pop culture. Skye—the daughter of the sixties folkadelic icon Donovan—had never been in a movie before this one. She'll soon secure her place in Gen X history by playing John Cusack's first love, Diane Court, in Cameron Crowe's *Say Anything*; she'll also turn up in *Wayne's World* as the Shakey's Pizza waitress who introduces Rob Lowe to Wayne and Garth's public-access show.

In real life Skye dates Anthony Kiedis of the Red Hot Chili Peppers before leaving him for Ad-Rock—Adam Horovitz—the Beastie Boys, who leaves Molly Ringwald to be with Skye, a chain of events that deserves to be unpacked as a ten-part historical miniseries someday. Horovitz and Skye are married in the early nineties; before they divorce in 1999, Q-Tip of A Tribe Called Quest immortalizes her on the Beastie Boys's "Get It Together" by rhyming her first name with "Chachi and Joanie." Keanu is destined for similar first-name-basis significance, but *River's Edge* is the first movie in which you can see why. His kicked-back performance as a high school burnout nagged by his conscience is still some of the best work he's ever done.

River's Edge plays at film festivals in 1986 and opens in theaters in 1987. Other films about teenagers from this same period—including *Pretty in Pink*, *Lucas*, *Ferris Bueller's Day Off*, and *Some Kind of Wonderful*—will launch the careers of actors such as Matthew Broderick and Winona Ryder and help shape lasting pop-cultural notions of what the eighties were like. But—notwithstanding John Hughes's occasional interest in class friction among high school kids—they're all pretty light films, filtered through adult nostalgia and invested in an upbeat notion of teenage life as fun and romantic.

If *River's Edge* is a teen movie, it's a teen movie the way 1979's teens-versus-cops classic *Over the Edge* and Penelope Spheeris's 1984 punk-house cult film *Suburbia* were teen movies, and it's set in a different eighties, shadowed by the fears of its moment. "We may be the generation that sees Armageddon," Ronald Reagan mused to the TV preacher Jim Bakker in 1980, during his first presidential campaign; everybody in *River's Edge* lives like that's a given. "The whole world's gonna blow up anyway," says the murderer, John Tollet, played by Daniel Roebuck. "Might as well keep my pride. You do shit, it's done, and then you die." *River's Edge* is like a depraved Family Crisis movie about the problem of teen nihilism; there are four Slayer songs on the soundtrack, alongside more punkish bands like the Wipers. When Kurt Cobain lists his top fifty albums of all time in a 1993 journal entry, only the Wipers will make the list three times. The Wipers song on the *River's Edge* soundtrack is an up-tempo rock song called "Let Me Know," but the ten-minute title track from their second album, *Youth of America*—a pitiless night wind of a song, deadpan and despairing—is the music that sounds the most like *River's Edge* feels.

When grunge comes along in a few years it'll sound like the *River's Edge* kids picking up instruments and learning another way to tell their secrets. It won't be long before models dressed like whimsical approximations of the kids in this movie are flouncing down runways for Marc Jacobs. *River's Edge* director Tim Hunter will go on to direct a few episodes of TV's *Twin Peaks*, which has echoes of *River's Edge* in it—it starts with another girl dead on the ground—but remains somehow a more hopeful vision of small-town life even though more of the show's local teens are doing sex work or involved in trafficking cocaine, which in the Twin Peaks universe comes from Canada.

In 1987, what *River's Edge* has to say about kids in America is received like a distress call from another world. But the story is based on true events that happened in the city of Milpitas, north of San Jose, in 1981. Marcy Conrad was fourteen, and Anthony Jacques Broussard was sixteen, and one day Broussard took Marcy Conrad to his father's house. They argued. Broussard raped Conrad, strangled her to death, and dumped her body in a ravine in the foothills east of town. The next day, when he told his friends what he'd done, they didn't believe him, so Broussard took them to the ravine and showed them the body. Soon other kids came to see it, too. This went on for two days. Finally two of the kids who'd been to see the body went to the police.

By the time Broussard pleaded guilty to first-degree murder in the attempted commission of a felony—rape—and was sentenced to twenty-five years to life in prison, he'd ceased to be the story. The story became about the kids who'd gone to see the body, and the kids who'd kept quiet about it.

"Youths Silent on Murder Victim Leaves a California Town Baffled," wrote the *New York Times*, in a story that doesn't quote one Milpitas high school kid until its thirty-first paragraph. Some Milpitas adults, the *Times* wrote, "blamed television, both its violence and what they saw as its inculcation of a sense of unreality, an inability to distinguish emotionally between a real act of violence and one on a flickering screen."

Only the *Washington Post* questioned the consensus, suggesting that for the kids involved, the problem was "not callousness, but fear and confusion. They were young people afraid of the police and without much guidance in how to balance loyalty and justice, how to confront an act of madness. One student who saw the body said he went home and stared at the ceiling all night."

At UCLA, a film student named Neal Jimenez reads the news stories about Marcy Conrad's murder and writes a screenplay about it.

"Most of the characters were based on people I had gone to high school with," Jimenez will say years later. "I thought it spoke to a mood that young people were feeling at the time—feeling detached from things and wanting to zone out."

When *River's Edge* comes out, the reviews are mostly positive, but even the critics who admire the film seem a little horrified by it. It's received as an indictment of a generation without morals or feelings, and it probably finds an audience for that reason—like Larry Clark's *Kids* a decade later, it shows empathy for a group of hard-partying teenage characters while depicting their seeming *lack* of empathy in a manner guaranteed to scandalize and excite art-house moviegoers. The posters for *River's Edge* pitch it as an exploitation movie—THE MOST CONTROVERSIAL FILM YOU WILL SEE THIS YEAR—and when it becomes a sleeper hit after opening in New York and Los Angeles, Island Pictures president Russell Schwartz suggests to the *New York Times* that it's finding an audience primed for "bleak chic" by recent movies such as *Blue Velvet* and *Angel Heart*.

But when asked about the movie's supposedly unfeeling characters in an interview a few years later, at least one cast member takes issue with the idea that the characters are unfeeling.

"God, that's not what it's about, man," Keanu says. "When I read the script, it wasn't robots I thought I was hearing. I heard pain and just so much emotion . . . People tend to make *River's Edge* sound like it is of the eighties, of the eighties disease and of the new youth. But

I think it's kind of timeless in terms of like the characters and their reaction to finding a dead friend on the ground . . . I don't think in the '50s Beaver would have run to the police and said, 'My best friend just killed someone—gee, Wally!'—you know, it wouldn't have happened that way."

River's Edge imagines the complicated reasons those kids had for taking part in the cover-up, and Keanu gives that Milpitas kid staring at the ceiling an authentically inarticulate voice. He's almost upstaged at first, though. As Lane, the manic right-wing punk who helps cover up the murder, Crispin Glover goes all the way over the top, punching syllables in that strange signature Crispin Glover cadence, audibly capitalizing entire words: "Do you think this car runs on GOD'S OWN METHANE?" Daniel Roebuck plays John, the killer, as a lumbering doomed Frankenstein. And Dennis Hopper is Dennis Hopper.

Hopper plays Feck, a twitchy older local who shares his pot stash with Glover. He's in it for the companionship; Lane, exploiting his loneliness, is in it for the weed. Hopper is there to add a sense of consequence for the characters that doesn't involve the police, along with an additional layer of suspense, tension, and weirdness. Especially weirdness—Hopper's love interest is an inflatable sex doll named Ellie, whose ear he whispers in and whose honor he defends. But Hopper, at the time an infamous near-casualty of the golden age of drug-taking, is also there to underline what the movie is saying more subtly through touches like Keanu's wardrobe—a tie-dye T-shirt under a denim vest with a skull and a peace sign on the back—that these kids' lives are what's left of the sixties, minus any sense of idealism.

Like a true hipster, Keanu dreams of moving to Portland. Another kid, Tony, has an even wilder idea: "We can just take all our parents' money," he says. "Take off. Discover America. Make like we're *Easy Rider* plus five."

Nobody in the scene seems to remember that the whole point of *Easy Rider*—it was on the poster—was that the protagonists went looking for America and couldn't find it anywhere. But nobody takes Tony seriously anyway, because for one thing, Glover's the only one with a car.

Ione Skye has a crush on her ex-hippie English teacher, whose name is Mr. Burkewaite, although when the kids say it, it sounds like "Berkeley." Burkewaite admits to his students that his peers "are executives now . . . everybody sold out," but insists that before that happened, "Fundamental changes were made—changes we now take for granted . . . We stopped a *war*, man"—and brags about "knocking a few pigs on their asses" at protests.

Some nerdy kid pipes up in objection to this last part. A rocker dude responds, "Oh, fuck off, Kevin—wasting pigs is radical, man." Nobody's really listening except Ione. Later when she tells Keanu she respects Burkewaite, he can't believe it: "You respect an *adult*?"

The only real legacy the sixties seems to have bequeathed society in *River's Edge* is that everybody gets high, including Keanu's mom and his little brother. Keanu's home is a space of chaos. Keanu's mother talks to his little brother like a sibling ("Why are you so *mean*?"), Keanu's stepfather is a disembodied, bellowing voice from the TV room. Keanu treats his stepfather like a guy who fucks his mom and eats her food: Keanu calls his stepfather a *motherfucker* and a *food-eater*. In *River's Edge* it's like the apocalypse has already happened on some symbolic level, vaporizing the bonds between people.

In *River's Edge* the dead girl's name is Jamie. She's played by Danyi Deats and she's already dead when the movie starts.

As in the Milpitas story, the kid who killed her takes his friends to see her body. He says he killed Deats because "she was talking shit." Glover takes the lead. He decides they need to cover up Deats's death. Something about that idea excites him: "It's like some fuckin' movie. . . . We've gotta test our loyalty against all odds. It's kind of exciting. I feel like Chuck Norris." When Roebuck hesitates, Glover chews him out for his lack of self-interest.

"It's people like you that are sending this country down the tubes," he says. "No sense of pride, no sense of loyalty, no sense of *nothing*, man. Why do you think there's so many welfare cases in this country? Why do you think Russia's gearing up to kick our asses, man?"

Keanu, grappling with the feeling that none of this is right, smokes dope at his house in front of his mom and his sister. Some old film noir flickers hazy on the living room TV. Keanu barely looks at it. TV is not to blame in this story—it's meaningless, its violence is weightless, it holds no sway. The kids can even anticipate the way the medium will trivialize their experiences: "Lane, Portrait of a Teenage Alcoholic," Ione says. "They could make a movie out of it."

Keanu leads the cops to the riverside to show them the body. Keanu is realistically teenage in his inability to articulate to the cops what he felt when he saw the body. His low affect makes visible the struggle to comprehend a horrible act whose only salient point is its total meaninglessness.

The movie is full of doll symbolism, starting with poor dehumanized Jamie, and Ellie the sex doll, who comes to a similarly bad end; when Keanu's little brother throws their younger sister's doll in the river, the sister makes a Popsicle-stick grave marker in the backyard and Keanu, empathetically, helps her get it to stand up. This ability to embody both slacker detachment and humane compassion is one of the things Keanu has to offer the movies, and *River's Edge* is the first movie to see that in him.

Ione and Keanu hook up, and for a few minutes of screen time the movie almost assumes the shape of a more traditional teen romance. They're the only two kids in town whose hearts still work and they manage to find love in a hopeless place. Their blossoming relationship is a flower sprouting from a Hellmouth.

She's the more experienced one, or at least that's how she talks. She teases Keanu—"Do you have to be drunk before you kiss a girl?" Keanu's lip quivers. She wants to go park and look at the stars. "We'll pick up a sixer on the way," she says. She's got plans for Keanu. An important thing about Keanu's gentle passivity as a romantic screen presence—here, and going forward—is that it hands an atypical amount of sexual agency to his female costars.

Keanu and Ione talk about their feelings, and their feelings about the feelings they know they're supposed to have about the girl who died. "I didn't even cry for her," Ione says to Keanu. "I cried when that guy in *Brian's Song* died!"

Ione says, "Sometimes I think it'd be a lot easier being dead."

"Aww, that's bullshit," Keanu says. "You couldn't get stoned anymore."

"I hear it's the same sensation," Skye says.

At Feck's house, Roebuck tells Hopper the real story about killing Deats and what it felt like to do it. As Keanu and Ione Skye make love in a sleeping bag on the grass, Hunter cuts back and forth between Roebuck's story—"I had total control of her," he says, admitting that he enjoyed it—and shots of Keanu on his back with Ione Skye on top.

This is only Keanu's sixth or seventh movie, depending on which projects you count as features, and yet a pattern is already developing. We're starting to see how he'll approach intimate moments like this one, how directors will use his sexuality on-screen, and how his atypical screen presence will scramble our expectations about how a leading man behaves.

The *River's Edge* scene is Keanu's second sex scene in a movie; the first one is with Olivia d'Abo in a movie called *Flying*. Released some places as *Dream to Believe*—and in others, once Keanu is more famous, as *Teenage Dream*, with Keanu's face as a dominant visual element in the VHS box art—it's really a movie about d'Abo's character, who suffers a knee injury in a car crash but refuses to give up her dream of becoming a gymnast, training in secret even after her alcoholic stepdad forbids it. Keanu is just the love interest—the goofy boyfriend whose feelings are hurt when d'Abo is too busy secretly doing gymnastics to give him her full attention. But once she finds the courage to stand up to her stepfather and her creepy boss, Keanu is right there supporting her in the big tournament scene, and afterward they make love for the first time—we know it's the first time because a sultry eighties song with lyrics about this being their first time plays on the soundtrack.

What's important about the sex scene in *Flying*, though, is that it's d'Abo who's shown undressing Keanu, taking the lead. She bends down into the frame to kiss *him*; symbolically she's the one taking *his* virginity. This makes sense in *Flying,* because d'Abo is the main character, and the movie is about her taking back control of her life, and making the decision to go all the way with Keanu is part of how that happens. And to an extent the *River's Edge* scene works the same way—Keanu's supposed to be the last kid in town with any innocence to lose, and the movie underlines that by showing us Ione taking the lead with him. The main point of the scene is the juxtaposition between Roebuck's ghoulish narration of his crime and the shots of Keanu and Ione making love; we're supposed to understand that Deats's murder and the kids' after-the-fact complicity in it have tainted everything, even this brief interlude of teenage abandon.

What's interesting about both these scenes in historical context, though, is that they're indicative of what Keanu's sexual persona is going to be like going forward, at least on-screen. Has any leading man so frequently been made love *to* in movies? He is made love to in *Feeling Minnesota* by Cameron Diaz (she pulls Keanu into the bathroom at the reception for her wedding to Vincent D'Onofrio; they do it on the floor, awkwardly) and by Charlize Theron in *Sweet November* (but only after he stops trying to take charge, lets her set the pace, and lets himself be vulnerable). In the pilot episode of Jay Mohr's 1999 movie-business satire *Action*, he plays himself, a Keanu Reeves who's surprised—not unpleasantly—when Mohr's date, played by Illeana Douglas, starts jerking him off during a movie premiere. And no actor has ever received so many involuntary blow jobs—from the vampire brides in *Bram Stoker's Dracula,* from the sex worker in *Generation Um...,* from two predatory millennials in Eli Roth's *Knock Knock.* The fact that he's so often depicted as the passive party in these exchanges will be a part of his appeal as a movie star and also part of why he remains an enigma even after becoming one; it puts anyone turned on by him in a position to imagine *taking* him as opposed to *being* taken.

This is an atypical way for a leading man to present on-screen; it's another way in which Keanu seems like the leading man of the future, unburdened by traditional alpha-male hang-ups and even by gender norms. In *The Matrix Reloaded,* there's an infamous sequence that cuts back and forth between shots of Earth's last remaining humans dancing at an extremely horny-seeming cavern rave in the underground city of Zion and a more private, intimate sexual encounter between Keanu's Neo and Carrie-Anne Moss's Trinity. Straight dudes love to goof on this part of the movie, but over time, as more gay and trans voices have entered the conversation around the *Matrix* sequels, the reputation of that moment has changed—particularly the shots of Keanu and Moss together, which visually resemble a love scene between two women even though one of the actors happens to be male.

In real life, after they film their love scene together, Keanu and Ione Skye go to IHOP for breakfast.

In *River's Edge*, by the time he slips away with Ione, Keanu has already gone to the cops and shown them where the body is. But when they grill him back at the station house he can't explain himself to them. A police detective with an open shirt and a receding hairline and an incongruous East Coast tough-guy edge gives him a hard time: "So you're standing there staring at your dead friend like it's all some kind of big joke, right? Some adventure. What the hell was going on in your head, Matt? Huh? Exactly what? What were you thinking about?"

Keanu doesn't have an answer. The police detective is looking for some kind of emotional response Keanu can't provide, and Keanu resents it, being asked for this proof of his humanity, because doesn't the fact that he's there prove that? Suddenly he's not giving a kicked-back performance anymore; before he jumps up and shouts at the detective and tries to leave, he's performing the refusal to give a performance, and his inarticulation is a kind of truth.

The detective makes him sit back down.

"Talk some more," he says to Keanu. "I find you very interesting."

Something similar will happen for Keanu himself after *River's Edge*. People will look to him to understand something about a certain kind of modern young person. *River's Edge* is prescient about more than just grunge fashion; in their disaffection and their simultaneous rejection of both sixties nostalgia and eighties conservatism, these kids are some of the first identifiably Generation X people put on film.

River's Edge seems to both capture a sensibility and call it into being, a full four years before the author Douglas Coupland's first novel gives their cohort a name.

Like Chris Cornell, David Cross, Michelle Obama, Jeff Bezos, Marisa Tomei, Nicolas Cage, Boris Johnson, and Lenny Kravitz, Keanu was born in 1964, which is technically the very end of the Baby Boom. From an actuarial standpoint, someone like Winona Ryder (b. 1971) is a more solid example of a Generation X actor. But generations are weird and slippery and subject to associative drift—it's hard not to think of Douglas Coupland as a Gen X novelist even though he was born in 1961, and it's hard not to think of Barack Obama as the first Gen X president even though he was born the same year as Coupland, and it's hard to think of Keanu as being more of a generational peer to Bill Clinton than to Winona Ryder. The theme of conflict with the sixties that runs through *River's Edge* is a paradigmatic Gen X thing—Boomers, after all, focused their wrath on lazy Gen Xers before they had millennials to kick around. Eventually Keanu will make some of the most Gen X career moves possible, including starting a proudly amateurish rock band that plays scruffily punkish music of no great ambition but accepts a major-label recording contract proffered by an industry desperate to reach a youth market they can't be bothered to understand—a transparently in-bad-faith deal all around. The traps he falls into are identifiably Gen X traps.

In 1987, the same year *River's Edge* comes out, an MTV station-identification spot casts Keanu even more explicitly as a generational representative. He's not identified as Keanu Reeves; this was before his name would have meant anything to most people. He plays a guy looking at the camera, holding a remote control, who proceeds to tell you a story in a disorganized and confusing way.

"The other day Arlene and I," he says, "we were driving up past the pancake house?"

He clicks the remote at the camera, there's a burst of static, and there's a cut to a different angle on him. "Her mother wanted her to deposit something at the bank, which I really can't stand, because"—more static, cut to Keanu behind the wheel of a large automobile, with Arlene, presumably—"you pull up, and this big, like, metal door, like, *lurches* out at you."

Click—he shows you the pancake house, and then—*click*—where it is in relation to the bank. Angle on Keanu, looking at Arlene/the camera, saying, "You wanna get something to eat?" He rewinds, shows us the barbecue they were at before the bank. "Things got pretty wild, and Benny, he, uh, started throwing things."

Click, static, back in the car, Keanu looking at Arlene/the camera again, saying, "You wanna get something to eat?" Arlene, she just looks at him. "I mean for all you know," he says, suddenly serious, "that teller may not even be human." Then—static, cut—it's night. Keanu's driving, rock music playing quiet in his memory.

"I look out the window," he says, "and they've, like, in the middle of the night they've repainted all the stripes on the road." The camera drifts off him and looks at the white lines of the highway as they flow by.

Cut back to Keanu, same shot as the opening shot, standing there looking at the camera. "And I'm like, I live in a town with one pancake house and two banks. And what the hell kind of place is that?" Keanu points the remote at the screen again, like *we're* TV and he's turning *us* off.

Cut to his thumb on the remote-control power button—which turns out to have the MTV logo on it, except upside down, and you'd have to be a total geriatric to see this (the logo's upside-downness) as anything but fantastic from a branding perspective, because one of the things being advertised in this spot, with its scrambled approach to mise-en-scène and narrative form, is the nontraditional nature of MTV as an information-delivery system, and even if Keanu isn't articulating that in any concrete way, he's playing a character who *assumes* he's making sense, in whose head all this skipping around seems as straightforward as A to B to C, and of course, in this sense this ad is dealing from the top and bottom of the deck, selling an idea of youthful irreverence to actual young people while also signaling to the kind of old people who buy basic-cable advertising that MTV has an at-this-point-in-history unique power to lull young consumers into hyper-receptivity to advertising by bracketing that advertising with content that speaks to them in an approximation of their own paddle-balling brain-voice, and the way Keanu tells his pancake-house story in this ad is supposed to make him seem like someone whose way of processing information is, like the patterns of visual interruption in a music video, somehow new and different and unprecedented, a kind of *cognitive foreignness* that Keanu is about to become the leading cultural avatar for—and then the announcer comes on and says:

"MTV—

Finally, a channel for the way *you* think."

7 | CRASH DUMMY

"I'm having too much fun, Lauren. This trip through space and time will be over on its own soon enough."

—KEANU REEVES AS CHRIS IN *PERMANENT RECORD* (1988)

"The seminal roles for him were *Dangerous Liaisons* and *Parenthood*," Keanu's then-manager Erwin Stoff would say years later of the work Keanu does after *River's Edge*, as the eighties give way to the nineties. "He purposely did not take starring roles that conflicted with those movies because he and I really felt the future was going to be defined by directors like Stephen Frears and Ron Howard, actors like Michelle Pfeiffer, Swoosie Kurtz, and John Malkovich. The whole idea at that point was not to keep starring in teen movies. I wanted him to have a real career."

Liaisons and *Parenthood* are unlike most of what he'd done before, but also unlike most of what he'd go on to do. His future would not really be defined by Ron Howard. In both movies, the main characters are adults who look at Keanu the way the movies looked at him around this time, as a useful idiot or a lovable one; these parts are just a bridge to something else.

In the meantime the teen movies trickle, bracketing the more grown-up parts. *The Night Before* is a kind of *Tiger Beat* version of *After Hours* set in downtown LA, with Keanu as a nerd who accidentally sells his uptight prom date to a pimp during a wild night he wakes up from and struggles to reconstruct. Keanu is at least charming in it, and authentically Keanuesque in flashes. Early on, when they've missed their exit and are clearly nowhere near the prom, Lori Loughlin says, "We're totally lost," and Keanu, beatifically unconcerned, answers, "Sooner or later we'll come to the ocean," and keeps on driving west.

Permanent Record, from 1988, is about a teenager named David, and the people David leaves behind when he dies by suicide, including Keanu. But first Keanu sneaks into a recording studio with David, played by Alan Boyce, and there in the recording studio is Lou Reed.

The year after *Permanent Record* comes out Lou Reed will sign to Sire Records and release a comeback album called *New York*, which will be literate and angry and focused and more than a little strident and will give anyone invested in a notion of Lou Reed as an artist of inexhaustible vitality an excuse to sweep years of wobbly Lou Reed product under the rug.

This is before *New York* happens, though, so by asking us to believe two cool high school kids in 1988 would sneak into a recording studio just to catch a glimpse of mid- to late-eighties Lou Reed at work, *Permanent Record* would seem to be asking a lot.

But one thing that's hard to explain to anyone who became conscious after the early nineties—and especially after the late-nineties dawn of the commercial internet—is the extent to which kids of the eighties lived, pop-culturally speaking, like squatters in the ruined castles of the sixties and seventies, forging a value system out of received wisdom and garbled myth and overly effusive *Rolling Stone* reviews of new albums by golden-age rock stars, a category that by the eighties had stretched to include Lou Reed.

The best scene in *Permanent Record* that does not involve Lou Reed is the long unbroken shot at the very beginning of the film, of a large group of high school kids hanging out by their parked cars on a bluff by the ocean in the morning. They're smoking cigarettes, listening to boom boxes, leaning on each other's truck beds. Their clothes nail the movie to the eighties but the cars suggest a never-ending seventies—old Volkswagen Beetles, a Honda from '74, a Toyota from '76.

The camera makes its way to the edge of the bluff, lingers on a girl doing her homework on a rock, pauses to look at the gray sea, then turns back, to watch the kids all getting into their cars and driving off to school. The bluff is where David will kill himself later in the movie but in this moment before we know that, the unhurried attention the scene pays to these kids doing nothing feels almost anthropological. There's also a little bit of *River's Edge* in these shots, images of a teen world functioning on its own terms with little or no adult supervision. The rest of the movie never recaptures the feeling of this passage, the sense of a story unfolding at its own pace, as opposed to one that's being staged for us, so we can learn something.

Keanu's next movie, *The Prince of Pennsylvania,* makes a little over three thousand dollars during its opening weekend in 1988; its undernourished kidnapping-plot story line takes forever to get going and the characters droop under the weight of their quirks. But it also contains probably the best eighties Keanu performance that isn't *River's Edge*, and like that movie it captures its time by zeroing in on young people stranded as much in history as by geography.

We're in coal country again, all junkyards and gray skies—the town is never named, but writer-director Ron Nyswaner is from Clarksville, where Jock Yablonski from *Act of Vengeance* died. A few years after *The Prince of Pennsylvania*, Nyswaner will write the screenplay for Jonathan Demme's *Philadelphia*, one of the first mainstream films to grapple with the AIDS crisis, and publish a memoir about the "sissy-boy-from-coal-mining-Pennsylvania shame" he carried with him from his teen years into an adulthood marred by addiction.

The Prince of Pennsylvania feels like it's telling half of Nyswaner's own story; by making the protagonist a straight nonconformist it circles truths it can't quite name. Keanu's character, Rupert Marshetta, even has a gender-nonconforming haircut, long on one side and shaved on the other. But in this story it's not a statement, just a provocation, inspired by some local biker-punk types Keanu's befriended.

Whatever's going on with Rupert's masculinity gets channeled into a series of clashes with Fred Ward, his Vietnam-vet coal-miner father, who doesn't know what to do with him.

As in *My Own Private Idaho,* Keanu plays a prince who rebukes the king. He kidnaps and ransoms his own father to give Bedelia a reason to sell a plot of land that Ward owns; he tells his older lover, Amy Madigan, that what he's doing is a revolution and she can get on board or not. But it doesn't work. After Keanu kidnaps Ward they find out he's already sold the land without telling anybody.

Once again the past can give Keanu nothing—Ward is no example to live by—and the present isn't much better. The school dance reproduces the capitalist ideology of the moment, like it always does. "You can't come in unless you're dressed from *Dallas* or *Dynasty,*" says the student at the door. Keanu crashes the place with his punk friends in their Mohawks and leather. Among the papier-mâché cacti and cardboard oil rigs festooned with Texas flags he dances with a girl he knows.

"We offend common rabble with our truth," Keanu tells her. "We *are* the truth."

"I don't want to dance anymore," she says. "You got my dress all yucky."

"Well, yuckiness *is* truth," Keanu says.

She fumes: "Can't you be normal for *three minutes*?"

In the spring of 1989 Keanu is on TV again, in an *American Playhouse* production of Richard Greenberg's *Life Under Water,* about white people in the Hamptons and the clever, acrid bon mots they trade. He's haughty and lonely in it, a pampered prince of the North Shore, and Sarah Jessica Parker is this girl he meets on the beach, who he can't believe isn't into him.

"I don't trust you any further than I can throw you," she says.

"You should," he replies. "I only tell nice lies."

"Like most intellectuals, he's intensely stupid," says John Malkovich's Valmont, in Stephen Frears's 1988 period piece *Dangerous Liaisons,* regarding the Chevalier Danceny, played by Keanu Reeves. In *Dangerous Liaisons,* it's the eighteenth century and no woman in Paris can resist John Malkovich, even though John Malkovich looks like Tommy Wiseau from *The Room*; Keanu's Chevalier is a "tragically penniless" commoner, a music teacher and a good-hearted dweeb. Jilted by her lover the Comte de Bastide, Glenn Close convinces Swoosie Kurtz to hire Keanu to tutor the Comte's new fiancée, Uma Thurman, hoping Keanu will deflower her before the Comte can. When that doesn't happen, Malkovich steps in to take care of things himself.

The movie has two ingenues in it—Thurman, only nineteen here, and Keanu, who's utterly unconvincing as a person from eighteenth-century France and (either in spite of that or because of it) is funny in this movie in ways he doesn't get credit for. Frears does give him one of the best on-screen introductions in Keanu history—at the opera, as the fancy Parisians in the audience survey the crowd through their spyglasses, the camera mimics their movements, scans left to right from the stage up into the luxury boxes, and as an aria reaches its crescendo it finds Keanu, just as a preposterous tear rolls down his face.

Years later a reporter will suggest that he seemed uncomfortable in the part, and with noncontemporary characters in general, and after a long pause he'll say, "Yeah, well—on *Dangerous Liaisons*, for example, they only gave me my shoes on the first day of shooting. I guess that's symbolic of the whole thing."

Twenty years after its release in 1989, Ron Howard's *Parenthood* will become the basis for a television series, but with its reassuringly dovetailed A-and-B-plot construction the movie already feels like TV. Keanu is Tod, who marries into Martha Plimpton's family, to mom Dianne Wiest's consternation—she calls him "that Tod," like a bad dog. He and Plimpton give each other skater undercuts in Wiest's bathroom, and at some point they fight and he calls her a bitch and they break up, but we don't see the fight, we only hear about it later, so Keanu remains technically innocent of having called Martha Plimpton a bitch in front of us.

He wears Wiest down and her family opens up to let him in. He's the only one who can penetrate the bubble of shame and anger that surrounds Joaquin Phoenix as Plimpton's brother, who's been wanking himself into a state of emotional distress that now looks prophetically Joaquin Phoenix-esque. If this *Parenthood* were a TV show, Keanu would be its charmed-doofus Fonzie, dispensing useful-idiot wisdom before wrecking the hot rod he refuses to give up.

"Can you do that again next week?" asks the guy at the drag strip. "The crowd loved it."

"Sure," Keanu says. "That's a good job for me. Crash dummy."

But by the time *Life Under Water* airs and *Parenthood* opens in theaters, the defining Keanu movie—of 1989, and of the next few years—has already been released.

The seed for *Bill & Ted's Excellent Adventure* is planted in 1983, in an improv class in Los Angeles, when Chris Matheson and Ed Solomon are given the prompt "Fifteen-year-old boys talk about world affairs." They begin naming zones of armed conflict and categorizing them as "bogus." The characters later become Bill and Ted; the idea becomes a screenplay, "Bill & Ted's Time Van," by Matheson and Solomon.

By the time the script sells, the time van has been replaced by a phone booth, so it won't seem like they're ripping off the time-traveling car from *Back to the Future,* which comes out in 1985. In due course a casting director summons all the young dudes to read for the parts of Bill and Ted. During the audition process Keanu hits it off with Alex Winter, a former child actor who shares his interest in books and motorcycles and the bass guitar.

Decades later the *Daily Mail* gets its hands on some tapes from the casting process. Keanu is mostly reading Bill and Winter's playing Ted, but even with their eventual roles reversed they already have a dynamic—when they're supposed to make each other laugh at some dumb joke, they actually laugh. When Winter's supposed to act delighted as Keanu does a little tap dance to "If I Only Had a Heart" while pretending to be wearing a heavy suit of armor, he actually seems delighted. They're utterly believable as two guys with joint custody of half a brain.

But the real revelation from the casting tapes is the footage of Winter and Reeves reading with other people. When Keanu reads with actors Gary Riley (best known as one of the hoods who discovers the dead body in *Stand by Me*) and *Teen Wolf*'s Matt Adler, there are no sparks. And Winter seems even more adrift playing Ted opposite a spike-haired Pauly Shore, who delivers every line straight to the camera like a teenager doing a show for his bedroom mirror, displaying the same endless self-amusement that will soon make the Wiez a brief but intolerable pop-cultural sensation as a VJ on MTV.

Once Keanu and Winter's obvious chemistry gets them hired, they make the in-retrospect crucial decision to play Bill and Ted—San Dimas high school knuckleheads, underachieving history scholars, and aspiring metal gods—as innocents without a mean bone. They're versions of *Fast Times at Ridgemont High*'s Jeff Spicoli minus the implied aroma of pot smoke and the aggressive ("You *dick!*") part of Spicoli that is identifiably Sean Penn's own prickliness poking through the character's skin. And unlike their most obvious successors, Mike Myers and Dana Carvey's Wayne and Garth, they aren't horny, either. Bill and Ted appreciate "babes" but they do not *schwing*. They are a child's idea of burnout dude-dom.

"The thing we'd discussed with each other going in, and then confirmed with the writers," Alex Winter will say in 2019, "was that these guys have never taken drugs. They're really virginal and they're really naive. So we didn't play them like stoner slackers—we played them like nine-year-olds. They get disappointed and then they get happy again and they get disappointed and they get happy again—it's a very childlike way of approaching the world."

The movie's plot is even dumber than its leads are supposed to be. Bill and Ted, from the SoCal suburb of San Dimas, play heavy metal music very poorly in a band called Wyld Stallyns. Ted's father, the local police chief, has vowed to send Ted to military school in Alaska if he can't pass his history final.

What nobody knows is that Wyld Stallyns are destined to become the most important band in human history. Sometime in the future, their music will usher in an age of galactic peace and prosperity, but none of that will happen if they part ways here—so humanity's supreme leaders send George Carlin back in time to help

Bill and Ted by loaning them a time machine so they can collect actual historical figures like Lincoln, Socrates, Genghis Khan, and Billy the Kid and bring them to present-day San Dimas, where the Mongol emperor lays waste to a mall sporting-goods store, Napoleon acts out at a water park, and Sigmund Freud ponders the shape of a corn dog.

The first *Bill & Ted's* is not a smart comedy. It's not even a smart *dumb* comedy. Winter and Keanu carry the whole thing on catchphrases and charisma. But there's a fundamentally hopeful message at the bottom of this cinematic Circle K nacho-basket—that it's okay if you're not yet the thing you're supposed to become, and you have all the time in the world to become it, even if you have no clue how to get there.

Shot in 1987—when Winter first meets Keanu, *River's Edge* hasn't even been released yet—the movie becomes one of many assets caught up in the bankruptcy of the producer Dino De Laurentiis's company, De Laurentiis Entertainment Group. It sits on the shelf until 1989 and is about to go straight to cable when it's acquired, by Nelson Entertainment, for the fire-sale price of $1 million; in order to release it, the studio has to loop a few lines of dialogue, because 1988 is no longer "the present." When the movie is released theatrically in April 1989, the reviews are most heinous. In a three-paragraph dismissal buried on page C12 of the *New York Times*, Vincent Canby calls it a "painfully inept comedy." The *Washington Post* writes, "More than anything, the picture looks paltry and undernourished. Even the warts on Lincoln's face look slapped on." In the *Los Angeles Times*, future Keanu interview-meltdown witness Chris Willman accuses the movie of "unabashed glorification of dumbness for dumbness' sake," referring to the characters as "inconsistent ciphers" and second-rate Spicoli clones.

"Some of it is okay, but I found Joan of Arc doing aerobics excruciating to watch," Ed Solomon tells *Cinefantastique* years later. "Our idea was to put Lincoln and Freud in a room together and have them play foosball, as opposed to the continuing pressure, which was, 'Lincoln should give a speech like his Gettysburg Address.' We always tried to do the weirder, less obvious choice."

Excellent Adventure goes on to make $40 million anyway, and Ted "Theodore" Logan becomes Keanu's first iconic character. For a long while after this every new Keanu performance will be evaluated on how Ted-like or not Ted-like he seems. When reporters meet him in a promotional capacity they will show up expecting Ted. Many of those same reporters will also write about Ted as something he has to live down or work off, an albatross like Mork or Opie or "Fight for Your Right to Party."

But Keanu started out as a bohemian Toronto theater kid; he probably would have said yes to Gus Van Sant and Francis Ford Coppola and Bernardo Bertolucci even without a highly quotable dumb-guy part to efface from his résumé.

It's possible the legacy of Ted frees Keanu of any obligation to serve up profundity when he does interviews, a part of the job he's turning out to be not super great at. But when you read a lot of the press he does after *Bill & Ted's*, he doesn't seem like he's hiding behind a happy-go-lucky persona. He's often struggling to be understood, or at least to come off as articulate, and when he gets frustrated, or acts weird, or clams up, or goes for a furious walk around the room, it's usually not because his interlocutor's line of inquiry has veered too far into the personal. It's usually because he's started hearing himself talk and is convinced that he sounds stupid. It's the self-consciousness of a smart kid who never got great at playing the game of school.

PART TWO
BOGUS JOURNEYS

8| NONTHREATENING BOYS

1991 ends up being Keanu's breakthrough year. He stars in three great movies, each of which is about two guys on a bogus journey, each of which overturns preexisting ideas about Keanu and his range while also slyly undercutting old notions of on-screen masculinity. It's one of the best movie years an actor has ever had; it's also the moment where he becomes a cultural icon independent of any individual movie, a pop star and an artist's muse and an artist in his own right all at once. In August he appears with Alex Winter on the cover of *Sassy* and in September he and River Phoenix are on the cover of *Film Comment*, a level of newsstand omnipresence that says something about the range of people he's now of interest to.

But before the first of his '91 films hits theaters, he's all over MTV in something that isn't a movie but looks exactly like one. The video for Paula Abdul's "Rush Rush" is the closest Keanu ever comes to being a pure teen idol—a painstaking re-creation of Nicholas Ray's 1955 teen drama *Rebel Without a Cause*, with Keanu playing James Dean to Abdul's Natalie Wood. It's an odd casting decision and even Keanu knows it. "Another regurgitation of icons and culture by the American media," he joked about the video in an interview that same year. "And I'm your guy, I guess, for that right now." Pop culture processes disruptive presences through reductive analogy, like Jean Cocteau said: "People love to recognize, not venture. The former is so much more comfortable and self-flattering."

James Dean died in 1955, at twenty-four, about a month before *Rebel* opened in theaters, two years before *On the Road* and Elvis's first single, and his ghost has haunted young male actors' press clippings ever since. If you are a Method dude and a bit of a feral creature, if your vibe is *poète maudit*, if you have trashed your trailer, if you are a person of coyly ambiguous sexual preference or someone who people enjoy imagining as such, if you wear smart-guy glasses to read surprisingly weighty books, if you're prone to losing sight of the line between performance and reality or are determined to blur and shatter that line, if you tell interviewers you want to eat and breathe and shit art—you get to be referred to as the next Next James Dean for at least half a year. It helps if you can actually act, but it's not required.

Keanu is known for pulling up to interviews toting a motorcycle helmet and struggling to articulate his responses to softball questions, so he seems to fit the New Dean profile, if you squint. But by invoking regurgitation, he indicates a grasp of the cyclical nature of these things. Dean was an actor whose raw energy sometimes felt too big for movies to contain; the way he bounces off the walls in *Rebel Without a Cause*, sometimes almost literally, represented a violent break with screen-acting tradition. His example inspired generations of iconoclasts, from Bob Dylan (who based the cover of 1963's *The Freewheelin' Bob Dylan* on an old photo of Dean in New York City) to Morrissey (who wrote an obsessive fan-bio about Dean in the seventies, put a picture of the actor on the cover of the Smiths' "Bigmouth Strikes Again" single, and pretends to weep at his grave in the video for "Suedehead"). Frank O'Hara wrote tributes to him, and so did Taylor Swift. But Dean also became the subject of Hollywood Boulevard souvenir-shop nostalgia and deceased-Boomer-icon mythology, available as a key chain or a T-shirt wherever fake Academy Awards statues are sold. And pop entertainment traded on his absence by conjuring a series of Deanesque troublemakers who could be more easily reconciled with a calm cultural mainstream.

You could argue that this process starts in the seventies 1950s of *Happy Days*, with Henry Winkler's greaser mascot Arthur Fonzarelli, who becomes a quasi-paternal figure and eventually a high school teacher over the series' long run. In 1991, it's happening on *Beverly Hills 90210*, a hit Fox TV series whose conceit—fresh-faced Minnesota kids acclimating to the fast life at a high school in California's toniest zip code—lets it thread the needle between nineties edge and eighties family-drama values.

In the first season Shannen Doherty's Brenda Walsh flummoxes her conservative Minnesotan parents by falling for Dean ringer Luke Perry's Dylan McKay, a prototypical complicated-bad-boy figure who keeps a copy of Byron's *Collected Works* in his '64 Porsche. Dylan starts out as a brooding outsider, but it's Doherty who ends up leaving the show and Perry who sticks around. Brenda's mother and father parent Dylan instead; over the years as he struggles with addiction and feuds with the Mafia his TV family keeps taking him back. In 2017, two years before Perry's death at age fifty-two, he'll turn down the chance to play Dylan again in Fox's *90210* revival, but he does play Archie Andrews's father in nearly fifty episodes of the campy teen series *Riverdale*, whose adult cast is knowingly stuffed with other culturally significant formerly young actors, including Skeet Ulrich and Molly Ringwald.

In *90210*'s penultimate Season 1 episode, sixteen-year-old Brenda has premarital sex with Dylan, a plot turn that so outraged local Fox affiliates that the show's writers quickly cooked up a pregnancy-scare episode to show Brenda's decision as having had consequences. Paula Abdul's "Rush Rush" is released as a single the same day this episode airs. A character like Dylan is one way of trading on the Dean archetype's rebellious resonance while soft-pedaling the challenge Dean and his characters posed to everyday life, and in the video for "Rush Rush," Keanu Reeves is another.

"Rush Rush," the first single off Abdul's second LP, *Spellbound*, is a sweeping ballad—Abdul calling to a dream lover as drum machines tick along at prom-night spotlight-dance tempo. In the videos she'd made to promote her debut album, *Straight Up*, Abdul had cultivated an overtly sexual image—"Cold Hearted," directed by David Fincher, repurposed the sultry "Take Off with Us" number from Bob Fosse's *All That Jazz*—so the gentleness of "Rush Rush" is positional, a pivot to sweetness. It goes on to become the longest-running number one single since Madonna's "Like a Virgin," logging five weeks at the top of the Hot 100.

The "Rush Rush" video was directed by Stefan Würnitzer, previously best known for En Vogue's "Giving Him Something He Can Feel." The imagery has that soft-edged early-nineties music video look, the same creamy translucence as David Fincher's videos for Madonna's "Express Yourself" or Aerosmith's "Janie's Got a Gun," a kind of light synonymous with functionally limitless record-company promo budgets. Like those videos, "Rush Rush" is meant to remind you of movies, but in this case it's meant to remind you of a specific movie. Keanu and Abdul reenact all the big beats from *Rebel Without a Cause*—the drag race, Griffith Observatory, the dark empty mansion, Dean holding a milk bottle to his face to cool his teenage rage, which as it turns out is a move no one else but James Dean can pull off, not even Keanu Reeves. Keanu copies other, smaller beats, like the way Dean walks with his hands in his pockets when he runs into Natalie Wood on the way to their first day of school, and there's even a restaging of the moment when the one guy in the car with the weird hat gives James Dean nonsensical directions to his new school, pointing at the sky and going "That way."

Even if you know *Rebel Without a Cause* you may not remember the guy in the car with the weird hat, and many young pop fans watching MTV in 1991 probably didn't know the movie at all, so the care Würnitzer takes in re-creating the source material is odd; the video has a parody's attention to detail, minus the jokes. At the same time it leaves out a lot of the things that made the movie what it was. There are none of the Oedipal overtones of the original, which Nicholas Ray allegedly conceived of after catching his son in bed with Gloria Grahame, Ray's second wife. There's no Sal Mineo character in the Paula Abdul version of *Rebel*, so there's no homage paid to the sequence where Wood and Dean and Sal Mineo's Plato—who's in love with Dean's character—hide out together in the old mansion, briefly becoming a surrogate family that's also a love triangle, dreaming in the dark that they can remake adulthood, until they're forced to confront that fantasy's unsustainability in the hard light of real life.

But the real problem is that Keanu just seems too *nice* to play Dean's iconically tortured Jim Stark. He lets his hair hang down in his face in a way that presents as rebellious in the context of the video's very nineties 1950s, but at no point does he seem like he presents any danger to Abdul or himself. In the opening credits of *Rebel*, Dean sinks to his belly in the gutter to examine a wind-up monkey, then makes a little bed for the monkey out of trash, as if the monkey represents every part of him that the cold adult world can't or won't nurture. In the "Rush Rush" video's version of the monkey-in-the-gutter scene, Keanu looks at the monkey like he's thinking, *Wow, what a great monkey*.

So he's a James Dean who'd fit right into the pages of Lisa Simpson's favorite teen magazine *Non-Threatening Boys*. Many other young actors of this moment might have done a better job channeling the hurt and anger Dean once brought to this role. The most obvious candidate is River Phoenix, Keanu's costar in *I Love You to Death* and *My Own Private Idaho*, who'll eventually go down as his generation's James Dean by dying young and leaving the question of his future potential unanswered.

Of course when an interviewer asked him about Dean in 1991, Phoenix said he'd never seen a Dean film, and suggested that Brad Pitt—then a newcomer who'd just given his breakthrough performance as the hitchhiker in *Thelma & Louise*—seemed to better fit the bill. The "Rush Rush" video couldn't have abided Phoenix's rubbed-raw screen presence, anyway. The movie was about establishing the social outsider as tragic hero; the video needed an actor who could soften that figure's sharp edges, converting tragedy back into fantasy. At the beginning of 1991, Keanu was at least briefly the man for the job—already enough of a star to step into the outline of a legend and fill it somewhat credibly, wise enough to immediately shrug it off.

FBI

9| DICK AND RONNIE KNOW THEIR JOBS (THE BOY LOOKED AT JOHNNY)

The Yugoslavian filmmaker Zoran Popović's film *Struggle in New York* documents performances staged in 1976 by members and former members of the New York chapter of Art & Language, a conceptual-art collective from the UK. In one segment of the movie, the musician Mayo Thompson, founder of the band the Red Krayola, stands in the corner of what looks like a Manhattan loft, playing an electric organ, and then Kathryn Bigelow steps up to the microphone.

She's wearing jeans and a tucked-in white dress shirt. She's tall and her hair is parted down the middle. She looks like Patti Smith as designed by Ralph Lauren. As Thompson and drummer Jesse Chamberlain lock into something like a groove, Bigelow begins to read from a notebook: "Let's not pretend. Most of the power and clout in the art world is in the hands of fascists of one kind or another." Her delivery is strident, declamatory, but she keeps shifting her weight from side to side. She never quite meets the camera's gaze. Something weird is going on at the corners of her mouth, like she's trying to suppress a smile—she's more sure of herself than she is of these words.

Bigelow was from San Carlos, California, a suburb south of San Francisco. She studied painting at San Francisco Art Institute and the

Whitney Museum, worked as an editor at Semiotext(e), made ends meet in New York by renovating lofts alongside other struggling artists—"I did the drywall, Philip Glass did the plumbing," she'd say later—and played a small part in Lizzie Borden's Afrofuturist sci-fi film *Born in Flames*. She first picked up a camera while assisting the poet-turned-performance-artist Vito Acconci on an installation, took to it immediately, and switched her focus from painting to filmmaking. She enrolled in Columbia University's graduate film program and started watching movies seriously and critically, absorbing everything from Sam Peckinpah's bloody revisionist Western *The Wild Bunch* to Rainer Werner Fassbinder's *In a Year with 13 Moons*.

In Bigelow's first student film, 1978's *The Set-Up*, two guys pummel each other verbally and physically for twenty minutes while the Columbia professors Marshall Blonsky and Sylvère Lotringer deconstruct the action in voice-over. "And the piece ends," Bigelow later recalled, "with Sylvère talking about the fact that in the sixties you think of the enemy as outside yourself, in other words a police officer, the government, the system, but that's not really the case at all; fascism is very insidious, we reproduce it all the time." You can draw a straight line from this meditation on one of action cinema's fundamental narrative building blocks, the fistfight, to Bigelow's subsequent work in narrative film, including *Point Break*, and not just because one of the guys doing the brawling in *The Set-Up* is a young Gary Busey.

Something interesting usually happens when a painter picks up a camera, but Bigelow is an artist who takes up the specific subcategory of action cinema as her medium. She's talked in interviews again and again about how staging stories on familiar genre territory lets you get the audience's buy-in before subverting their expectations. In her first feature film, 1981's *The Loveless*, codirected by Bigelow and Monty Montgomery, a starved-for-kicks motorcycle gang (whose leader is played by Willem Dafoe, a stage actor making his own feature-film debut) terrorizes a small town. It's a quasi-Lynchian neo-noir that collapses the distance between actual biker-exploitation movies like *The Wild One* and *The Wild Angels* and Kenneth Anger's fetishistic use of biker iconography in *Scorpio Rising*. Bigelow's second feature, *Near*

Dark, is a punk vampire movie that eventually bends into the shape of a Western. And her first mainstream film, the police drama *Blue Steel*, upends a standard cop-hunting-serial-killer story by making the cop a woman, played by Jamie Lee Curtis. "My interest," Bigelow would say later of the movie, in which at one point a fiber-optic camera ogles the oiled surface of a .45 as if its lines are the curves of a Bond girl, "was to sexualize the gun."

After *Blue Steel* Bigelow and her then-husband, the director James Cameron, decide to rework a screenplay by W. Peter Iliff about a hodad FBI agent who learns to surf in order to infiltrate and bust a gang of surfers whose day job is bank robbery. Iliff's script, *Johnny Utah*, has been kicking around for a few years. When Ridley Scott almost makes the film in 1986, Johnny Depp, Val Kilmer, Charlie Sheen, and—intriguingly, confusingly—Matthew Broderick are all supposedly contenders for the lead. But when it comes time to cast Johnny in her version of *Point Break*, Bigelow knows she wants Keanu for the part.

"We had this meeting," James Cameron will tell *Premiere* in 2002, "where the Fox executives were going, 'Keanu Reeves in an action film? Based on what? *Bill & Ted*?' They were being so insulting. But she insisted he could be an action star. . . . I didn't see it either, frankly. I supported her in the meeting, but when I walked out I was going, 'Based on what?'. . . . But she worked on his wardrobe, she showed him how to walk, she made him work out. She was his Olympic coach. He should send her a bottle of champagne every year, to thank her."

History has vindicated Bigelow on this one: It's easier to imagine *Casablanca* without Bogart, *Saturday Night Fever* without Travolta, or *Ace Ventura* without Jim Carrey than it is to imagine *Point Break* without Keanu at its center, even though Keanu is neither the most obvious action star she could have cast, nor (at this point in his career) the most dexterous or verbally limber one.

In Bigelow's hands, though, *Point Break* isn't just about a surfing FBI agent. It's about a man who's spent his life moving from one insulated world to another—the bubble of a college-football program, then federal law enforcement, with a catastrophic knee injury during a Rose

Bowl loss in between—without making any time for self-discovery. Soon he's tempted by the freedoms of the surfers he's supposed to be investigating, particularly the magnetic surf guru and Zen bank robber Bodhi, played by a preposterously golden-god-like Patrick Swayze. Like the protagonists of Bigelow's later war films *Zero Dark Thirty* and *The Hurt Locker*, Johnny Utah has a conditional identity and no evident life outside the job. So *Point Break* doesn't need an action hero as much as it needs a protagonist who can believably convey an existential need that the life of a waterman might fulfill, whose source code can plausibly be overwritten by contact with Bodhi's gang. It needs a Johnny Utah who seems like he's still learning how to walk.

Johnny's underrealizedness becomes a big part of the film's cult appeal. A clip of Keanu self-righteously delivering the line "I am an FBI agent" to Bodhi—hitting every letter of the acronym hard, *eff, bee, eye*—has become a meme, a YouTube clip with over 133,000 views, a key piece of evidence in the case against Keanu as an actor. At each performance of *Point Break Live*, a campy theatrical adaptation of the movie first staged in Seattle in 2003, one lucky audience member is chosen to wear a wet suit and read all of Johnny Utah's lines off cue cards. "This method," the program reads, "manages to capture the rawness of a Keanu Reeves performance even from those who generally think themselves incapable of acting."

But in the context of the film, Keanu's performance is exactly right. Toward the end of the movie, Bodhi warns Keanu about one of his associates, a genuinely bad dude named Rosie who runs with a group of guys the script calls "surf Nazis." What Swayze says about Rosie is: "He's got this gift of blankness," which in context means Rosie is without remorse and capable of anything. At this phase of his career, Keanu has a gift of blankness, too. In *Bill & Ted's* he used it to comic effect, to play a dude blessedly unburdened by knowledge of the world; Bigelow's the first director to recognize that Keanu's aura of psychic vagueness can also serve as an external indicator of an internal void.

Any questions about whether Keanu can hold the screen in a movie like this one dissolve during the opening credits, which serve as a hero's introduction. The first full shot of him, newly hard-muscled in a rain-wet black T-shirt, sporting a Zoolander pout while racking a shotgun at an FBI target range, is like a memo to his fan base, alerting them to update their daydreams. The gun has officially been sexualized.

Years later, in the liner notes to the 2009 "Pure Adrenaline Edition" Blu-Ray of *Point Break*, Keanu Reeves will describe the movie as the story of "a total control freak" who's transformed after "the ocean beats him up and challenges him. . . . He becomes as amoral as any criminal. He loses the difference between right and wrong." This is not really what happens in *Point Break*, but the fact that even Keanu can misread it says something about how easy *Point Break* is to misread.

Point Break is about an agent of the establishment who has to become a cool guy in order to do the work of the establishment, but once he becomes a cool guy he begins to reject the establishment's ideas. It's also a story about a character deciding between two versions of masculine community. The first of those is the Los Angeles FBI office, where blustering alpha-male intimidation is the order of the day. When an academy-fresh Keanu shows up for his first day of work, chipper in a Pat Riley power suit, his new boss—played by the great, squirrelly character actor John C. McGinley—immediately tells him that whatever he learned at Quantico has no meaning.

"You know nothing," McGinley says. "You know less than nothing. If you knew that you knew nothing, that would be something." It's the first junk-food koan in a movie that will be full of them—but when McGinley catches Keanu grinning and goofing around during his spiel about what makes a great FBI agent, the subtext zags in another direction.

"You're a real blue-flame special, aren't you, son?" McGinley sighs. "Young, dumb, and full of cum." Keanu smirks, taking this—or the general annoyance with which McGinley says it—as a compliment.

"Full of cum" is definitely one way of putting it—McGinley's by-the-book rhetoric notwithstanding, the Los Angeles FBI office appears to be a bubbling stockpot of repressed sexual energy for which interoffice banter acts as a safety valve.

McGinley takes Keanu to a room where a bunch of blindfolded

FBI agents are diving for bricks in an indoor pool. Indoor pool water is water without waves, domesticated water, which means these FBI guys are cut off from salt and sun and the pleasure and danger that water will represent in the movie going forward. One of the guys in the pool is Gary Busey, playing Angelo Pappas, a veteran agent who's spent years hunting a crew of highly professional, highly elusive bank robbers who pull their jobs wearing rubber Halloween masks of four former US presidents (Reagan, Carter, Johnson, Nixon). Then they vanish, Busey puts it, "like a virgin on prom night."

Busey starts to show Keanu some security-camera footage from the Ex-Presidents' last job, and a couple of dim-bulb agents materialize, saying they need to take the tapes, "if you guys are finished jerking off watching MTV." (That said, when those agents show up to take the tapes, Busey and Keanu are looking at a freeze-frame of a guy's butt, on which a tan line tells a story, so you almost can't blame them for raising an eyebrow.) One of the agents refers to Busey—whose thing with the Ex-Presidents has clearly turned him into a bit of a joke around the office, and may be the reason Busey appears to have decades of experience on practically everyone around him but no evident seniority—as a "hard-on." Later, while he's explaining his belief that based on the seasonal rhythm of when they work and when they don't, the Ex-Presidents might be surfers, knocking off banks to underwrite their nomadic quest for the perfect wave, Busey will show Keanu a bar of Mr. Zog's Sex Wax, traces of which were found at the scene of the Ex-Presidents' last job, and Keanu, picking up the lingua franca of this place already, will say, "You're not into kinky shit, are you, Angelo?" and Busey, leering, replies, "Not yet."

If you're determined to respond to *Point Break* like it's a joke—or a series of inadvertent or coded disclosures—all this locker-room talk is where the joke starts. It's a signal to put on your irony-colored glasses and commence communally snickering at the testosterone-juiced spectacle that's about to unfold. But although there are absolutely moments in *Point Break*, particularly once Patrick Swayze shows up, that throb with a palpable get-a-room kind of energy, you can't successfully enjoy *Point Break* as a pure camp spectacle without sort of deliberately misapprehending what it's trying to do.

There's a huge difference between the homoeroticism of *Point Break* and the homoeroticism of (say) *Top Gun*, and the difference is in what the two movies know about themselves, or don't know. The scene in *Top Gun* when Val Kilmer's Iceman and Tom Cruise's Maverick, who've just bested the Soviets in close-quarters air combat, banter about who's going to ride whose tail, inadvertently undercuts all the high-tech death-dealing and swaggering hypermasculinity the movie's worked so hard to sell us, giving us no choice but to retroactively read the amped-up jingoistic spectacle of the film we've just watched—with its beefcakey beach volleyball scenes set to leadingly titled Kenny Loggins songs—as two hours of teeth-gritting sublimation. It makes *Top Gun* seem obtuse, like David Cross as Tobias Fünke on *Arrested Development,* closeted even to himself, endlessly and obliviously tripping over his own phrasing.

The fact that *Top Gun* lends itself so readily to this specific ironic reinterpretation—from the monologue a young, amped-up Quentin Tarantino delivers as a party guest in 1994's now-known-solely-for-this-one-scene *Sleep with Me,* insisting that it's a movie "about a man's struggle with his own homosexuality," to the present-day fan-edit trailers on YouTube recasting it as a star-crossed romance—feels like a mistake, a bobbing boom mic of innuendo breaching the top of the frame. Somehow everybody read the script, from Tony Scott to Tom Cruise to the Department of Defense (which according to a 1986 *Time* magazine article vetted the screenplay for problematic content before authorizing the navy to accept $1.8 million of *Top Gun*'s production money "for the use of Miramar Naval Air Station near San Diego, four aircraft carriers and about two dozen F-14 Tomcats, F-5 Tigers and A-4 Skyhawks, some flown by real-life top-gun pilots," then set up recruiting stations outside theaters to catch young men before their gung-ho buzz faded) without picking up that what was happening between Cruise and Kilmer was kind of a *vibe.*

In *Point Break,* however, from the moment Patrick Swayze first shows up on-screen dipping his fingers sensually into the curl of a wave that is also cocooning and caressing him in seductive slow motion—the idea that Keanu is inexorably drawn to this guy isn't inadvertent subtext. It's text. This isn't to say that *Point Break* is literally or intentionally about repressed homosexuality any more than *Top Gun* means to be. But it's the story of a man who feels a previously unacknowledged yearning for a specific kind of physical, visceral experience after he meets another man whose whole existence is about chasing that kind of experience. It's about the extent to which he's willing to acknowledge that yearning and let it remake him before societal constrictions get in the way, and in that sense the movie is operating in territory that stories not specifically about gay romance seldom find reason to explore.

It turns out being an undercover federal agent is a lot like being an actor preparing to play a part. You find somebody to shadow—in Keanu's case it's Tyler, a tough surfer girl (and Bodhi's ex-girlfriend) played by Lori Petty, with a rap sheet full of crimes that sound like hair-metal song titles, from "Excessive Speed" to "Indecent Exposure in a Moving Vehicle." Then you learn to tell a version of your own life story for dramatic effect, using your own truth as part of your performance. Keanu talks Petty into teaching him to surf by telling her things about himself—that his parents died in a car wreck, that he's been a little bit adrift since that happened, that he's begun to realize his goals have always been other people's goals, that he feels the pull of the ocean. It sounds true because most of it is.

Petty's Tyler has short hair and a gender-ambiguous first name. When zipped into matching black wet suits she and Keanu look like two iterations of the same idea. Jamie Lee Curtis said that when she and Kathryn Bigelow were working on *Blue Steel* together, Bigelow talked to her about Sigourney Weaver's performance in *Aliens*, "and how a woman in a man's world almost doesn't look like a woman on the surface." We're maybe supposed to see Petty as someone who's adopted some traditionally masculine postures to hold her own in the male-dominated world of Swayze and his gang. There's a brother-sister quality to her chemistry with Keanu. In bed Petty sleeps draped sideways over his body and he stares broodingly at the ceiling. On Keanu's nightstand there is an alarm clock shaped like a football helmet, like something you'd find in a little boy's bedroom.

At one point Keanu and Petty show up to a house party at Swayze's place. The suspense in the scene is how Swayze will react to seeing Keanu with his ex-girlfriend. But Bigelow creates a moment that's entirely about Swayze and Keanu exchanging meaningful looks. The camera moves through a crowd of buzzed beach bums making goony faces at the camera, turning us into a guest at the party. Swayze is dancing with a tipsy woman. He holds a shot glass of tequila in his mouth and tips it into hers. He dips her low on the dance floor and she bends away from us, off in her own world. Bigelow cuts to the reverse shot. Petty is looking away from Swayze, who only has eyes for Keanu.

Later Petty and Reeves follow Swayze and his crew to the beach for an impromptu surf session. Keanu catches his first real wave. Swayze shouts, "Isn't that the best feeling on Earth?" Then Bigelow cuts to Petty, floating somewhere nearby, laughing like everybody else is laughing, but far enough away that she needs her own separate shot—a third wheel, on what's suddenly a first date. Of course, after this, she and Keanu make love on the beach for the first time, but it's significant that this intensification comes after Swayze takes Keanu surfing for the first time. The surfing scenes are all about the guys, just like later when Keanu watches the four Ex-Presidents surfing together and realizes by watching how they move together as a unit that they're the bank-robbery crew he's chasing—a moment that's about his solving the case in his head, but also about his perceiving their brotherhood and knowing he'll never be part of it by virtue of being FBI. Maybe everything that feels overheated and verging-on-camp about Keanu and Swayze's relationship is just Bigelow, who's coming from a similar outsider's perspective, imagining and exaggerating the intensity of the bonds between men—bonds catalyzed by physical risk and forbiddenness and forged in spaces she'll always be excluded from.

***

Bigelow has said she keeps coming back, in all her work, to "the moment where the main character goes through the looking glass and can never return." In *Near Dark* the glass is almost literal—when Lance Henriksen's nomadic vampire clan descends on a seedy country roadhouse to massacre the punks and bikers inside and feed on their blood, the probationary vampire Adrian Pasdar hesitates, then crosses the line into savagery, by leaping through a window to catch some poor redneck who's trying to escape.

Pasdar is in love with one of Henriksen's acolytes—Mae, played by Jenny Wright—but he's also a little bit compelled by Severin, Henriksen's psychotic enforcer, played by Bill Paxton. Severin, who takes what he wants from the world, represents the allure of the vampire lifestyle, which *Near Dark* imagines as a hypermasculine space that exists outside the social strictures that prop up traditional masculinity.

In *Near Dark* the vampires have to be destroyed because they're a threat to Pasdar's humanity specifically and to humanity in general by dint of being vampires. *Point Break* complicates its central character's dilemma by raising the possibility that the world on the other side of the looking glass might actually be more peaceful and principled. There's violence in Swayze's world, but it's ultimately territorial, animal violence, the violence of necessity and survival. Recall the gang's career stats as bank robbers, per Busey in the first act: twenty-seven jobs in three years, not one fatality. We've seen them intimidate the civilian customers at the banks they rob and commit property crimes of escalating violence. But they're mostly crimes against capital. The violence of the FBI proceeds from an assumption of morality, but when the showdown comes it leaves Keanu unsure of who's on the right side.

Midway through *Point Break*, Keanu and Busey lead an FBI raid on a scummy crash pad occupied by a group of urban-primitive surfers. As is often the case, we know something Keanu doesn't—these guys aren't really the Ex-Presidents, although one of them is Rosie, who's a kind of liaison to Bodhi's crew. They're no good, though—we've already seen them try to kick Johnny Utah's ass once, for surfing their beach without permission, a situation resolved only by the timely arrival of Bodhi, who doesn't think much of them: "Brains are wired wrong, they're into bad shit," he tells Johnny. "They only live to get radical. They don't understand the sea, so they'll never get the spiritual side of it."

The raid starts with Keanu pulling out a little mirror on a stick, catching a glimpse of a naked woman in the shower while he's trying to figure out who else is inside the house. The surf Nazis realize they're about to be raided and go for their guns. Busey almost gets shot at the front door. The next three minutes are all blood and screaming and flying glass and chaos and pain. A surf Nazi the credits call "Tone" (Anthony Kiedis, in Union Jack board shorts) shoots himself in his own Reebok. The naked woman from the shower throws Keanu against the wall and knees him in the nuts. Keanu tackles a guy through a window—a callback to Pasdar's exit from the biker bar in *Near Dark*—and they fight on the lawn. The guy gets the upper hand and manages to push Keanu's face within inches of the spinning blades of a lawn mower (as if trying to violently and symbolically destroy Keanu's mask) before Busey intervenes.

All of this turns out to have had no purpose, including Keanu shooting a guy in a Venice Beach tank top who turns out to be the first person Keanu has ever killed on the job. The punk in the sleeveless flannel, played by Tom Sizemore, turns out to be an undercover DEA agent. He's been working this crew for months. His wife is fed up with him, makes him "sleep at a Ramada Inn" when he's not working. And he happens to know the surf Nazis can't be the Ex-Presidents because the last time the Ex-Presidents hit a bank, these guys were in Fort fucking Lauderdale.

"It's been paper targets until today, huh? It's no different, Johnny," says Busey, by way of reassurance. "Just a little more to clean up. You did all right today. You did real good." Keanu's not so sure. He winds up staring at himself in the surf Nazis' cracked bathroom mirror, wondering whom he's looking at.

"This was never about money for us," Swayze tells Keanu, before the Ex-Presidents pull what turns out to be their last bank job. "It was about us against the system. That system that kills the human spirit. We stand for something. To those dead souls inching along the freeways in their metal coffins—we show them that the human spirit is still alive!" It's a manifesto; Swayze sees the Ex-Presidents' crime spree as nothing short of a program of mass psychic liberation. In *Die Hard* Hans Gruber demands the release of his imprisoned "revolutionary brothers and sisters" in Northern Ireland, Quebec, and Sri Lanka in exchange for the lives of the Nakatomi Plaza hostages. He's a former member of a West German radical group, but eventually the movie reveals that he's now just a regular bank robber using the language of political terrorism as a smoke screen. He knows about "Asian Dawn," the Sri Lankan group, because he read about them in *Time* magazine. Ideologically he's just another eighties sellout in a power suit. This tidies the moral universe of *Die Hard* significantly. We can root for Bruce Willis to fuck Gruber's whole plan up regardless of where we stand in relation to the cause of international leftism.

In *Point Break* that clarification never comes. Swayze does deviate from his own program during the final bank heist. He orders his guys to raid the vault, something they've never done on previous jobs. One of the Ex-Presidents gets shot right away, by an off-duty cop who's been on the floor with the rest of the hostages. His decision leads indirectly to the deaths of two more Ex-Presidents down the road. And in order to force Johnny to help him hit the bank Swayze puts Lori Petty in a position to potentially be killed by Rosie, the one who has the gift of blankness, so he's at least an *accessory* to violence. But he never betrays his fellow Ex-Presidents to save himself. He even has to be told to leave one Ex-President's dead body behind in Mexico instead of stopping to bury him.

There's nothing obligating Keanu to put Swayze down, apart from his self-identification as an *eff bee eye* agent and his duty to the ethical abstractions of the job and the fact that he's the protagonist and Swayze is the bad guy. In the *Fast and the Furious* movies Paul Walker starts out as the Johnny Utah character who becomes emotionally involved with the crew of outlaws he's supposed to be infiltrating, but the series takes this conceit to a crowd-pleasing conclusion by having Walker's character resign from the LAPD to become part of Vin Diesel's street-racing *familia*. *Point Break* doesn't go that far. But in the film's postrobbery coda, when Keanu finally catches up to Swayze on the Australian coast as the storm of the century prepares to batter the beach, Keanu lets him paddle out for one last ride instead of arresting him, which of course is a way of letting Bodhi die in the ocean instead of going to prison. Then Keanu tosses his badge into the waves, confirming that whatever's been brought to the surface in him by this experience can't be put away. If this is an action movie, it's an action movie in which action becomes a means of shedding a false self. If it's a romance, it's also a tragedy—about two lovers who give each other the gift of freedom but don't get to share it.

MALE
CALL

10 | THE BOY WHO CAME DOWN FROM THE HILL

"I think Keanu and I are the nicest guys on the planet—with the exception of George Bush and Ronald Reagan."

—RIVER PHOENIX

In *My Own Private Idaho* River Phoenix plays Mike, a young street hustler who suffers from bouts of stress-induced narcolepsy, and Keanu is Scott, who's a more worldly and experienced hustler but also turns out to be the slumming son of the mayor of Portland. Together they turn tricks with men and occasionally with women and then go looking for Mike's long-lost mother, first in the United States and then in Rome, where Scott meets a girl and leaves Mike to travel on by himself. In *Private Idaho* as in Van Sant's first two features, *Mala Noche* and *Drugstore Cowboy*, the open road is like outer space—a place where anybody can abandon anybody, just by letting go. To love somebody is to risk being left by the side of the road, the way the laughing Mexican youths in *Mala Noche* do to Tim Streeter when they make off with his car, or the way Matt Dillon and his family of pharmacy robbers do to poor Heather Graham, whose body gets left behind in the drop ceiling of a motel room after she ODs in *Drugstore Cowboy*. In *Private Idaho* we know early on that Keanu's Scott stands to inherit a fortune on his next birthday, and in the course of the movie we can see him pulling away from River, gearing up to sell out and leave the street behind. This is a movie in which two guys sleep with strangers for money and nothing really bad happens to them, and yet there's a tension, because you know at some point Keanu's going to break poor River's heart.

***

In 2008, after wrapping Van Sant's *Milk*, James Franco hangs out with the director in Portland. They walk the locations where Van Sant shot *Idaho*; later Van Sant shows Franco raw footage from the movie, material only Van Sant and his editors have ever seen. Van Sant's in a different place as a filmmaker than he was in 1991; he's been nominated for an Oscar for directing *Good Will Hunting* and he'll get another one for *Milk*. But he's also become increasingly enamored of long unbroken shots in the meditative and/or patience-taxing spirit of the Hungarian maestro Béla Tarr, and before *Milk* he's spent the early 2000s making *Gerry*, *Elephant*, and *Last Days*, movies Roger Ebert once described as a trilogy about "the camera following white guys to their doom." Franco and Van Sant start talking about how Van Sant cut the *Idaho* footage in the nineties and what the movie might look like if it had been cut by the Van Sant of today. Eventually Franco—who's referred to River Phoenix as his favorite actor and *Idaho* as Phoenix's best performance—leaves Portland with Van Sant's footage and his permission to recut it in some arty Gus Van Sant–meets–Béla Tarr–meets–James Franco kind of way.

At this time James Franco also happens to be the new face of Gucci by Gucci Pour Homme, a men's fragrance—notes of cypress, violet, bergamot, jasmine, tobacco, and patchouli—which Franco helps them sell in TV ads where he walks around a luxury apartment in a black suit, reciting the lyrics to Bryan Ferry's "Slave to Love." Franco convinces Gucci to help finance his *Idaho* project, and eventually he creates not one but two "new" films using Van Sant's raw material—a twelve-hour behind-the-scenes documentary called *Endless Idaho*, and *My Own Private River*, an impressionistic alternate *Idaho*, exactly as long as the original but built from unused takes and deleted scenes. *Private River* is a perfect James Franco joint, a sincere expression of Franco's admiration for Phoenix and his equally sincere love of exploitive conceptual-art stunts involving the images of hot dead movie stars, an act of fandom and a bootleg resurrection, like the car-crash imagery and blow-up dolls in his James Dean tribute art show *Rebel* or the Brad Renfro commemorative switchblades he sold through the art quarterly *THE THING*. Because New Line Cinema still controls the rights to *My Own Private Idaho*, Franco can't officially release either of these films, but in 2012 he gets permission from River Phoenix's brother, Joaquin Phoenix, to screen both movies publicly, as part of an exhibit at the Gagosian Gallery in Los Angeles. After that screening, Joaquin Phoenix asks James Franco not to show the films again.

Endless Idaho is now a hard movie to see, but since 2015 *My Own Private River* has been quasi-legally available on YouTube, where it's been viewed over one million times. As a deep dive into Phoenix's performance its murk is affecting, but by reducing Keanu to a supporting player it removes the dynamic that made the original both wobbly and tragic—the sense that Keanu and Phoenix are actually characters from two separate movies who've crossed paths temporarily on the way to something else. It lives online next to a collection of *Idaho*-inspired video art that's more straightforward in its intentions—an ever-growing ecosystem of tribute videos by fans who've recut *Idaho* in tribute to Phoenix and Keanu's friendship and to Scott and Mike as a fictional couple. By boiling the movie down to a series of embraces, looks, and painful, halting words, and setting these images against a range of emotive pop songs—"Young and Beautiful" by Lana Del Rey, "Daddy Issues" by the Neighbourhood, "You Found Me" by the Fray, "Dreaming of You" by Cigarettes After Sex, "Kiss Me Through the Phone" by Soulja Boy featuring Sammie, and even "Lullaby" by Nickelback—a new generation of fans have retconned *Idaho* as a true bromance with a happy ending.

***

Phoenix is six years younger than Keanu but they have a lot in common. They both play music; they both have parents who drifted on the breeze of the sixties. (Phoenix's parents spent time in the Children of God, a cult that fused free love, apocalyptic Christianity, and—allegedly—institutionalized sexual abuse; River once told *Details* magazine he'd first had sex at age four.) Keanu has never had as much chemistry with a costar as he does with River in *Idaho*, and he's never been as fearless and free with his body. There is no Keanu sex scene as intimate as the moment in *Idaho* when the Portland cops catch Keanu and River in bed together and Keanu tries to freak them out by tenderly tugging the hairs on Phoenix's nipple.

"He's like my older brother, but shorter," Phoenix once said of Keanu. You can—or at least, you could, back then—imagine them growing old on-screen together.

"I really would like to do Shakespeare with River," Keanu once said in a joint interview. "We could do *A Midsummer Night's Dream* or *Romeo and Juliet*."

"I'll be Juliet," River responded.

They meet while Keanu is making *Parenthood*, playing Martha Plimpton's boyfriend and eventual husband. Martha Plimpton's real-life boyfriend at the time is River Phoenix, brother of Joaquin, who's playing Plimpton's brother in the movie. For two guys other than Keanu and River this could have been a source of tension, but instead it's the foundation of a friendship. The first time they're in a movie together it's a couple of years later; the movie's called *I Love You to Death*. Tracey Ullman and Kevin Kline play a married couple who own a pizza parlor, River Phoenix is a pizza cook who's in love with Tracey Ullman, and when Ullman finds out Kevin Kline's been cheating on her and decides to have him killed, it's River Phoenix who arranges for two local lowlifes to take care of it. One of the lowlifes is Harlan, played by William Hurt, and the other one is Marlon, played by Keanu Reeves.

This movie gives Keanu one of the best entrances of his career. River Phoenix goes to a bar to talk to Hurt and Keanu about killing Kevin Kline. Because he's arranging a murder he shows up in disguise. He's wearing a fedora and a fake mustache. He looks like Spike from *Peanuts*, Snoopy's brother who lives in the desert and talks to cactuses. When he finds William Hurt, Hurt is facedown on the baize of the pool table and you can see his pink scalp through his thinning blond hair. Only the pool cue still carefully perched between his thumb and forefinger suggests that he's awake. Hurt is not necessarily the first actor you'd think of for the part of an area hippie who dabbles in murder for hire, but his wardrobe does a lot of work. He's wearing flip-up granny sunglasses, a brass bracelet, and a silver ring with a turquoise stone, and he's got a full beard that you can just tell smells like bong water. If there were a Newman's Own–type face on the side of the box that nitrous oxide canisters come in, it would look like William Hurt in this movie.

And then, from under the pool table, like the disembodied arm of the lurking Once-ler in *The Lorax*, comes Keanu's hand, holding the cue ball, and then Keanu himself, in a velour pullover. He's got a ring in his nose and a pot-leaf neck tattoo. His haircut looks self-administered and he appears to be as red-eyed high as anybody's ever been in a movie. He may not actually be Method stoned in this scene, but the moments that follow are some of the finest stoner acting of his estimable stoner-acting career. William Hurt says, "You know my cousin Marlon?" And River Phoenix says, "Of course I do. How are you, Marlon?"

And then there's a pause. A pause long enough that if you felt like it you could pick up a copy of Walter Benjamin's *On Hashish* and read the part where Benjamin writes, "Now the hashish eater's demands on time and space come into force. As is known, these are absolutely regal. Versailles, for one who has taken hashish, is not too large, or eternity too long," and put the book back on the shelf in the time it takes Keanu's Marlon to register that River Phoenix is talking to him. "What," he finally says, with perfect idiot contempt, like he heard the question but has no interest in wasting energy on a response.

Keanu's one of many moving parts in the farce that follows. Everybody keeps trying to kill Kevin Kline, but nobody can actually get it done. This is one of the last times for a while that we'll see Keanu as a true ensemble player on-screen. He's about to make *Point Break*, which will make him too famous to hang out at the edge of a movie without his presence being a distraction. In *I Love You to Death* he looks like he's really enjoying his final moments on Earth as a character actor. It's also an important movie for Keanu because it's the one he and Phoenix are making when they get the script for Gus Van Sant's next movie.

When it comes to them it doesn't look like a screenplay usually looks. It's a seventy-two-page document set in various eccentric early-Macintosh fonts. It pulls together ideas from other scripts Van Sant's worked on and put aside over the years—a movie about gay street hustlers, dropped after Van Sant discovered John Rechy's books on similar subject matter, a road movie about two of the characters from *Mala Noche*, and an adaptation of Shakespeare's *Henry IV* and *Henry V*, specifically the parts of those plays that Orson Welles stitched together in *Chimes at Midnight*, which retold the Henry plays from Falstaff's perspective. Parts of *Private Idaho* are essentially a queer, grunge *Chimes at Midnight* remake, right down to the casting of a director—William Richert, who made *Winter Kills* and River Phoenix's *A Night in the Life of Jimmy Reardon*—in the Falstaff part.

The hustlers in Van Sant's script don't see themselves as gay, despite what they do for money. But Van Sant still assumes no big-name actor at the turn of the nineties will want to get anywhere near this project. He plans to give the part of Mike to a friend named Mike Parker, who's described in a 1991 *Rolling Stone* profile of Van Sant as having formerly been "a Portland runaway, living in youth shelters, hanging out in a bowling alley, taking drugs and turning the occasional trick." For Scott, the mayor's son, Van Sant is leaning toward a Philadelphia-born actor named Rodney Harvey, who's appeared in two films by Warhol's Factory alumnus Paul Morrissey and who played Sodapop Curtis in the TV version (Rob Lowe played the part in the movie) of *The Outsiders.* (In *Idaho* he ends up playing Gary, the hustler who helps Keanu drag an unconscious Phoenix out of Grace Zabriskie's house.) Bruce Weber even shoots publicity photos of Van Sant and a shirtless Parker at a motel in Santa Monica called the Shangri-La, photos Van Sant intends to use to announce *Idaho* as his next film and Parker as its star.

Van Sant sends the script to Keanu and Phoenix, figuring they're going to pass. River Phoenix's agent Iris Burton—who discovered

Phoenix and his younger brother, Joaquin, busking outside a mall in Century City in 1981—finds the material distasteful and won't even show it to her client. Van Sant makes contact with River and Keanu directly and has better luck.

"I don't know, man, Gus Van Sant gave me a call," Keanu tells *Us Weekly*'s Dario Scardapane in 1991. "I thought it was an amazing script. Just in terms of narrative, man, there's cows, *bang! bang! bang!*, porno shops, salmon swimming, blow jobs, money-exchanging, and then I bust out in Idaho, *smash!* And then Shakespeare. It's *Henry IV* and I'm, like, doin' voice-overs on camera. Like soliloquies. I have all these soliloquies."

Van Sant thought of Keanu playing Scott—whose scenes involve a lot of pastiched Shakespearean dialogue—because he's a fan of *Bill & Ted's Excellent Adventure*. "They had their eloquent way of speaking—a false eloquence, their own valleyspeak," he'll say later. "So I thought of it as characters who are speaking in their own secret language when they're together—it's their way of having fun."

It turns out Keanu's been wanting to do a low-budget movie when he hears from Van Sant. He is very into the Shakespeare aspect of the piece. He's been telling interviewers he wants to play Mercutio or Prince Hal someday, and Scott Favor is Prince Hal, pretty much—a ruler's black-sheep son who's fallen in with an old lush and his crew of malcontents, dallying before he returns to a life of wealth and power. Invoking the geography of Portland, whose upper-class enclaves tend to sit higher up, Van Sant refers to Keanu's character as "the boy who came down from the hill."

"Well, he's probably me," Van Sant told Graham Fuller. "I can use my own background as an example for Scott's background, and I did sometimes with Keanu, too. Keanu grew up with a well-off background himself and used that when he was figuring out how to play the part. We tried to work out who Scott was. At times he was maybe both of us, Keanu and me."

The casting of two teen idols will add an additional subversive spin to moments like the newsstand scene, where a wall of gay-porn magazine covers comes to life, with Keanu and River among the preening, posing models. But Keanu and River's participation also means Van Sant gets to make *Private Idaho* as a $2 million movie for New Line Cinema. At the time New Line is best known for the *Nightmare on Elm Street* movies, and Van Sant liked the idea that his movie about men having gay sex for money would play in multiplex malls the way the Freddy Krueger films did. But New Line has just launched a specialty division called Fine Line, and *Private Idaho* ends up being the first Fine Line movie, which puts it on the art-house track—although in an interview included on the Criterion edition of the movie, the director Todd Haynes tells Van Sant that he remembers stories about unsuspecting young girls going to see the movie in theaters and freaking out at the sight of Keanu kissing a man.

"We were driving in a car on Santa Monica Boulevard, probably on the way to a club, and we were talking really fast about the whole idea," River Phoenix will say later, about how they decided to do the movie. "We were excited. It could have been like a bad dream—a dream that never follows through because no one commits, but we just forced ourselves into it. We said, 'Okay, I'll do it if you do it. I won't do it if you don't.' We shook hands. That was it."

In 1990, in *Interview*, Dennis Cooper—who says he's asking because his friends want to know—asks Keanu, "Are you gay or what?" Then he says, "C'mon, make it official."

Interview prints his response as follows:

"KR: No. [long pause] But ya never know."

Somehow his answer leaves the question hanging in the air. It never really goes away, and he never says things designed to make it go away, because to do that would imply some negative connotation to his being something other than straight. Of course, answering a question like Cooper's with a "no" that sounds like a "maybe" is also alluring; it dispels no one's fantasies.

When he's asked about his decision to do *Idaho* in spite of the risks the role's sexual content could pose to his image, his answer is "Who am I, a politician?" But according to Lance Loud, writing in *American Film*, Keanu "recoils when asked how he prepared for his hustler role. 'I didn't have to suck dick, if that's what you mean!'" But

Keanu's research process—which begins as soon as he arrives in Portland, still tan from shooting *Point Break* in Hawaii—does involve some direct experience with the hustler lifestyle.

"I took River and Keanu down to where boys prostitute themselves and we'd sit on the corner and just watch," Scott Green said in *Lost in Hollywood*, a sensationalized posthumous Phoenix bio by John Glatt.

Sometimes, according to Green, they did more than watch.

"River didn't pull 'dates,'" Green said, "but he did get into the johns' cars with me so he could see me make the deal. Sometimes River would even talk to them, saying what he would and what he wouldn't do. But after we agreed to the deal I'd say, 'I'm sorry. We can't do this.' And we'd jump out of the car leaving these guys wondering what the hell was going on."

The only shot in Franco's *My Own Private River* that seems to catch the private Keanu involves one of these interactions. Phoenix, in red-lensed shades and a peacoat, finishes lighting a cigarette and falls into step on the sidewalk with Keanu, who's wearing an orange patterned disco shirt tucked into black jeans and carrying a red gym bag. He puts his arm around Phoenix. He's chewing gum. Two movie stars, flattened into anonymity by a long lens, just a couple of hustlers on the street. It's starting to rain, and some of the people around them have umbrellas open. Keanu motions to River like *C'mere a minute* and veers off the sidewalk. In the street a white Mitsubishi van slows down and Keanu walks up to the driver's side. The windshield reflects gray sky so you can't see the driver as he rolls down the window. Keanu runs his non-gym-bag hand down his chest. He touches his nipple and then his stomach and then his dick through his jeans. He turns away from the van, his hand still on his crotch, and starts laughing as he walks away. River, who's also walking away from the van, says, "Twenty bucks," and at that moment Keanu makes eye contact with the camera, like he's just remembered he's being watched, or has known that all along and is curious to know what was captured.

Not long before the movie starts shooting, Van Sant buys a six-bedroom house in Portland Heights. It's the former residence of the industrialist James W. Cook; it has views of Mount Hood, Mount St. Helens, the Willamette River, and downtown Portland. During preproduction Phoenix and Reeves begin crashing there, along with other members of the cast and crew. Eventually Van Sant goes back to sleeping at his old apartment downtown and lets his actors have the run of the Portland Heights place. They stay up all night playing music together, sometimes joined by Flea from the Red Hot Chili Peppers, who plays William Richert's sidekick in the film. (Van Sant would later shoot the Chili Peppers' video for "Under the Bridge," another visual poem about a handsome straight guy caught up in street life and drugs.)

There's a photo from around this time of Keanu, River, Rodney Harvey, Mike Parker, and Scott Green—a former Portland street kid who's credited in *Idaho* as Van Sant's assistant and appears in the film telling a grim story about a pickup gone bad—hanging out on the front porch of a house. They look less like the cast of a movie and more like a grunge band on a cigarette break during recording sessions for their breakthrough album. If they're a band, Phoenix and Reeves are the irresistibly mediagenic lead singers. Later on, promoting the movie together, they trade inside jokes in interviews and embrace, disheveled and unselfconscious, in pictures shot by Bruce Weber, a photographer who is to hot, straight-presenting young guys what Ansel Adams was to Yosemite.

A blind item that appears in *Movieline* magazine during production alludes to a *Private Idaho* actor getting deep into character by "shacking up with drug-using streetfolk." Later, in a 1991 *Rolling Stone* profile of Van Sant, Keanu tells David Handelman that the scene around the movie wasn't actually all that wild: "We smoked a little weed once in a while, sipped some red wine." But Matt Ebert, a production assistant who worked with Phoenix on Nancy Savoca's *Dogfight* and then on *Idaho*, will later tell one of Phoenix's biographers about "rampant heroin use" by members of the *Idaho* cast. "He would come up to visit me and we would do drugs together," Ebert says of Phoenix. "Let me tell you, it did not take him long to go from, you know, a casual user to having an intense drug problem."

River Phoenix isn't the only cast member from *Private Idaho* who didn't make it out of the nineties alive. After the movie, Rodney Harvey struggles with heroin addiction and spends time in jail. In 1998, he overdoses on heroin and cocaine and is found dead in a Hollywood hotel room. A Partnership for a Drug-Free America PSA produced that same year intercuts a head shot of a young and beautiful Harvey with a series of photos of him eaten alive by heroin. A friend talks to *Premiere* about Harvey's time on the *Idaho* shoot: "He told me all about that little shebang," the friend says. "About how those guys hit it like nobody's business. Seven in the morning, pulling needles from their arms. He said they'd walk from the house to the set after shooting heroin all night."

There's home-video footage floating around of Phoenix and other *Idaho* cast members hanging out at Van Sant's house during this period. It's easy to find on YouTube; a lot of it involves Flea jamming on bass while a slightly butterfingered Phoenix plays along on acoustic guitar. But there's also a series of videos documenting a rambling late-night conversation between Phoenix and hustlers-turned-actors Mike Parker and Shaun Jordan.

Phoenix moves in and out of a dimly lit room, smoking and wearing sunglasses. He's wearing a button-down shirt but he has a towel around his waist. He trades stories with the hustlers, posturing in conversation like a seasoned drug user. When one kid mentions having a sixty-dollar-a-day crank habit, River says, "A dime bag makes you incredibly neurotic—I can't imagine," like a true man of the world. He's researching his role, or is already lost in it. You can see him constructing a personality in real time, absorbing the hustlers' stories and responding with anecdotes of his own, mimicking the matter-of-fact way they discuss fucking and being fucked, talking about using the pull-out method with his girlfriend and getting an erection in a gay porn store, before adding that the idea of gay sex "turns my nuts in loops." Sometimes he seems like he's bluffing; sometimes he seems unsure of the truth; sometimes he just seems fucked up.

What you don't get in these videos, or in Franco's *Private River*, or in any of the coverage of Phoenix's and Harvey's eventual drug-related deaths, is any sense of Keanu's level of participation—if any—in the riskier extracurricular aspects of the *Idaho* shoot. Maybe he did nothing. Or maybe, like Scott Favor in the film, he existed within a social space and lived by its rules and then walked away. The movie wants something different from Phoenix than it does from Keanu—unguarded helplessness versus glib disregard—and may have taken a greater toll on Phoenix.

Most of the Shakespeare stuff that attracted Keanu gets cut; somewhere on YouTube you can find a remarkable seven-minute scene between Keanu and William Richert based on the play-within-the-play from *Henry IV, Part 1*. With Richert's gang as an audience, Richert and Keanu take turns acting out Keanu's confrontation with his disapproving father. When Keanu plays Scott's father it's some of the most remarkable physical acting he's ever done. He contorts his body, pretends his chair is a wheelchair he's confined to, twists his face into a mask, bellows his lines. It's over-the-top but it's fascinatingly over-the-top; you almost never see Keanu go off like this. But it's also Keanu playing a person who's performing; the theatricality of the moment shields him from its implications.

Van Sant's camera can't take its eyes off Phoenix, whether he's flopping narcoleptically on highway blacktop or cackling at *The Simpsons* in a john's hotel room. Its relationship with Keanu is more ambiguous and unresolved; Van Sant's camera admires him from an almost intimidated distance. We see Keanu's Scott the way Mike sees him. In the published version of the screenplay, which is significantly different from the shooting script, there's a scene where Mike wakes from one of his blackouts, sees Scott watching over him, and thinks, in voice-over:

"The first time I met Scott, I had a feeling he was a sort of comic book hero. He was always saying the right thing at the right moment, and standing up for me when there was no reason to. Look at his face now, when the sunlight shines off his lower lip, like it is the face of some sort of statue. Strong and soft at the same time . . . I'd make a bet with anybody right now, that Scott is a saint or a hero or some such higher placed person."

It's worth noting that there are only two actual sex scenes in *My Private Idaho* in which Keanu participates—one with Chiara Caselli in a farmhouse in Italy, and then a threesome in a hotel room with Phoenix and Udo Kier—and both feel like a testament to Van Sant's inability to pierce Keanu's airspace. Both scenes are staged as a series of quick-cut tableaus in which the actors are holding an erotic pose as if they're being shot with a still camera. It's as if the movie's imagination fails when it's called upon to picture what sex with Keanu would actually be like.

As written, the emotional peak of Phoenix's character's story line is a confrontation in the middle of the movie between Mike and his brother, played by James Russo, who turns out to also be Mike's father. After Phoenix shoots the scene he doesn't feel like he's delivered the big moment he's supposed to deliver, and he comes up with another idea.

There's a night scene later in the film where Keanu and Phoenix sit by a campfire. In the script, Mike makes a pass at Scott because they're bored. It's a small moment without much dialogue. Phoenix decides to make something bigger out of it. He and Keanu work out some new lines. He asks Van Sant if they can shoot it late in the schedule so he can engineer a more cathartic performance. It ends up being the last thing they shoot in America, on a soundstage in Seattle, before the production moves to Italy.

"He had decided," Van Sant tells Graham Fuller years later, "that that scene was his character's main scene and, with Keanu's permission, he wrote it out to say something that it wasn't already saying—that his character, Mike, has a crush on Scott and is unable to express it—which wasn't in the script at all. It was his explanation of the character."

Phoenix even blocks the scene himself, requesting limited coverage—one wide shot, one medium shot, close-ups for River and Keanu. They're sitting next to each other by the fire, about a foot apart. What happens between them rewrites the movie, transforms what's already been captured on film, calls things by a name.

Phoenix starts to talk about where he came from, everything he didn't have—a good upbringing, a normal family, a normal dad, a normal dog.

"You didn't have a normal dog?" Keanu asks.

Phoenix says he didn't have a dog at all. He keeps going. There's something he wants to say.

"What do I mean to you?" he asks. Keanu says he's Phoenix's best friend, which is less than Phoenix wants to hear. He gets even quieter.

"That's okay. We can be friends," Phoenix says.

Somewhere in the distance a coyote howls. Keanu either realizes what Phoenix is getting at or has known it all along and realizes he has to acknowledge it. He shifts his weight so he's facing Phoenix.

"I'll only have sex with a guy for money," Keanu says to Phoenix. "And two guys can't love each other."

"Well, I don't know," Phoenix says. "I mean, for me—I could love someone, even if I wasn't paid for it. I love you and you don't pay me."

Suddenly the space between them is a gulf. Keanu's lying back against his bedroll, real casual. Phoenix almost has his head between his knees. Keanu looks away, like someone who is accustomed to people falling in love with him, and says, "Mike . . . ," and Phoenix says, "I really wanna kiss you, man."

Keanu sighs. He moves over a little and pats the patch of ground that movement opens up. He beckons Phoenix to come over to where he is and pulls him into an awkward, halting embrace, stroking his hair a little. Strong and soft at the same time.

They never kiss. Van Sant will say later he stopped short of directing them to do it, that he felt weird staging a kiss between "the two boy heartthrobs." They try it only once and the take ends with Keanu and Phoenix "barking at the moon."

Phoenix creates a James Dean moment for himself with this scene. It doesn't ask for the same amount of emotional nakedness from Keanu, but what it asks for is something more complicated. Scott has another life to go back to and Mike only has this one; part of the distance between them is that Scott can leave anytime he wants. Years later when James Franco recuts this scene for *My Own Private River* he leaves out all the painful words but includes a shot of Keanu holding Phoenix in which Keanu is staring past him, into the fire, his mind on something else.

In Italy they part ways, and at the end of the film Scott shows up back in Portland, wearing a fine suit and tie and an overcoat, riding in a limousine. His father is dead. In Shakespearean fashion he also banishes William Richert's Bob—"My old psychedelic teacher"—who goes off and dies of loneliness. Keanu's father's funeral takes place in a park and from his seat at the funeral Keanu can look across the park and see Bob's gang of hustlers throwing him a wild outdoor wake.

The movie ends like it started, on the highway. Phoenix passes out. A salmon-colored car pulls into frame and a guy gets out and pulls him into the car. We don't see the guy. Years later when someone asks Van Sant who the guy in the car is supposed to be, Van Sant says, "It's me." But the script says it's Scott; many of the fan videos that close with this image seem to take it on faith that it's Keanu. In the artistic community that recuts *My Own Private Idaho* the notion of the movie being a love story is canon; the big aesthetic question facing each fan-editor is whether to end on Phoenix alone on the asphalt and let the story's essential tragedy breathe, or succumb to the urge to suture Scott and Mike back together with a dreamy pop song and a judicious edit, contriving an ending where Scott rescues Mike from the entropy of the road—or one where Keanu symbolically does the same for River.

On the night before Halloween at the Viper Room, a Hollywood nightclub then owned by Johnny Depp, Phoenix downs a drink that turns out to contain a dissolved mixture of cocaine and heroin. He collapses on the sidewalk outside the club and Sunset Boulevard scenesters in costume watch him convulse as his brother, Joaquin, makes a frantic 911 call that will be played days later on *Inside Edition*. At Cedars-Sinai the doctors massage his heart. At 1:51 on Halloween morning a doctor pronounces him dead.

It's maybe not Keanu's first great loss but it's the one that will define him going forward, for years. *Private Idaho* itself deepens and complicates the legacy of *Wolfboy* by casting Keanu as a more or less straight guy for whom gay sex and maybe even queer love are not entirely out of the question. But Phoenix's death does as much to shift the perception of Keanu as a whoa-dude meat puppet than any movie he makes in the nineties; it's the beginning of the conception of Keanu as a stoic sufferer that reaches its apex decades later with Sad Keanu.

It's also a defining loss in terms of Keanu's public image because it's the only one he's ever really talked about. He doesn't go around bringing it up, but sometimes people ask him about it, the way a French reporter does in 1993, and he gives them something like an answer.

"River was an exceptional person, incredible . . . Where is my Juliet? Bullshit, fuck!"

Then, after a long silence: "He was a really good guy."

11
KEANU IS AN EVIL ROBOT DOPPELGANGER AND A BREAKFAST CEREAL AND A MAN WITH A DOG'S FACE

For a while before it's finished the title of the *Bill & Ted's* sequel is in flux. The studio isn't sure they want to release a movie called "Bill & Ted Go to Hell." Eventually the decision is made to call it *Bill & Ted's Bogus Journey*. Sometime before that happens, Keanu Reeves and Alex Winter sit in directors' chairs in their Bill and Ted outfits and talk to MTV's movie-news show *The Big Picture* about the title.

Winter starts naming the kind of intentionally boring titles only a risk-averse studio could love—"Bill & Ted 2," "Another Bill and Ted." Keanu pretends to fall asleep, as if bored unconscious by these ideas, and then he pretends he's waking up angry, shouting, "No, no, no, no, no," shaking his hair in his face, shaking a fist, squirming in the chair they've put him in.

Winter says, "What was another one—'Bill & Ted's Excellent Adventure Number Two'?"—and Keanu moans in dismay at this one and grabs two handfuls of his own hair, and Winter says, "'Bill & Ted's Excellent Adventure: The Sequel,'" and Keanu starts growling like a dog, and Winter says, "We're fond of that one. 'Bill and Ted Are Back' . . ."

His teeth still doggishly gritted, his tone and cadence now channeling the carnival-barker voice of Primus's Les Claypool, Keanu

interrupts: "*And then there was a cereal! And then there was* [inaudible], *and then you could buy the toys, and then*"—he starts pounding tightly clenched fists on the arms of his chair, headbanging, sputtering nonsense syllables, "*dingdadingdadingdading,*" which—as he starts miming the operation of a giant cash register with both hands, moving like a big, dumb machine—becomes "*Ching cha-ching cha-ching ching ching* . . ."

Winter says, "K-Tel Presents Bill & Ted . . ."

". . . *ching, ching, ching,* RING IT UP FOR SALE!" Keanu says, and finally goes quiet.

There really is a Bill and Ted cereal in stores around this time. Bill & Ted's Excellent Cereal is technically a tie-in with *Bill & Ted's Excellent Adventures*, a short-lived CBS Saturday-morning cartoon whose first season features Keanu, Winter, and Carlin voicing their *Bill & Ted's* characters. Its arrival on grocery-store shelves marks the first and presumably last time the comedian and counterculture icon George Carlin's likeness will ever appear on a cereal box. The marshmallows are shaped like musical notes and the oat squares are cinnamon-flavored, like Apple Jacks. Many years later in an interview, the director and licensed-breakfast-food connoisseur Quentin Tarantino will declare it "better than Lucky Charms."

The MTV footage feels like an archetypal nineties moment—Keanu and Winter as unruly young artists, full of Cobain-in-the-membrane rage and boredom at being dragged back into a cash-in sequel, sneering at commercial imperatives. But in a 2019 interview Alex Winter will remember the moment differently. If he and Keanu seemed disgruntled that day, he'll say, it had less to do with playing Bill and Ted again and more to do with the gap between the script they'd signed up to do and the movie they found themselves making. Money was tight and many scenes were cut at the last second; the word OMIT appeared on so many pages of the shooting script that Winter and Keanu took to calling the movie "Bill and Ted's Omitted Adventure."

"We were really excited about doing it," Winter will say, "and put a lot of effort into building the story with the [writers] and figuring out what we were doing. We would have incredible ideas, like super-cinematic ideas, and then a lot of stuff just started getting yanked. [Keanu] was really disheartened by that."

Bogus Journey may not be everything it could have been, but it's still crucial to what we might call Keanu's 1991 Trilogy. All three of the 1991 Keanu movies are in one way or another love stories about men. *Point Break* and *Private Idaho* both take place in extralegal underground milieus where the codes of traditional masculinity can be renegotiated, but in both movies that renegotiation is temporary and ultimately society's rules win out—Bodhi chooses death and glory because the only alternative is jail, and Scott Favor accepts his destiny in the straight world, turning his back on Mike and the dangers of street life. *Bogus Journey* dares to suggest that something else is possible—that two guys can love each other without it having to end in tragedy and separation. We know Bill and Ted are destined to somehow inspire a utopian future where people are excellent to each other; it's possible to believe despite evidence to the contrary that these two dummies might really invent a new reality, if only because they're able to imagine a world less hung up on monogamy.

But before that can happen, like all messiahs, Bill and Ted have to die in the desert.

Once again we find them first in San Dimas, future rock gods still so undistinguished they can barely get on the bill at the Battle of the Bands contest where they're supposed to somehow deliver a performance that changes the world. As in the first movie, they're living with the threat that life will come between them. They're still dating the princesses they brought back from the Middle Ages; the princesses are medievally traditional and being unmarried they do not, as it were, sleep over. Ted, ruefully: "Our girlfriends are most chaste."

One night Bill and Ted each take a knee and propose to their respective princesses, with gumball-machine rings and poetry. They give almost the exact same will-you-marry-me speech, except Winter's speech includes a poem about the sea and Keanu's poem is about the forest. What Bill says at the end of the proposal is "Will you marry us?" The princesses are being asked, as a duo, to marry Bill and Ted, as a unit, forming a kind of quadrouple. On some level Bill and Ted's bond is presented here as existing independent of and maybe superseding the institution of marriage. The notion that Bill and Ted might have to part ways in order to devote themselves to their princesses never comes up, because it's unthinkable.

Meanwhile in the utopian future, a music-hating, Bill-and-Ted-despising stock villain named De Nomolos—which is "Ed Solomon" spelled backward—has siezed control of Bill and Ted University as part of a plot to eradicate Bill and Ted's rock and roll utopia before it comes to pass. The second step involves a secret weapon—two evil robot duplicates of Bill and Ted. "We're total metalheads," Keanu's Evil Ted says. He and Winter's Evil Bill peel their faces back like rubber masks, revealing the grinning robot heads underneath—a cross between the skeletal face of a Terminator and one of those clear plastic novelty telephones from the nineties.

Winter's and Keanu's performances as Evil Bill and Evil Ted are a fascinating repudiation of the first movie—Winter's great as an evil version of himself, but Keanu might be more unnerving, because his Evil Ted feels like the kind of monster Keanu that Keanu might conjure in order to scare himself. Evil Ted's grinning emptiness is a nightmare of corruption, an externalization of the fear of discovering something without empathy living inside your skin. When Evil Bill and Evil Ted show up at Bill and Ted's apartment, Bill is unrattled—they've met themselves before, after all, toward the end of the first movie. But only Bill shakes his duplicate's hand. Keanu doesn't shake hands with Evil Ted. It's as if Keanu can't stare directly into another Keanu, as if he knows that on some level this would be ontologically dangerous.

Evil Bill and Evil Ted drive Keanu and Winter to the desert and hurl them off a cliff, and for a while they're dead and the movie becomes an odyssey through the afterlife. Meanwhile Evil Bill and Evil Ted head back to terrorize San Dimas, attempting to force themselves on the princesses before trashing Bill and Ted's apartment. Evil Ted slam-dunks its own head on their indoor basketball hoop and Keanu smiles up at his own body from a floor strewn with smashed plates. The film becomes its own critique—Evil Bill and Evil Ted are crude, exploitive sequels to themselves, disrespecting the characters and what they stand for.

In Purgatory they meet the Grim Reaper, played by William Sadler in white-faced homage to Bengt Ekerot's Death in Ingmar Bergman's *The Seventh Seal.* Sadler's scenes are the part of the movie that everyone remembers, but after the montage where Bill and Ted beat him at Battleship,

Clue, magnet football, and Twister, he becomes a one-note sidekick as underwritten as the shanghaied historical figures in *Excellent Adventure*. It's the story line about the false Bill and Ted that means the most, because it stages a confrontation between Keanu Reeves and falsehood as a *concept*.

***

As scripted, the movie's finale would have been a callback to the first movie, with Bill and Ted recruiting Einstein, Sitting Bull, Leonardo da Vinci, Betsy Ross, and Joe Louis from the afterlife to San Dimas to help them battle their robot doppelgangers. The filmed version skips this beat entirely. Instead Bill and Ted make it to Heaven, where God introduces them to an alien who builds them two more robot duplicates out of hardware-store materials, evening the odds in Bill and Ted's imminent confrontation with their alternate selves and upping the total number of Bills and Teds in this movie to three apiece.

These are cobbled-together, get-the-job-done robots compared to De Nomolos's Evil Bill and Evil Ted. They look like macaroni art. But when the robots square off with Evil Bill and Evil Ted at the Battle of the Bands in San Dimas, even Evil Bill and Evil Ted have to agree that the robots are excellent, because despite being evil, Evil Bill and Ted are still a Bill and Ted at heart.

The end of the movie will be a celebration of the banishment of false selves—even Pam Grier, as the administrator in charge of the Battle of the Bands, will turn out to have been George Carlin all along. The real Bill and Ted will use their time machine to go off with the princesses and return to the stage seconds later, having magically practiced for sixteen months, among other things—now Winter has a ZZ Top beard and Keanu has a Vandyke, and they're both carrying babies in backpacks. Maturity has been painlessly achieved.

But first Bill and Ted take up their joysticks and deploy the robots, and as their destruction approaches, Evil Bill and Evil Ted say, "Catch you later, Bill and Ted," and Bill and Ted say back, "Catch you later, Bill and Ted," and the good robots punch the evil robots' heads clean off, and the heads spin through the air, shooting out sparks like fireworks, and the crowd cheers and even Death has to laugh.

***

Keanu will not have River Phoenix to grow up with, but he has Alex Winter, the only other person on Earth who truly understands what it's like to have been Bill or Ted—who grasps what Winter described in a 2012 interview as the "bad acid trip aspect to having your face on a cereal box."

Winter was a child actor who spent the early years of his career on the Broadway stage; by the time *Bill & Ted's* opened in 1989 he'd become more interested in working behind the camera, and had already written and codirected his first short film, *Bar-B-Que Movie*, a low-budget *Texas Chainsaw Massacre* parody starring members of the Texas psychedelic-art-noise-punk band the Butthole Surfers. The success of *Bill & Ted's* got Winter and his writing partner Tom Stern in the door at MTV, where they created a short-lived half-hour sketch-comedy series called *The Idiot Box*. In the early nineties Winter and Stern wrote a horror-comedy script called *Hideous Mutant Freekz*, which they envisioned as another potential star vehicle for the Butthole Surfers. When the opportunity to bankroll an R-rated movie built around the band responsible for albums such as *Locust Abortion Technician* and *Hairway to Steven* failed to entice a single movie studio, Winter and Stern retooled the idea and sold it to 20th Century Fox as a pure teen comedy.

The fate of this movie—which by the time it's released is called *Freaked*—is sealed by a regime change at the studio during production, even before it bombs at test screenings. It opens on only two screens, in October 1993, and while the reviews aren't uniformly terrible, it flops in a way that guarantees a movie almost instantaneous entry to cult-film Valhalla. It's a feature-length extrapolation of the surreal sketch-style material that bracketed music videos on *The Idiot Box*—Tod Browning by way of Primus, the Residents, Lloyd Kaufman, and Frank Zappa, whose legacy Winter would celebrate in a 2020 documentary. But it also takes the character-assassination themes of *Bill & Ted's Bogus Journey* a step further by depicting movie stars as greedily complicit tools of planet-defiling capitalism, and celebrity itself as a hideously disfiguring medical condition. It's Winter's most pointed commentary on the specific out-of-body experience of being Bill S. Preston.

Winter stars in *Freaked* as Ricky Coogan, the obnoxiously famous leading man of the *Ghost Dude* movie franchise, whose main character's Bill-like catchphrase is "Boo, dude." Under pressure from an obviously evil multinational corporation, Ricky agrees to headline a Central American publicity tour promoting an obviously toxic pesticide called Zygrot-27. During that trip, he winds up in the wrong part of the jungle and is kidnapped by Randy Quaid, the proprietor of an amusement-park freak show that breeds its own talent by dousing people in Zygrot-27 until they mutate.

Exposure to these chemicals turns Coogan into a hunchback with squirting pustules and half a gargoyle's face. He takes refuge among Quaid's other creations—including Rosie the Pinhead, the Worm, a sock puppet voiced by Bobcat Goldthwait, a bearded lady played by Mr. T, a guy with an eternal flame shooting out of his ass, and a young John Hawkes as a bovine-human hybrid called Cowboy—and eventually joins them in an uprising against Quaid and his enforcers, a pair of machine-gun-toting Rastafarian eyeballs named Eye-and-Eye. The first line is "*Yeah*," as bellowed by Keanu's future *Johnny Mnemonic* costar Henry Rollins, who sings the title song with Blind Idiot God. The special makeup effects are by Screaming Mad George, the Osaka-born gore genius whose résumé includes contributions to *Predator* and *Bride of Re-Animator* and the unforgettable roach-motel death scene from *A Nightmare on Elm Street 4: The Dream Master*. And the best cameo, with all due respect to Mr. T, Bobcat, Morgan Fairchild, and Brooke Shields, is Keanu Reeves's uncredited appearance as "Ortiz, the Dog Boy."

If you didn't know it was Keanu, you wouldn't know it was Keanu. He's unrecognizable even in close-ups thanks to a full face of Lon Chaney–style fur and delivers his lines in an absurdly fang-mouthed Latin American accent. Ortiz is the leader of the freak insurgency, a beret-wearing revolutionary who wears his mutated status with pride, not shame—unlike some of the other denizens of Quaid's freak show, Ortiz doesn't want to be cured of his freakdom. Keanu says he based the character on "Che Guevara, Fidel Castro, and Tom Jones."

Winter's superdeformed Ricky physicalizes a hip star's fear of being warped beyond recognition by success, a very nineties hipster concern. And Ortiz comes off as an expression of Keanu's own relationship to fame. He's both noble and feral, refuses to heel for authority, and expresses no desire to be anything but a dog-boy, even if it costs him society's acceptance. If Ricky is everything Alex Winter doesn't want to be as a famous person, Ortiz might be a vision of the kind of uncompromising and iconoclastic star Keanu *does* want to be. By the time *Freaked* sneaks in and out of theaters in the fall of 1993, Keanu has started filming *Speed*, a movie that will boost his public profile in a way that he'll openly struggle with. As much as his *Freaked* role represents a chance to make an anticareerist punk-rock gesture and clown around with Alex Winter some more, it also feels like a declaration of intent—he's using his last moments before stepping on the bus to action superstardom to play a character who refuses to dial down what makes him unusual. And doing the part in full fur represents a chance to craft a performance in which his face—and by extension the idea of "Keanu Reeves"—is not a factor, before his skyrocketing recognizability makes that basically impossible.

In the absurdist *Bill & Ted's* universe getting rid of your false self is as easy as asking God to introduce you to an alien who'll help you build a robot to punch your doppelganger's head off. In real life, but specifically in a movie star's real life, the false self—the notion of you that exists in the mind of the public, the up-to-no-good portrait painted of you by the gossip blogs, and also the false version of you that *you yourself* put out into the world in order to keep your true self private—can be harder to kill. *Freaked* is Keanu putting on a mask to show us who he really is and what he doesn't intend to let go of, no matter what mutation-inducing corporate chemicals he's about to be exposed to.

The freaks try to escape Randy Quaid's compound disguised as milkmen. Winter tries to join them and Keanu responds with the movie's most quotably ridiculous line: "Twelve milkmen is theoretically possible—thirteen is ridiculous!" He and Winter get into a knife fight; then Keanu spies a squirrel and runs off to chase it.

12| OPERA ENVY

In April 1992, a Simi Valley jury acquits the four Los Angeles police officers who were videotaped beating a Black motorist named Rodney King during a traffic stop. The night the verdict is announced, Los Angeles erupts in riots and Keanu rides around town on his motorcycle. The uprising continues the following night and Keanu finds himself out in it again: "I had to pick up a friend around 12:30 that night and the air was electrified," he says. "It felt lawless. Like a Western town where no one wore their badges on the outside. Guns everywhere."

Like nearly everyone else who's seen the King videotape, Keanu can't believe the verdict went the way it did. But when he talks about it his thoughts zoom outward, to the broader issue of man's inhumanity to man.

"Some people don't like to feel that they're in the same boat with you," he says. "They'd like to have more room in the ocean and pick your teeth with your bones."

Point Break confirms that Keanu can carry an action movie, if he chooses to; his choice is to not do that. Instead he works with esteemed directors such as Francis Ford Coppola and Bernardo Bertolucci in movies that make more creative use of his screen persona when they acknowledge it at all. It's not that he wants to bury Johnny Utah, exactly, but he's petitioning to reopen the question of what kind of actor he's going to be. He'll spend most of the nineties in restless motion, trying on and discarding answers to that question, until *The Matrix* comes along in 1999 and temporarily squares the circle.

Winona Ryder brings James V. Hart's screenplay for *Bram Stoker's Dracula* to Francis Ford Coppola. Coppola wants to make the film with Ryder as Mina Murray; for the part of the solicitor Jonathan Harker, Mina's fiancé, he wants to cast Ryder's boyfriend, Johnny Depp. Depp has been shaking off the suspended-adolescence phase of his career around this time, skipping out on TV's *21 Jump Street* to play sexy leather-clad weirdos for Tim Burton (in *Edward Scissorhands*) and John Waters (in *Cry-Baby*). But when Columbia Pictures tells Coppola that Depp's not a big enough star, Coppola asks Winona whom she'd cast, and she suggests Keanu.

The seemingly pretty important question of how Keanu's whole deal will translate to a Gothic period piece apparently never comes up. "I wasn't so sophisticated about what that [persona] was," Coppola will admit later. But he knows he wants to populate his movie with other attractive young stars like Ryder. Hart's script goes back to the core of the Dracula mythos—it pulls its story directly from Stoker's 1897 novel, rather than the influential 1920s stage adaptation that shaped most modern Draculas. But it's also a revisionist, sexed-up take on the material; Keanu, an actor who missed his calling as a movie publicist, tells the UK magazine *Smash Hits* that it's a film about "vampires, submission, rape, domination, bestiality, guilt, Biblical overtones, Satan, God, Christian motifs, the dead, the undead, blood, murder, revenge, opera, classicism and oral sex."

As a kid, Keanu trick-or-treated in a Dracula cape his mother sewed. He's a fan of the original Max Schreck *Nosferatu*—"with Dracula's long fingers and the shadows and all that interplay," he says—and admires Nicolas Cage's unhinged performance as a vamp-bitten yuppie literary agent in *Vampire's Kiss*. Besides, it's Coppola, with the great cinematographer Michael Balhaus shooting, and a supporting cast that includes Anthony Hopkins and Tom Waits along with

Gary Oldman as the Count. What actor could resist a chance to run away and join this circus?

Keanu's costar Sadie Frost—who wrote in her own memoir about the strange experience of playing a vampishly sexualized Lucy Westenra for Coppola shortly after the birth of her first child—described the production as "a whirl of parties and attention." In a 2005 interview, Keanu made it sound like a dream: "It was great to be in that environment: going for a run in the morning, looking at the stars at night, going into Francis's research library, spending time with him," he said. "You know—watching Tom Waits sing 'Waltzing Matilda' to Winona at the piano, Winona crying. It was a beautiful life. *Les enfants du paradis.*"

He's invoking Marcel Carné's *Les Enfants du Paradis*, a three-hour epic shot in occupied France and released in 1945, about a courtesan, played by the French actor and singer Arletty, who seeks her own path while juggling various suitors, including a criminal and a long-suffering mime. Among other things, it's one of the most romantic depictions of the lives of artists in the history of movies, setting its central melodrama against the backstage culture of the theaters on Paris's so-called Boulevard of Crime, back when Keanu's chosen profession had an air of colorful disrepute. ("An actor!" sniffs the criminal Lacenaire, after he spots Arletty dancing with his rival. "What a breed! I can see why they're buried at night.")

Keanu brings up the Carné movie a lot in interviews around this time—making Kenneth Branagh's *Much Ado About Nothing* while living with his castmates in a villa in Tuscany, working for scale, and cooking his own food will remind him of *Les Enfants du Paradis*, too. ("We had a place to eat, a place to sleep, and a place to play as humans," he'll say. "We get to frolic in our joys and passions and everyone's humor was brought out with open hearts.")

As a chance to be an *enfant* among *enfants*, a guest at the party, *Bram Stoker's Dracula* is irresistible. But it's also an auteur project helmed by a somewhat preoccupied auteur. The profile of Coppola that Janet Maslin files for the *New York Times* on the eve of *Dracula*'s release is all about the director's eagerness to cultivate a reputation as a team player. There's a sense that the film is on some level also a chance for Coppola to put a stake in a legacy of troubled, costly productions that goes back to *Apocalypse Now.* The *Times* piece runs a few months after Coppola files for bankruptcy for the third time, aiming to resolve "a complicated decadelong series of financial and legal problems" stemming from the making of his 1982 bomb *One from the Heart.* Maslin quotes Columbia Pictures chairman Mark Canton describing Coppola, approvingly, as being "particularly concerned that he could be a good citizen in terms of his responsibility report card" while making *Dracula.*

But the material also brings out Coppola's experimental side. To avoid delays due to weather and other vagaries of filming on location, he shoots most of the movie on soundstages, but decides against building elaborate sets, letting Eiko Ishioka's wildly inventive costume designs establish the look of the film instead. He's intent on using practical effects—smoke and mirrors, forced perspective, camera tricks dating back to the silent era—instead of modern CGI, and when his visual-effects team balks at this plan, he fires them and puts his son Roman Coppola in charge of executing his ideas.

The sequence where Mina and Harker get married in Romania while Dracula attacks Lucy in her London bedroom is cut like an arch self-reference to the climax of the original *Godfather*, which juxtaposes the baptism of Connie and Carlo's son Michael and the Corleone family's soldiers knocking off the rest of New York's dons. In that sequence the first shotgun blast immediately follows the priest asking Michael Corleone if he renounces Satan; in *Dracula*, Keanu and Winona sip sacramental wine before the wolf tears Lucy's throat open and a geyser of Kool-Aid-red blood floods the room.

All this creative invention makes for a movie without one boring scene, but it also means Coppola can only devote so much of his attention to coaxing a performance out of Keanu, who shows up to set exhausted after his *Point Break*–to-*Idaho* year. Keanu will say later that he was plagued by self-doubt. He will come away from the movie thinking of himself as its weakest link, and it will weigh on him. "I was bad in [*Dracula*]," he'll tell David Ritz a few years later. "I didn't have the juice. My colleagues in the cast—Anthony Hopkins, Winona Ryder, Gary Oldman—were beautifully operatic. I wound up with opera envy."

The movie's least convincing practical effect is Keanu's English accent, and the script does him no favors by making Harker narrate much of the first act, even if that's how Stoker did it in the book. The standard English pronunciation of the name of Hungary's capital city is *Boo-da-pest*. Hungarians say *Boo-da-peshht*. As Harker, Keanu says *Bee-ooh-da-pest*, which sounds like pure San Dimas. It's not the last time he'll play a part he's not quite right for or struggle to maintain an accent other than his own, but he's never struggled this visibly; his subsequent reputation as a bad or at least a severely limited actor will rest largely on *Dracula*.

"He tried so hard," Coppola will say later. "That was the problem, actually—he wanted to do it perfectly and in trying to do it perfectly it came off as stilted. I tried to get him to just relax with it and not do it so fastidiously. So maybe I wasn't as critical of him, but that's because I like him personally so much. To this day he's a prince in my eyes."

There's no counterintuitive case to be made for Keanu's Harker accent. But his wobbly line readings don't ruin the movie; if anything, they obscure what's otherwise one of his most underrated performances. Harker is a strange figure in Stoker's book, which violates one of the basic tenets of Hollywood storytelling by spending a bunch of time up front with a character who isn't really the protagonist. Coppola told Keanu to think of Harker as "the first yuppie"; the first few pages of the novel, written as extracts from his diary, are essentially a chatty Yelp review of Transylvania, with remarks on hotel decor, wine, and local cuisine ("I had for breakfast more paprika, and a sort of porridge of maize flour which they said was 'mamaliga,' and egg-plant stuffed with forcemeat, a very excellent dish.").

Stoker is already building suspense in these pages—when Harker departs by coach for Dracula's castle, he notices the townspeople crossing themselves as he pulls away. But the character's job in the story is to be incognizant, then helpless; it would have been malpractice on Keanu's part to try to make Harker into a dynamic hero or a nutjob who could compete with Hopkins's boisterously morbid Van Helsing, or Waits bouncing off the walls of a rubber room as Dracula's trotured familiar, Mr. Renfield. Like the rest of the suitors who join Van Helsing's Crew of Light, he's destined to lose this Gothic game of Mystery Date to Oldman's Dracula, who starts out as a desiccated husk but lands in London as a frock-coated storm of irresistible sexual energy. (In his granny glasses and top hat, the person Oldman resembles most, ironically, is Johnny Depp.)

Some actors are good at making us believe they know more than they're saying, but Keanu may be at his best when a part calls for him to know less than we do. In the book Harker's meeting with Dracula is a confrontation between modernity and the bloody ancient past. Harker's journey from London has taken him across lands the Count tells him have been "fought over by the Wallachian, the Saxon, and the Turk," but when he gets there he shows Dracula pictures of the Carfax estate property "taken with my Kodak" (a brand name that was almost a decade old when Stoker's novel was published).

But there's also an unmistakable sexual overtone to their interactions. Stoker had, let's say, a complicated relationship to his own sexuality. He wrote passionate letters of devotion to male friends, as well as to Walt Whitman; he was close to Oscar Wilde, and his wife, Florence Bascombe, had been engaged to Wilde before marrying Stoker. After Wilde was prosecuted for "gross indecency with male persons" and ultimately sentenced to two years' hard labor, Stoker purged all direct references to Wilde from his writings. *Dracula* was published just two years later; its characterization of the Count as a fiendish aristocratic predator echoes the way Wilde was portrayed in court by the prosecution, while Harker—who seems almost hysterically blind to the nature of his host's interest in him—comes off like Stoker recasting himself as an innocent victim of unclean lust. The movie steers right into this: the moment where Dracula loses his composure after Harker cuts himself shaving is in the original text, but having Oldman finish shaving Keanu's throat before licking his blood off the straight razor is a flourish unique to the adaptation.

The Harker-in-Transylvania section of the film is another short, perfect Keanu Reeves movie hiding inside another film, a camp-horror sex comedy about an erotic Mr. Magoo, the oblivious object of everyone else's lust. Not until he sneaks out to explore the hidden depths of Oldman's castle and becomes a captive snack for three of Dracula's brides does he realize he's been on the menu all along. But as much as these scenes are about sex—the act as a Victorian hang-up, and Keanu's own sexuality as a blank canvas reflecting the erotic attention of all interested parties—they also play like a devilish visual metaphorization of what it might feel like, at this moment, to be Keanu Reeves, actor-turned–movie star. From the moment he arrives on Transylvanian soil he is never in control and he's constantly being watched, by wolves in the night and eyes in the sky. Everything on-screen helps tell a story about isolation and loss of agency—the chair that dwarfs Keanu at Dracula's dining-room table, the Count's slippery shadow reaching across the wall to clutch at him, the way Dracula whips out a sword when offended and pins him to the right side of the frame. Later Oldman will exit a scene with a whirl of his cape, and the room he leaves Keanu alone in will be plunged instantly into shadow, full dark across a wide screen, with Keanu's worried face floating disembodied in front of it. The film frame itself becomes a prison; then the darkness swallows Keanu, too.

13 | TRANSUBSTANTIATION WEDDING

Keanu Reeves and Winona Ryder are perfect for each other, so they can never be together—not in real life, or even on-screen, where there's always some force keeping them apart, whether it's an ancient vampire or their own issues. They both become icons as soon as they're even halfway famous, known for their hip taste in books and music, their healthy distrust of the path of least resistance, their lack of facility with accents, and their predilection for black clothes. In 2006's *A Scanner Darkly* Keanu plays a guy with two personalities, neither of whom can get over Winona. "How do you make it," he wonders, "with that kind of sweet, unique, stubborn chick?" The person he's asking, by the way, is one of the neurologists he's supposed to be talking to about his rapidly deteriorating brain—that's how important and unanswerable a question it is and will always be, to a certain breed of nineties man.

In 2018, Winona Ryder drops a historical bombshell in *Entertainment Weekly*, revealing that the scene in *Dracula* where she and Keanu get quickie married in Romania so Keanu can get over his sexy ordeal as a prisoner of Dracula's brides may have technically been a legally binding wedding to Keanu. The ceremony in the film is the only sequence not shot on a soundstage in Culver City; Coppola reshot the scene just south of Koreatown, on Valentine's Day, in an actual Greek Orthodox church, with an actual Greek Orthodox priest doing what might have been the actual honors.

Winona mentions this while promoting *Destination Wedding*, a sour but well-written romantic comedy with a strange gimmick—the only actors in it who have any dialogue are Keanu and Winona as Frank and Lindsay, prickly longtime singles who bump narcissisms at the Paso Robles wedding of Frank's brother, who's also Lindsay's ex. The movie captures the way cynical people can forge a connection in spite of themselves by *Get a load of this guy*–ing everyone else around them. They don't have anything nice to say, so they sit by each other. It's sitcom-y but Winona and Keanu's friendship makes it play.

Ryder may never have another relationship as infamous as her early-nineties engagement to her *Edward Scissorhands* costar Johnny Depp, who famously gets WINONA FOREVER tattooed on his bicep, and then, as if fact-checking himself, changes it to read WINO FOREVER when they go their separate ways. That moment is a defining one in her story as a star, as well as in Depp's. But her by-all-accounts-platonic relationship with Keanu lasts longer, and might mean more. They circle each other, intersecting periodically, reuniting on-screen about once a decade, both a little older and a little sadder around the eyes, two human indicators of time's passage. Like Keanu, Winona comes from hippie DNA. Her mother attended the first Human Be-In at the beginning of the Summer of Love. Timothy Leary was Winona's godfather; her father, Michael, was Leary's archivist and palled around in San Francisco with sixties icons like Allen Ginsberg. Winona's middle name is Laura, after *Doors of Perception* author Aldous Huxley's wife, another family friend. Winona starts acting at twelve and makes an impression just a few years later in her first feature-film role as Corey Haim's platonic best friend in *Lucas*, which comes out in 1986, the same year as Keanu's first big movies.

But she really clicks in darker projects that upend stereotypes of movie teendom. Against the advice of her agents and her parents she agrees to be in 1989's *Heathers*, a black comedy about a high school princess and closet bohemian who sours on the vapid "Swatch dogs and Diet Cokeheads" in her peer group, hooks up with Christian Slater—playing a motorcycle-riding rebel the script calls Jason Dean—and starts knocking off the popular kids, staging their murders to look like teenage suicides. And in Tim Burton's *Beetlejuice* she's the self-consciously spooky Lydia Deetz, a landmark character for Goth representation in cinema.

When magazines and newspapers begin writing about Winona, nearly every piece invokes Leary, Huxley, the Zen preschool she attended in San Francisco, and her family's stint at the Rainbow commune near Mendocino, framing her as a kind of second-generation counterculture celebrity and also a bit of a kook. Winona is a prototypical nineties hipster with a nineties hipster's affinities and aversions, but when she starts getting profiled in mainstream magazines it's not yet the nineties, so in a lot of her early press you can feel American celebrity journalism struggling to process a new and unfamiliar breed of Young Actor Coming of Age.

Her first *Los Angeles Times* profile, from 1989, reads more like a treatment for an independent movie about a manic pixie dream girl who turns a lonely *Los Angeles Times* reporter's world upside down: "Riding shotgun, Winona Ryder kicked up her feet on the dashboard and pumped up the volume on KROQ-FM, ebulliently crooning to the Dead Milkmen's 'Punk Rock Girl.' It was time for her favorite pursuit—exploring abandoned houses."

Vogue packs the descriptors "offbeat," "disarming," "quirky," and "eclectic tomboy" into a single sentence that ends by describing her as "part Annie Hall, part Holly Golightly." She shows *Premiere* her dog-eared copy of J. D. Salinger's *Catcher in the Rye*, in which she's underlined Holden Caulfield saying the goddamn movies can ruin you, and swears to *The Face* that if anyone ever tries to make a film of Salinger's book, "I would rent a plane or a helicopter and drop bombs on the set, destroy it. In my lifetime I'll see that it's just not done." She takes guitar lessons from LA punk legend turned actor John Doe on the set of 1989's *Great Balls of Fire* and plays the title role in Mojo Nixon and Skid Roper's video for the novelty rockabilly song "Debbie Gibson Is

Pregnant with My Two-Headed Love Child," which ends with Ryder, as Gibson, giving birth to a visually disturbing homemade Muppet and then enjoying a tasty burger. MTV refused to play it; Ryder called it "my favorite role to date."

Like Keanu, she works a lot as the eighties give way to the nineties; she cites exhaustion when she drops out of Coppola's *Godfather III* just before it starts shooting in 1989. Like Keanu, she's cast by great auteurs in some parts that give her trouble. Not everyone can buy her as a proper lady of the Victorian era when she turns up in Coppola's *Dracula*, or of New York's Gilded Age in Martin Scorsese's *The Age of Innocence* in 1993. In *The New Biographical Dictionary of Film*, David Thomson—clearly a fan, for the most part—writes politely that Ryder "may have lacked some of the technique required for period." The writer Masha Tupitsyn takes it further in an essay called "Famous Tombs," about Ryder's relationship with Johnny Depp and the fatalistic impulse behind Depp's notorious WINONA FOREVER tattoo. In her heyday, Tupitsyn writes, "Ryder was employed not to play a range of characters well—the way actors are traditionally expected to, and the way we knew Ryder wasn't especially good at doing—but to reflect something about a particular time and mood."

You could drop Keanu's name into that sentence for Winona's and the assertions would still track. Keanu struggles to find good parts at the end of the nineties, finds *The Matrix* in 1999, and starts the new century having brought the action-hero and gentle-Zen-pilgrim aspects of his star persona into temporary harmony. Meanwhile Winona makes at least one movie a year throughout the nineties. She dates a string of rock stars—Courtney Love famously says at one point that you're nobody in the music business unless you've feuded with her or slept with Ryder—and the rock stars she dates write songs about her, and so do more than a few rock stars she's never even met. These songs—a canon that if you believe the legends eventually grows to include Beck's "Lost Cause," Ryan Adams's "Cry on Demand," and the Old 97's' "Rollerskate Skinny"—are just one of the ways pop culture works through its Winona obsession. She voices Lisa's archrival on *The Simpsons* back when *Simpsons* voice cameos still mattered, makes out with Jon Stewart on *The Larry Sanders Show*, lip-syncs as Jon Spencer in a Blues Explosion video, and kisses Jennifer Aniston's Rachel on a *Friends* episode. She ends the decade by producing and starring in a movie version of Susanna Kaysen's memoir *Girl, Interrupted*; she gives a sharp, sensitive performance, although Angelina Jolie's showier, Oscar-winning turn as a fellow patient is all anyone can talk about.

Then in late 2001 she's caught shoplifting $5,500 worth of clothes from a Saks Fifth Avenue in Beverly Hills. She's arrested holding Demerol and Diazepam in liquid form, Vicoprofen, Vicodin, Percodan, Valium, morphine sulfate, and Endocet, which contains oxycodone. She's sentenced to counseling and community service; the fact that Ryder had a prescription for all the drugs apart from the Endocet leads authorities to her doctor, Jules Mark Lusman, a surgeon who's accused in a 2002 report by the California State Medical Board of providing narcotics on a "cash-and-carry basis" to a clientele of "wealthy and/or famous drug-seekers" in a manner the board compared to "the sub-plot of a Raymond Chandler novel." As a result of Ryder's arrest, Lusman lost his license to practice medicine, and Ryder lost face. But she also lost time, a precious commodity for an actor subject to Hollywood's prejudices against women over thirty. Her comeback in the late 2000s is somehow both welcome and ignominious—in J. J. Abrams's 2009 *Star Trek* reboot, then-thirty-one-year-old Zachary Quinto plays Mr. Spock, and Ryder plays his mother, because she's *thirty-seven*. Darren Aronofsky's *Black Swan* at least gives her a real role to play, albeit as an embittered former ingenue cracked by the pressures put on prima ballerinas. She's fared better lately on TV, in *Show Me a Hero* and *The Plot Against America* and as the mother of a child lost to another dimension on *Stranger Things*. But as an archetypal Gen X movie star, her struggle to hold her position in the twenty-first century mirrors the limited cultural footprint of Gen X as a whole. "Playing the nineties," Tupitsyn writes, "*was* Ryder's part, for once they ended, her specificity did not carry over."

When Keanu and Winona meet again in a movie it's 2006. In *A Scanner Darkly* Ryder plays Donna, a hung-up dealer carrying on a fitful but unconsummated relationship with the non-cop side of Keanu's split personality. The fact that it's Winona's image haunting Keanu's unraveling brain space and transfixing him on the surveillance tapes he studies in order to understand his own actions adds a layer of meaning; it feeds our sense that *Scanner* is Keanu dreaming of Keanu's own predicament, the disorientation of an actor who can no longer access his true self. Winona and Keanu do drugs together and it's exactly what you imagine Winona and Keanu on drugs would be like. Keanu wants only to connect—"It's like you know me. You can *read* me"—and Winona refuses to be touched. At the end of the movie, Keanu's supervisor, Hank—a character we've only seen in disguise up until now—turns out to be Donna, and Donna turns out to be a fellow cop named Audrey. She's been helping to manipulate Keanu all along, but she's also the only one in the film who feels bad about it.

Destination Wedding's Frank and Lindsay are appealing characters in the way TV's equally misanthropic Jerry Seinfeld (the character) and Elaine Benes were. But the only-two-speaking-parts conceit never stops feeling stagey and unnatural, and the notion that these characters are brittle because deep down they're lonely gets garbled because we never forget we're looking at Keanu Reeves and Winona Ryder, and this makes their isolation play like a type of isolation specific to the lives of stars, who rarely *aren't* moving through a world where everyone else is an extra. It's rocky as a movie but works beautifully as a shipper daydream about two generational icons growing old together on the installment plan. They will always be alone but they will always have each other.

14 | PLASTIC ROOTS OF THE BODHI TREE

Of the Keanu Reeves movies that no one particularly loves, my favorite is probably Bernardo Bertolucci's *Little Buddha*, a collision of auteur and actor and subject matter as unlikely in 1993 as it would be unthinkable today: The life of Prince Siddhartha, the pre-enlightenment Buddha and probably the most significant South Asian human in recorded history, brought to the screen by the director of *Last Tango in Paris* and the guy who played Johnny Utah. Bertolucci will say later that he'd initially envisioned his Siddhartha as a younger version of the legendary Indian film director Satyajit Ray, whose face was handsome and thoughtful and a little bit severe. He sent casting directors to India, but according to Bertolucci, all the actors they found "looked either like mini-Rambos or mafiosi."

Keanu enchanted Bertolucci the moment they met: "Indian illustrations and Indian epic movies, pop art, the things you see on the walls of the tobacconist of Vishnu and Krishna—they are all like Keanu," Bertolucci will say later, while promoting the film. "He has a kind of beauty that's not Eastern or Western. You're not sure what it is, except pure kitsch."

But in the early nineties, Keanu is not a counterintuitive choice for the part because of his ethnicity; he's a counterintuitive choice because he's *Keanu*, dude. The *Washington Post* calls Keanu's Siddhartha "the wackiest bit of casting since George Burns played God." It's the first thing people find hard to understand about *Little Buddha*, which comes at its subject from a range of odd angles. Parts of it are an art film about spiritually alienated Westerners struggling with the emptiness of their own lives. Parts of it are Bertolucci anticipating latter-day George Lucas, following adorable kids with cosmic destinies. Parts of it are an admirably quixotic attempt to dramatize some of the universe's most elusive and painful truths using only reaction shots of Chris Isaak. And for the length of one extraordinary sequence toward the end of the film it's the best illustration of what Keanu does in movies—or, more specifically, of how he *is* in movies, and how much he can convey without doing a whole lot.

He's already preparing for Siddhartha when he goes to Italy to play Don John in Kenneth Branagh's *Much Ado About Nothing*, in which Keanu delivers actual Shakespearean dialogue on-screen for the first time while wearing only leather pants. He has books on Buddhism shipped to the house where he and the cast are living, a Tuscan villa where Mona Lisa herself supposedly grew up. (Keanu always does the homework; when Gus Van Sant told him and River Phoenix to read John Rechy's *City of Night* as prep for *My Own Private Idaho*, Keanu inhaled Rechy's whole oeuvre.)

While making *Much Ado*, Keanu also gets to know the barrel-chested Shakespearean actor Brian Blessed. Blessed was the Duke of Exeter in Branagh's *Henry V*, Old Deuteronomy in the original West End production of *Cats*, and Prince Vultan, lord of the bird-men of Sky City, in 1980's *Flash Gordon*. When he meets Keanu he's in his fifties and has just made his first attempt to summit Everest without supplemental oxygen. He also meditates every day. Keanu asks Blessed to teach him a few things, and so the future Prince Siddhartha sits meditating in the hills of Tuscany with the former Prince Vultan. One day, while Keanu's meditating, he begins to feel like his body is "as big as a valley." His arm feels like it's eighteen miles long.

Is this an actor's process, or a spiritual quest? In Keanu's life, at this moment, maybe these two things aren't that different. He's preparing to play a pampered prince who emerges from his castle and discovers the world of suffering, disease, and death; as he gears up to make the movie, attempting to write the story of Siddhartha into himself on the cellular level, he subjects himself to something similar. In Bhutan he trains with the film's technical advisor, the Tibetan/Butanese lama Dzongsar Khyentse Rinpoche. In Kathmandu he gets furious diarrhea from monastery food; later, he stands by the river and watches a cremation.

"The parents were placing wood on a funeral pyre," he'll say later, "where a woman's body was burning . . . The sun setting on the temples . . . Saddhus chasing monkeys . . . Children playing with the dogs who were running around the fire . . . Life in all its diversity! The old, the young, Indians, tourists, pain, joy . . . There, I felt something of Buddha, something of the cycle of being. Birth, death, birth, death, birth, death. In the West, we do everything we can to distance ourselves from the sight of death."

It costs $35 million to make this film about a famous ascetic. Reporting for the *Los Angeles Times*, the travel writer Pico Iyer notes a call sheet listing "208 Members of the Court, 50 Court Guards, 36 Palanquin Porters, 12 Grooms, 11 Indian Girls and 8 Kapadi Players," with "Special Requirements" that include "10 Horses. Props: Palanquins (minimum of 3). Lunch: for 140 people (and for 350 extras)." Bertolucci flies in five hundred hairpieces from London to coif his extras, and pasta for the Italian plasterers working to restore the ancient city of Bhaktapur to fifth-century standard.

To play Siddhartha in the scenes where he grows a castaway's beard and survives on mud and bird droppings, Keanu drops weight by fasting. At night he has dreams, he tells the writer Kristine McKenna, of stuffing his face with bread and cheese, of rolling naked in the dirt and pouring red wine on his head. He doesn't sleep much but his mind feels electrified. He gives this electrified state of being a name. He calls it the "white zone."

The parts of *Little Buddha* that don't involve Keanu take place in the present. Chris Isaak is a Seattle architect who comes home from work one day to find his wife, played by Bridget Fonda, sitting with two Tibetan Buddhist monks in his austere postmodern house. "They were just admiring the emptiness of the room, sweetheart," Bridget Fonda says.

Isaak and Fonda play it cold and disconnected—from each other, from their own emotions. The monks think Fonda and Isaak's son may be the reincarnation of a newly dead Tibetan lama. Chris Isaak thinks he'll have another scotch. This is Isaak's second feature as a lead actor after Lynch's *Twin Peaks: Fire Walk with Me*, in which he investigated a pre–Laura Palmer killing with Kiefer Sutherland and wound up lost in space. After this he'd be an appealingly noncommittal and self-deprecating metapresence in the role of "Chris Isaak" on *The Chris Isaak Show*. But here his acting is all head tilts and eye rolls, James Dean legacy stuff as the squirm of self-consciousness. The great performance in *Little Buddha* is by Fonda, who has the least to do—when their son accepts an invitation to travel to Bhutan and meet other potential lamas, it's Isaak who chaperones the trip and Fonda who stays behind in cold, blue Seattle. She finds the corners of small moments anyway. When she drops off her son at the local Dharma Center and can't get away fast enough, as if recoiling from its churchy atmosphere or her own guilt, she indicates depths we never see.

Fonda and her son read a children's story about the life of Siddhartha, to help him—and her, and us—understand the history of Buddhism, which is where Keanu comes in. When Keanu's Siddhartha first steps outside the king's house to greet reality he's wearing a gold medallion and blousy pants. He looks a little like Aladdin and a little like Liz Taylor in *Cleopatra*. As Siddhartha he's lean and delicate and—there's no real way around this—sort of painted brown, or at least bronze, and his accent brings to mind the voice Hank Azaria used as Apu on *The Simpsons*, so in this case it's a relief when he can't really maintain it and lapses into talking like Keanu. He's also wearing eyeliner. It's the first time he's tried to pull off a physical transformation like this, and one of the last; after this he'll mostly leave the white-zone routine to athletes like Christian Bale.

Anyway: any non-Indian actor in their right mind would pass on this movie if it came up today, but Keanu as a pure-kitsch Siddhartha does perfectly suit the film, which is less a life of the historical Buddha and more of a fantasy seen through the eyes of a child reading a storybook. Siddhartha is also a classic Keanu character. Like Scott Favor in *My Own Private Idaho*, he's a son of privilege lured out of the palace and into the streets, where pain and struggle await. And like Neo in *The Matrix*, his story is about seeing the truth, and the responsibility that comes with that, and what can change in you when you're confronted with a vision of the world as it really is.

Soon enough he learns about sickness, and the fact that it precedes death for almost everyone. "Show me death," he says. He watches the ashes of a dead man float down a river in a bowl, a body being washed and placed on a pyre and put to the torch. Keanu weeps, broken open by what he's seen. He makes it his task to escape the cycle of reincarnation, chops his hair into a kind of feathered wedge, bids a tearful goodbye to his horse and his manservant, and posts up under the bodhi tree. Iyer writes that Bertolucci's location scouts found a perfect tree for this scene, located next to a perfect river, "but not, alas, at the perfect distance from the perfect river (so they raised the tree onto a platform and gave it plastic roots)."

It's here under this fake tree that Keanu does his best work in this film. That sounds like a backhanded compliment, since this is a scene where Siddhartha does nothing but sit still with a beatific half smile on his lips. But it's also an example of Keanu doing something we now know he's really good at—being the unchanging human presence at the center of a visual maelstrom, the object in the picture whose presence gives artificial realities a sense of stakes and scale. The meditation sequence in *Little Buddha* is a before-the-fact distillation of the role he'll play in *The Matrix*, as the oncscreen figure who'll keep us from feeling lost or alienated no matter how much uncannily postreality imagery the movie throws at us.

In the Siddhartha story, Mara, the demon who lives rent-free in every meditator's head, tries to tempt him into breaking his concentration. Five lissome young women appear before Keanu and take turns in a swing, their long hair brushing the Bodhi tree's gnarled roots. One of the brides spills a jug of water and a reflecting pool forms at Keanu's feet. An audience appears—Isaak and Fonda's son and two other children who've been identified as potential lamas, who share the screen with Keanu for the first time in the film. They settle among the tree's roots to watch what's about to happen.

The face of Mara rises growling out of the pool of water. The wind rises, the air turns to ash, the brides' alluring flesh crumbles and blows away with the dry leaves. The storm swirls and the kids seek shelter behind the tree trunk. Now a wide shot. Keanu is still meditating but the pool in front of him is now an angry sea. Lightning crashes. Waves break at his feet. Fireballs rocket toward him. The sea and the sky turn red. In the red fog an army of demons appear in silhouette. They nock flaming arrows and rain fire on him but the flames turn to petals that drift harmlessly to the ground. It's archetypal Keanu—he just sits there watching everything unfold and not reacting, our serene and contemplative focal point against a backdrop of all illusory catastrophe and danger the movies can throw at him.

In real life Keanu couldn't quite hack the lotus position, something Bertolucci didn't find out until after he'd been cast. But Keanu's meditation face is great because it's so unserious. He looks like he's trying not to laugh.

15 | THE SPACE OF FREE ACTION

In 1989, a few months after *Bill & Ted's Excellent Adventure* comes out and radically alters his reality, Keanu is up in the Berkshires, earning decent reviews as the jester Trinculo in a Shakespeare and Company production of *The Tempest* where André Gregory from *My Dinner with Andre* plays Prospero. It won't be the last time he responds to a career crossroads by zagging toward the stage.

"I saw a lot of plays with my stepfather when I was younger," he says in 1992, "and the theater became my first love. There, you're really performing. You're a real actor, not some meat puppet."

Back in 1985, when Keanu is balancing an about-to-pop film and a TV career with classes at Leah Posluns Theatre School in Toronto, an instructor named Lewis Baumander directs him as Mercutio in *Romeo and Juliet*—a role he'll describe decades later as "one of the breakthrough moments of my life." (Baumander later points out that Mercutio is also the one character in the play who doesn't seem to have parents.) When Keanu accepts a star on the Hollywood Walk of Fame in 2005, he talks about none of his movies by name but mentions Mercutio twice. "But Hollywood was calling, Hollywood was calling," he says, and the "But" is suggestive, as if some other scenario might have appealed if Hollywood had not been so determined to have him.

Baumander and Keanu stay in touch over the years. When the artistic director of the Manitoba Theater Centre, Steven Schipper, calls Baumander in 1993 wondering if there's a part that could lure Keanu onto their stage, Baumander remembers his old friend's obsession with Hamlet.

The fact that it's Baumander asking doesn't quite explain why Keanu agrees to do it. When he's asked by the *Toronto Star* to speculate, Baumander points out that Keanu is "at the right age to play Hamlet—29—and it's been suggested to him by Kenneth Branagh and Kevin Kline, who've both played Hamlet, that now is a good time to play Hamlet," which doesn't quite explain it either.

Maybe it has a little to do with redemption, after the unintentional laughs and scathing reviews that greeted his Don John in *Much Ado About Nothing*. Maybe it's about setting a personal goal that isn't about his personal brand, and reasserting some power over his career by building this into the schedule. Maybe, symbolically, it's about stopping the fucking bus for a minute—or proving it won't explode if he does.

When they discuss logistics, Baumander floats the possibility of staging a Manitoba Theatre Centre production of *Hamlet* in New York, or in London as "a Richard Chamberlain 'I have arrived' kind of number," but Keanu opts to do it at the actual Manitoba Theatre Centre in Winnipeg. Symbolically, by choosing to do theater in Canada he's returning to the inception point of his acting career, to when he was being measured by a different set of values from the ones he's increasingly being held to, as movie star and meat puppet.

***

A news item in 1993 in the *Independent*—a pickup from Keanu's Cannes press-conference appearances supporting *Much Ado*, with the headline "He's a Star, but Is He an Actor?"—quotes him saying he's currently trying to decide between "playing a SWAT operative in an action story" for his next project and starring in a friend's movie where he'll play a composite of "Apollo, Dionysus and Bacchus." He is also quoted describing the experience of reading the novel *Dr. Faustus* by Thomas Mann as follows: "I'm like, *Wow, fuck*."

He chooses the SWAT movie—it's *Speed;* you know it, there's a bomb on a bus and the bus can't slow down—but even once it's finished and he's out in the world promoting it, he still seems to be struggling with the decision. *Entertainment Weekly* puts him on the cover along with the words "The Next Action Hero?" and when Keanu meets the writer Melina Gerosa at Little Frida's (described in the story as a "lesbian coffee shop in West Hollywood") he gives *EW* an interview worthy of the question mark in its headline. When he's asked to name his favorite action movies, he names three historical dramas by British directors, the newest of which came out in 1981: "I like the action scene in *Excalibur*, the fighting scenes in *The Duellists*, um, *The Three Musketeers* with Oliver Reed."

By the story's second paragraph he's dismissed the idea that he wants to be the next Stallone, Schwarzenegger, or Willis: "I don't have any ambition to do that," he says. But in 1994 even that answer won't stop people from asking the question, as if the choice isn't entirely his. It's the beginning of a transitional phase for American action movies. Schwarzenegger—whose next movie, *True Lies*, due out later that summer, will be his last collaboration with James Cameron—is still a box-office draw, and so is Stallone, whose film *The Specialist* will make $170 million in the fall. Dolph Lundgren and Jean-Claude Van Damme have *Man of War* and *Timecop*—two of their very best bad movies—in the pipeline. But none of these four guys are getting any younger, and to varying degrees they're all hitting the diminishing-returns point of their leading-man careers. The man who should be the breakout action star of 1994—Brandon Lee, son of Bruce—has been dead, after an accident on set, for over a year when his would-be breakthrough film, *The Crow*, comes out in May. John Woo's just made his first English-language movie, *Hard Target*, with Van Damme, and Jackie Chan's US breakthrough *Rumble in the Bronx* is only a year away, but mainstream American movies haven't assimilated Hong Kong action cinema as an influence yet. Nicolas Cage's face remains firmly attached to his head.

So in 1994, as if scrambling to nominate any plausible successor to the genre's waning icons, Hollywood builds a lot of action movies around counterintuitive, nontraditional, so-crazy-it-just-might-work leads. Alec Baldwin remaking Sam Peckinpah's *The Getaway* and fighting crime as pulp-fiction hero *The Shadow*? Sure! Ray Liotta as a wrongfully convicted marine stuck on a futuristic prison island in *No Escape*? Why not? Jeff Bridges as a former IRA terrorist turned bomb-squad cop trying to catch his old compatriot Tommy Lee Jones in *Blown Away*? I guess! Meryl Streep as a history teacher whose strained marriage to David Strathairn takes a back seat to a white-knuckled white-water-rafting adventure in *The River Wild*? Uh, sure—it's Meryl Streep! Of all the talent thrown at the action-movie wall in 1994, it's Keanu who seems most likely to succeed—but at first, he's ambivalent about signing on to play *Speed*'s Jack Traven. In that *Entertainment Weekly* interview, Keanu remembers reading an early draft of the script that read like "*Die Hard* mixed with some kind of screwball comedy."

A last-minute rewrite by script doctor Joss Whedon pivots Jack away from loose-cannon-cop cliché, and only *Speed*'s opening sequence hints at the standard action comedy it could have become. When Keanu Reeves and Jeff Daniels and the rest of their SWAT team show up to deal with a sabotaged elevator full of people and somebody asks if there's anything that can stop the elevator if it falls, Keanu cracks, "Yeah—the basement," and for a minute you can imagine a version of this movie where he and Jeff Daniels do a lot more high-fiving.

In the *Speed* we're actually watching, Jack Traven has no backstory, no apparent attachments other than Daniels. His haircut gives him an ex-military vibe but the film never confirms that or anything else. He's just a problem-solving machine. He wears a digital watch and chews gum without a wasted movement. When Jeff Daniels quizzes him about how to resolve a hypothetical hostage situation, Keanu's solution is to shoot the hostage, and when they're clearing passengers off the elevator and the lady in the very back of the car is too scared to climb up and out, his solution is to shout at her to move, and when Dennis Hopper shows up as the guy who rigged the elevator and holds Jeff Daniels at gunpoint, rendering the hostage question literal, Keanu shoots Daniels in the leg.

"[B]y cutting himself loose from the precious object through whose possession the enemy kept him in check, the subject gains the space of free action," wrote the philosopher Slavoj Žižek, who saw this notion of radical sacrifice as a means of liberation from existing social reality as the thread connecting *Speed*, Freud, Abraham, Toni Morrison's *Beloved*, the fictional Turkish crime lord Keyser Söze killing his own wife and child in *The Usual Suspects*, and the part in Mel Gibson's *Ransom* where Gibson takes the money he's supposed to give his son's kidnappers and instead says he'll give it to whoever kills the kidnappers for him.

And yet—after Keanu is given a medal for shooting his own partner—the rest of the movie will be about him solving problems in ways that refuse to disregard human frailty. When he shows up in flannel, khakis, and a white T-shirt for the movie's second act, known in philosophical circles as The Part with the Bus, he looks like a guy, not a SWAT cop, and once he's on the bus, the first complication he has to deal with is a passenger who turns out to be a gun-toting fugitive who thinks Keanu's there to take him out. In order to resolve this situation Keanu has to put his gun down, symbolically relinquishing his identity as police and the authority that comes with it. "I'm not a cop right now," he tells the guy with the gun. "We're just two cool guys."

It's working, until another passenger, a construction worker, decides to be a hero and tackle the guy with the gun, which leads to the bus driver getting shot and wounded, which leads to the rest of the movie, in which Sandra Bullock's Annie takes the wheel and acts of individual heroism become less important than collective action by the bus riders as a community. Even the guy with the gun, ostensibly a criminal, gets reintegrated into the society of the bus when he helps Keanu escape from being trapped under the bus's wheels.

In a world whose everyday mechanisms can be weaponized against the individual—the elevator is a guillotine and the bus is a bullet—survival takes more than the "big, round hairy cojones" Keanu gets complimented on by a passenger after one particularly close call. It requires Keanu's Traven to nurture and support Sandra Bullock so she can do the work of driving the bus, validating her feelings of guilt after a passenger gets killed: "You were glad you were still alive . . . You should be glad. We all are." And when Jeff Daniels gets blown up and Keanu begins to flip out, exercising the stereotypical male prerogative to explode with anger, it's Bullock who says focus, come back, we need you. So *Speed* is a perfect action movie for Keanu because it's about a tough guy who, in order to do his job and save the bus passengers and himself, has to learn to be cooler to other people, to be more Keanu-like. What's being posited here is a new model for what kind of action an action hero takes, and by extension a new way for Keanu to function within this genre that everyone in 1994 is so eager to see him dominate, whether or not he's excited to do so.

The consensus that's formed around *Speed* since 1994 is that it's where Keanu—having spent a few years punching above his weight for Coppola and Bertolucci—finally internalized the lesson of *Point Break*, accepting his destiny as a buff yet compassionate action hero for the nineties. Which is not a narrative Keanu has ever seemed eager to accept. A few years later, when he's prompted by the journalist Chris Heath to name the movies he's most proud of in a *Rolling Stone* cover-story interview, Keanu will reel off the following top-ten list, plus an honorable mention:

"*River's Edge*, *Permanent Record*, *Bill and Ted's*, *I Love You to Death*, *Little Buddha*, *Tune in Tomorrow*, *The Last Time I Committed Suicide*, *The Matrix*, *The Devil's Advocate*. I like a lot of *Johnny Mnemonic*. I like the version of *Feeling Minnesota* that's not in the movie."

The fact that *Private Idaho* doesn't immediately spring to Keanu's mind may be the most interesting thing about that list, but Heath notes the conspicuous absence of *Speed*. Keanu replies that the good thing about making *Speed* was how little space it took up in his head, which left plenty of room on the old hard drive for the fifteen hundred lines of Shakespeare he was busy trying to learn. He'd walk around on closed-down freeway overpasses between takes, soliloquizing.

When Heath asks him what this tells us about *Speed*, Keanu's answer is "It ain't Shakespeare."

What *Speed* really tells us is how little actual acting Keanu has to do in order to be compelling in a movie, which cannot be a comfortable truth. But it's possible *Speed* understood Keanu better than Keanu understands *Speed*.

16 | THE LAZIEST BOY IN SCHOOL

"An art critic I know named Tim Martin recently commented, 'When Keanu performs, it's as if he has a foot of Robert Bressonian space around him,'" the artist Stephen Prina told the *Los Angeles Times* in 1994, "and he does have a peculiar detachment that doesn't allow for the kind of psychological relationship you have with a traditional method actor."

Writer-director Robert Bresson felt that traditional film actors projected personality, character, and emotion in ways that short-circuited the audience's own ability to empathize. Beginning with 1951's *Diary of a Country Priest*, he instead sought out nonprofessional actors—in *Notes on the Cinematograph*, he even eschews the word "actor," referring to his cast instead as "human models"—whom he coached to deliver lines with minimal inflection. I think he would have liked Keanu.

In 1994 everyone wants to talk to Stephen Prina about Keanu, because in 1994 Prina is teaching a twelve-week course on Keanu's films at the ArtCenter College of Design in Pasadena, California, and just about everyone writes about this like it's the most out-there, hilarious thing they've ever heard—unchecked postmodernism at its most laughably defundable.

Prina finds himself in the somehow extremely appropriate pop-art position of being jeered at by both the *National Enquirer* ("Here's proof that education ain't what it used to be") and *The New Yorker*, via a Talk of the Town piece by Susan Orlean. Orlean is actually way snarkier than the *Enquirer*, writing that Prina "taught courses on major dudes like Fassbinder and Pasolini in previous years," and that the class "is actually twelve gnarly weeks of culture, sociology, anthropology, and philosophy, plus there's, like, a lot of homework."

The, like, subtext of Orlean's dispatch is that this class is total bullshit. But when Prina's students discuss *Bill & Ted's* they do it through the lens of Foucault's *Nietzsche, Genealogy, History*, and when they talk about *I Love You to Death* they do it in the context of *The Philosophy of Andy Warhol*, and so on. If it's total bullshit, it's no more total bullshit than any other art school class.

People magazine quotes one of Prina's students: twenty-seven-year-old Keith Mayerson, "who keeps a log of 'Keanu sightings, ' confides, 'I [stood beside him at a urinal] at a club once.' But that magic moment"—snark again—"is not, to Mayerson, a critical component of the course. 'It's really about looking at pop cinema and deconstructing what's interesting about it,' he says. But just what *is* it about Keanu that students want to discuss? 'He's a hero for the slacker generation,' Mayerson says. 'He's a little vacant, a little inarticulate, but he's still beautiful and still gets the girl.'"

These stories tell us a lot about where Keanu was in 1994 as a cultural figure. He's both a figure of fun and increasingly the subject of some pretty high-end thinking. As Chuck Stephens puts it in the San Francisco *Bay Guardian* in July, Keanu "is our shared experiential dilemma, a public-service koan, a fragment of nonsense in which the lysergic bubble of meaning bursts and blooms."

Not everything being written about him around this time is that thoughtful. *Speed* opens on June 10, 1994. It's the number one movie in America that weekend and will end up being the seventh-highest-grossing movie of that year, behind *The Lion King*, James Cameron's *True Lies*, and *Forrest Gump*. (*Little Buddha*, released in late May to positive but befuddled reviews, is the eighteenth-biggest movie in America during *Speed*'s opening weekend.)

In late June, Samuel Reeves is tried and sentenced. The *Star* screams "Speed Hunk Keanu's Long-Lost Dad Jailed on Drug Rap." The *National Enquirer*'s story about the sentencing—"'Speed' Star's Nightmare as Dad Is Jailed in Cocaine Bust"—even quotes Keanu, via the highly suspect recollections of "a buddy."

"Drugs are truly evil," Keanu's buddy quotes Keanu as saying, "I don't even use them, but they've turned my life into a nightmare. They took my best friend, River—and now they've put my father in prison for 10 years. If I only had the power to stamp deadly drugs out of existence, I'd do it in a second!"

It doesn't sound true. It sounds like bad screenwriting. It's hard to imagine Keanu saying the words "If I only had the power to stamp deadly drugs out of existence" out loud. It's hard to imagine Batman saying those words.

In August a British tabloid, the *Daily Mirror*, publishes a story compiling evidence of Keanu's supposedly wild existence—his jailbird father, but also his many bike wrecks and his dead friend River Phoenix. A few paragraphs in, there's a reference to "rumors about his sexuality."

The story goes on to describe, in curious detail, Keanu's supposed relationship with the openly gay billionaire record executive David Geffen, with whom (the *Mirror* alleges) he's been seen "painting the town red at parties and going on wild shopping sprees." The *Mirror* quotes a source saying they've been spotted at Barney's, "giggling like schoolboys as they tried on mounds of £350 shirts."

Just before Christmas the French celebrity weekly *Voici* takes things a step further, reporting that Geffen and Keanu have actually gotten married in a private ceremony—"the first gay marriage in the history of show business"—at a restaurant in Los Angeles. The alleged officiant is a rabbi and the guests include Steven Spielberg, Cindy Crawford, and Elizabeth Taylor.

The details change as the story makes the rounds. By the time Keanu finds out about it he's up in Winnipeg rehearsing for *Hamlet* and the story is that he and Geffen got married on a beach somewhere in Mexico.

There's no evidence to support the Geffen-Keanu rumor but it doesn't go away. It shows up as a blind item in George Christy's column in the *Hollywood Reporter* just before the end of the year. Christy, the first American journalist to go near the story, later says, "In Europe, they reported the rumor as fact. I decided to mention it in the column, and I feel pretty stupid for doing it, because I'm not interested in rumors. Financial, sex, and health gossip is always below the belt. I write a positive column."

Gay marriage will eventually become the law of the land, and there's nothing inherently homophobic about the suggestion that Keanu and David Geffen have tied the knot, but the conceit that they've done it in secret frames their hypothetical love as something sordid and embarrassing—it contains the notion that *they themselves* find it sordid and embarrassing, and takes for granted that Keanu turning out to be gay would be fatal to his career.

Keanu appears on the cover of *Out* magazine's July/August 1995 issue ("The Straight Issue") and when he's asked about Geffen, he says, "I guess I have to say I've never met the guy." They don't meet until years later, when Steve Martin's play *Picasso at the Lapin Agile* opens at the Geffen Playhouse in Los Angeles. Carrie Fisher, who's sitting with Geffen when the meeting happens, claims Geffen's first words to Keanu were, "Was it as good for you as it was for me?"

Also in August, in a *Vanity Fair* cover story tied to *A Walk in the Clouds*, Keanu waves off the suggestion, floated by the writer Michael Shnayerson, that there might be some utility to shooting the gay rumors "down cold," perhaps in the pages of *Vanity Fair*.

"I mean, there's nothing wrong with being gay," Keanu replies, "so to deny it is to make a judgment."

It's the righteous answer, if not exactly the one *Vanity Fair* is looking for. But of course the other reason a story like this one isn't worth denying is that it's a conspiracy theory, and an on-record denial is rarely enough to make a conspiracy theory go away. It's the midpoint of the nineties and Keanu has reached that tier of celebrity where his own account of the events of his life will be only one of countless unfolding narratives; not denying the Geffen story is an acknowledgment that nothing can be done about this.

Tabloid bullshit abhors a vacuum, but so does art. That zone of mystery created by Keanu's refusal to define himself on the spectrum of sexuality also encourages more creative interpretation. Because we're always at a distance with Keanu, held at bay by that "peculiar detachment" Prina identifies, the bond we form with him is more emotional, based in longing and imagining. We fill the gaps in our understanding of him with an imagined version of Keanu that is determined by our desires. His performances are the same way—he gives us only so much, and we imagine what isn't conveyed, how much is present, and maybe even felt, but unexpressed.

Keith Mayerson, the art student who told *People* about peeing next to Keanu at a urinal, goes on to become an accomplished artist who shows his work all over the world. He paints pop-cultural icons in muddy earth tones that shift the overall effect of each image away from "pop," turning his subjects into figures dredged up from a dream. In his *Hamlet 1999* series, he paints pictures—or more properly, pictures of pictures—of John Lennon and the Beatles, Abe Lincoln and George Washington, Superman and Kaneda, Jimmy Stewart hanging from the rooftop in *Vertigo* and Kyle MacLachlan in royal robes at the end of *Dune*, Daffy Duck and Dave Bowman—and, over and over, Keanu.

He paints Keanu from the cover of *Rolling Stone* next to a *Life* magazine cover of Ham the Astrochimp. He paints Keanu stopping bullets with a wave of his hand in *The Matrix*, and Keanu and Agent Smith hanging on wires in front of a green-screen backdrop while shooting *The Matrix*. He paints Keanu with River Phoenix, and Keanu alone.

Mayerson's greatest Keanu-related artwork is *Pinocchio the Big Fag*, exhibited as a series of watercolors and ink drawings in the spring of 1994 and later collected as a book. The project began life as what Mayerson later called a "bad Cole Porter–like musical," recasting the Pinocchio story as a bawdy coming-out metaphor; in the finished book Pinocchio's nose takes on what the *New York Times* politely calls "a new, erogenous identity," and the supporting characters he encounters on his journey to unashamed queerness include representations of Montgomery Clift, Jodie Foster (as the Blue Fairy, in a Yale sweatshirt), and Jesse Helms. On the front cover of the book version, Pinocchio is self-penetrating with his own nose, which loops from his face to his rectum like the handle of a coffee mug.

But *Pinocchio the Big Fag* is more dreamlike than pornographic, and while the delicacy of Mayerson's drawings helps with that—they're like pages from William Blake's *Songs of Experience* as reimagined by Raymond Pettibon—the fictional presence of Keanu helps, too.

Geppetto brings Pinocchio to life by cutting off his own penis and squirting blood on a piece of wood. He sings about wanting a masculine son, but Pinocchio scandalizes him by walking like a girl as soon as he wakes up. Cast out to wander the world, he's asleep in a subway station when he meets a boy named Lampwick. In the original Pinocchio story it's Lampwick who takes Pinocchio to Pleasure Island, where he stays too long and turns into a donkey. In the Mayerson version Lampwick is Keanu Reeves. The first time we see him in the book he's backlit by the sun, one hand down his unbuttoned pants. The caption reads, "Lampwick was the laziest boy in school."

Mayerson's borrowed images mark him as a Keanu fan. In a double-page spread illuminating the lyrics to the song about Pleasure Island, the central image is a pencil sketch of Keanu that is clearly based on a 1993 photograph of Keanu in Malibu—the one where he's naked except for a few necklaces and a T-shirt that he's holding just below waist height so you can see his pubic hair but not his penis. In the picture Pinocchio is floating in a river and Keanu is undressing on the riverbank to come join him. Later we see Keanu making tender love to a grateful Pinocchio on a sphincterlike lily pad while boys in an orgy writhe all around him.

Eventually they're parted, and when they find each other again Keanu is a donkey with a donkey dick.

Mayerson could have drawn any actor into his story, but Keanu, as a subject, seems to make sense somehow. Because he doesn't seem to particularly identify as straight or gay, he's open to whatever ideas people want to project onto him. His own preferences are private and amorphous and available only to us in fantasy; the sense we get is that he'd be into whatever we're into doing with him. The Bressonian space around Keanu as a public figure as well as an actor leaves room for us to imagine. His public life becomes a collaborative art project, a story without an ending that isn't finished until we invent one.

17| THEY SAVED KEANU'S BRAIN

In 1995's *Johnny Mnemonic* Keanu is less natural-seeming than he's ever been, but this time it works in his favor; he's extremely believable as a man who's hacked away the nonessential parts of his brain. He plays a futuristic data courier smuggling 320 gigabytes of contraband information inside his head. Everyone wants what's in there and is willing to kill him in order to get it, but the movie also portrays 320 gigs as a potentially mind-destroying amount of information for the human brain to store, which is funny if you've ever filled up two iPod Classics with 320 gigs of illegally downloaded rap music.

Johnny—no last name this time, he's just Johnny—is the first truly internet-poisoned human in movie history. At one point he shouts, "I need to get online!" like a pissed-off teenager whose iPad has been confiscated. He's a hero with very specific hardware requirements: "I need a Sino-Logic Sixteen, Sogo Seven data gloves, a GPL stealth module, one Burdine intelligent translator, and Thompson eye-phones."

That last phrase is, of course, pronounced like they say it in Cupertino, which is one of the many things about the future that this movie gets accidentally yet eerily right. As *Johnny Mnemonic*'s expository opening crawl explains, it's the second decade of the twenty-first century, corporations rule the world, a pandemic threatens life on earth, and the streets of major cities are full of masked protesters. The rest is science fiction.

The script for *Johnny Mnemonic* was adapted by William Gibson from his own short story, published in *Omni* magazine in May 1981 and later anthologized in Gibson's collection *Burning Chrome*. Gibson is a supremely visual writer who uses plot to keep his characters moving from one textural experience to the next. In the original short story this is how Gibson describes Johnny Mnemonic walking into a bar: "Muscle-boys scattered through the crowd were flexing stock parts at one another and trying on thin, cold grins, some of them so lost under superstructures of muscle graft that their outlines weren't really human." He's great on futuristic argot and tactile sensation and the physical details of the world he's building; movies that stayed true to his books would be deadpan art films requiring a Pentagon black-box budget for production design. Which—minus the big budget, anyway—is what the *Johnny Mnemonic* movie is supposed to be like, at first.

Gibson develops the script in collaboration with its eventual director Robert Longo, a painter and one of the biggest noises to emerge from the very noisy New York art world of the 1980s. When he and Gibson start talking the only thing on Longo's résumé that you could really call a movie is *Arena Brains*, a thirty-five-minute satire of New York art-world culture with just enough narrative to fill a coke spoon. Which doesn't mean Longo can't do "action." He's best known at the time for his "Men in the Cities" paintings, life-size human figures based on photographs he takes of his friends and associates jerking their bodies around in response to loud noises or Robert Longo whipping tennis balls at them. He then paints them in office attire—black suits, white shirts, black ties, like John Wick in advance.

Longo and Gibson envision a self-aware, lo-fi genre piece in the vein of Jean-Luc Godard's *Alphaville*, which is very much a Godard movie that happens to be a sci-fi movie and not the other way around. "We went in and asked for a million and a half," Gibson tells *Wired* in

1995, "and they laughed. It wasn't until we started asking for much more that they started taking it seriously." They end up making it for TriStar Pictures on a budget of $26 million.

Johnny—described in Gibson's original story as "your basic sharp-faced Caucasoid with a ruff of stiff, dark hair"—is a role Keanu was born to play. But *Johnny,* as a film project, marks the first time Keanu's growing fame derails a movie and turns it into something it was never meant to be. What it's meant to be is an intentional cult film, abetted by a dizzyingly hip supporting cast—Ice-T as the leader of a band of antitechnology revolutionaries, Udo Kier as Keanu's data broker, the Japanese superstar Takeshi Kitano as a Yakuza boss, Henry Rollins in nerd-emoji glasses as an underground body-modification surgeon. Longo describes the sets they build in Toronto—including a leaning tower of televisions, part of a secret city built from straight-world junk—as "*Batman* directed by Fellini," magical and campy and cheap.

Then two things happen. The first thing that happens is another TriStar movie, *Mary Reilly*—directed by Stephen Frears, with Julia Roberts as a Victorian housemaid who realizes that all is not well with her scientist employer Henry Jekyll—runs into production delays, leaving TriStar without a big movie on the schedule for May 1995. And the second thing is that *Speed* comes out and makes $100 million in seven weeks. TriStar realizes that Longo and Gibson's modest sci-fi-art-whatever project is just a few turns of the wheel away from being a cyberpunk action blockbuster featuring the star of *Speed.* They've already made Longo cast Dolph Lundgren as the villain, a murderous cyborg preacher who worships technology; later, when the film is being edited, they take it away from Longo and recut it into something approximating popcorn-movie standards, albeit the kind of popcorn movie where Keanu mind-melds with a cyborg dolphin.

The released version of *Johnny*, Keanu tells an interviewer while promoting *A Walk in the Clouds*, is "not the film that I made . . . [F]or three and a half months I played a character who didn't consciously want his memory back, so six months later we re-shoot a scene where I say: 'I want it all back,' which goes at the beginning of the film, and then at the end of the film, where my character used to make the ultimate sacrifice . . . he ends up in this stupid virtual reality world where this big fish ends up trying to save me and mankind."

This phenomenon—where Keanu signs on to make one kind of movie which then becomes a very different kind of movie, often *as a result* of Keanu agreeing to be in it—is a thing that will continue to happen to Keanu and becomes an ongoing source of frustration, as in his *Rolling Stone* interview with Chris Heath, where he says he prefers "the version of *Feeling Minnesota* that isn't in the movie." It's probably an occupational hazard you have to deal with if you're a big or even biggish star, but few actors talk as openly as Keanu does about how much it sucks.

"The way that power most manifests itself is this: not in the material you see on screen (that's something the studio decides) *but in the way that material is treated*," William Goldman wrote years ago in *Adventures in the Screen Trade*, and in Keanu's case this cuts both ways. You try to go make something weird and marginal and un-obvious, something you believe in, and then that project gets hammered into a more obvious shape so that the studio can capitalize on the very box-office potential that you set out to productively squander on something cool.

The theatrical cut of *Johnny Mnemonic* ends up being neither a particularly bold art film nor a particularly crowd-pleasing action movie. It slips in and out of theaters between May and July of 1995 and grosses just over $19 million, which would have been a minor miracle had it cost $1.5 instead of $26 million. In 1999, *The Matrix*—another dystopian-future cyberpunk-indebted movie starring Keanu Reeves as a guy with a data port in his brain—will outgross it in four days.

The only alternate version of *Johnny Mnemonic* that exists is the Japanese cut, which adds a few minutes of extra footage of Takeshi Kitano, who's a huge movie and television star in Japan. We'll probably never get to see the permanent-midnight version of *Johnny* that Longo and Gibson initially envisioned, although Longo has mused about cutting the existing movie down to its best hour or so and bootlegging it as the black-and-white art film it was always meant to be. As the Yakuza on Johnny's trail put it: "Narrow the bandwidth! Go low-rent!"

***

On the outside the Manitoba Theatre Centre is a Brutalist concrete block that resembles a minimum-security prison. The no-frills theater itself is designed to breed intimacy, blurring the line between actors and audience, orchestra and balcony. Once he arrives in Winnipeg Keanu keeps the line between actor and audience pretty unblurry. He walks to work in the snow and mostly dines alone at night, taking his food to go whenever other restaurant patrons seem too interested in his presence. One local paper sets up a hotline for readers looking to report Keanu sightings. Keanu does no interviews and no one from the theater is allowed to talk to the press. The phone rings off the hook with calls from *A Current Affair* and other tabloid TV shows, whose producers beg in vain for scraps of Keanu information.

And yet Keanu can't escape his persona by fleeing to Canada. He is now too famous to pull off the out-of-town tryout. People buy subscriptions to the MTC just to see Keanu's *Hamlet*. Fans from as far away as Australia and Japan buy tickets for multiple shows. The full three-and-a-half-week run of the play—twenty-two thousand seats in total—has sold out before the box office even opens. Over the course of the run the crowds of fans waiting at the stage door for a glimpse of Keanu get bigger and bigger.

Later Baumander will say that he "started off with one key thought, which was: Keanu *is* Hamlet." Hamlet knows he has to avenge his father by killing Claudius, the king of Denmark, but delays this action, due to neurosis or pangs of conscience or an overabundance of caution, for four whole acts. By coming here to do Shakespeare on the Canadian prairie, Keanu is doing more or less the same thing—delaying. He's chosen Shakespeare and Actors' Equity wages over a number of other opportunities, including a $7 million offer to be in Tom Clancy's *Without Remorse* and—most intriguingly—the part of Robert De Niro's bank-robbing partner Chris Shiherlis in Michael Mann's *Heat*. Keanu seems born to play one of Mann's hypercompetent stoic outlaws one day, and it's fun to imagine his take on Chris, the gambler who can't fully internalize De Niro's philosophy of nonattachment because he's too in love with his wife (Ashley Judd) even after she betrays him with Hank Azaria. Instead, the role goes to Val Kilmer and Keanu goes north. It's an important decision even though it's probably the wrong one and marks the beginning of a shaky period, parts-in-movies-wise.

When the show opens no tickets are provided to members of the press and video cameras are banned from the building. Keanu's agents reportedly wait to come see him until they get word that the show isn't a disaster. Which it isn't. Not everybody's sold on Keanu in the part. The *Vancouver Sun* praises his "emotional sensitivity" and "sleek and assured athleticism"—at one point, Keanu throws his sword and leaps from a twelve-foot parapet—but avows that "repeatedly throughout the evening, Reeves is undermined by his own lack of classical theatre technique" and never achieves "the fusion of sound and meaning so vital in communicating Shakespeare to audiences." But Roger Lewis, from London's *Sunday Times*, describes Keanu's performance as one of the three best Hamlets he's ever seen, mixing the "sheer virility of Larry Olivier's melancholy Dane" with "the Peter Pannishness, the little-boy-lost quality" of Mark Rylance's.

"The audience was quiet throughout," reports the *Winnipeg Sun*, "except to chuckle when he greeted Rosencrantz and Guildenstern as 'my excellent good friends.'"

The play concludes its run on a Saturday night in January. Another guy puts on the wool ski cap Keanu's been wearing around town and runs to a waiting car as a decoy, so that Keanu can slip out unnoticed and meet his castmates at the bar, to say goodbye.

In *Johnny Mnemonic*, when Johnny is forced to take refuge in a community of grubby techno-revolutionaries in the "Free City of Newark," he looks across the river at New York and delivers a rant for the ages:

> You see that city over there? That's where I'm supposed to be. Not down here with the dogs and the garbage . . . and the fucking last month's newspapers blowing back and forth! I've had it with them! I've had it with you! I've had it with all this! I want room service! I want the club sandwich, I want the cold Mexican beer. I want a ten-thousand-dollar-a-night

> hooker! I want my shirts laundered . . . like they do at the Imperial Hotel . . . in Tokyo.

The speech, written during shooting by Gibson in response to Keanu's request for "something more projective" to say, is a wink at Keanu's celebrity. It's Johnny morphing into a pampered star throwing a tantrum about the size of his trailer, and it's Keanu making fun of the kind of famous actor he never wants to be.

Doing *Hamlet* is a way of demonstrating—to us, or maybe to himself—that he's not that kind of guy. It proves he's willing to forgo big money and big-movie perks in order to take on one of the toughest challenges that exists for any actor. But it doesn't redefine him. He never does Shakespeare again, or live theater on this scale. He spends years filling his brain with Shakespeare's words and says them onstage every night for a few weeks and then it's over and he gets in a car and drives away, to face the question of what to do after *Speed*, which hasn't been answered and hasn't gone away. In the end doing *Hamlet* hasn't solved anything except Keanu's desire to do *Hamlet*. He winds up more or less where Johnny does at the end of Gibson's original story, wrung out and as confused as ever by the question of what to be, or not to be:

> And it came to me that I had no idea at all of what was really happening, or of what was supposed to happen. And that was the nature of my game, because I'd spent most of my life as a blind receptacle to be filled with other people's knowledge and then drained, spouting synthetic languages I'd never understand. A very technical boy. Sure.

18| QUATTRO FORMAGGI

What makes a man start a band? Let alone a man who's already famous for doing something else? Let alone a man who's basically as famous *as you can conceivably be* for doing that other thing? It's an almost impossible landing to stick. For every Drake or Jenny Lewis or Miley Cyrus—all child performers who changed tracks in early adulthood and never really tried to have it both way—there's a Shatner, a Seagal, or a Bruce Willis, and for every "Party All the Time" there's every other Eddie Murphy song. It's hard enough to write one song, let alone one good song, let alone twelve songs good enough to convince people you're not just a preening dilettante who craves more direct access to an audience's adoration and/or doesn't hear the word "no" often enough.

And yet: in 1991, when he's somewhere between *Point Break* and *Dracula* and old enough to know better, Keanu starts a band. The way it happens is simultaneously totally normal and totally Hollywood. One day Keanu's in the supermarket. He sees a guy in a Detroit Red Wings jersey and starts talking to him about hockey. The guy in the jersey is an actor named Robert Mailhouse. When he meets Keanu he's in the middle of a two-year run on *Days of Our Lives* as a police officer named Brian

Scofield, a performance that will win him the Soap Opera Digest Award for Outstanding Comic Relief Role in 1992. Chances are you've seen Mailhouse on TV, whether you know it or not—he goes on to play a philandering hospital administrator on *Melrose Place* and a detestable network executive on Aaron Sorkin's *Sports Night* and the gay man Elaine tries to convert to heterosexuality on *Seinfeld*, and by the mid-2000s he's earned TV's most distinguished working-actor merit badge by guest-starring on three different shows in the *CSI* universe. But after hockey brings them together, the thing Mailhouse and his fellow actor Keanu Reeves bond over isn't acting. It's music. Mailhouse plays the drums. Keanu has been known to fool around on the bass. At this point in his life Keanu has finally abandoned his hotel-hobo lifestyle and rented an actual house in Los Angeles; he and Mailhouse start jamming there with Gregg Miller, a singer and guitarist who's also a part-time actor.

So begins the story of Dogstar, a professional rock band that forms and eventually tours the world and puts out two major-label albums, all because it's really hard to make new guy friends in your thirties, even if you're Keanu Reeves. Especially in Los Angeles, where you kind of have to take up a hobby—it's why people play street hockey, which is another thing Keanu starts doing around this time. Whatever the other guys are thinking, for Keanu this is just a hang, at least at first, and even once it becomes more than that, he approaches the whole situation in an admirably un–Thirty Seconds to Mars–esque fashion. He's not the lead singer, for one thing—he's just the bass player. Off to the side, head down, Joe Rhythm Section keeping time. He never seems eager to have this work interpreted as an extension of some larger artistic practice. He is not a restless "creative" seeking a bigger canvas on which to paint. At no point does he seem motivated by a desire to hyphenate his job title. He wants to play some music with some friends, so he starts a mediocre band whose mediocrity he ameliorates by never once insisting that people pretend they're great. "We're terrible," he says cheerfully in 1993. "We've played about ten times now and though we're getting better, we play better in a garage. But I say, better to regret something that you have done than regret something you haven't done."

Of course, Keanu deciding to be a sideman in a mediocre rock band is like a kid covering his eyes and declaring himself invisible. It's impossible for him to disappear. And the fact that Dogstar is a hobby and not a project doesn't mean it's not an expression of Keanu's own neuroses and his relationship to stardom. He meets Mailhouse the year *Point Break* comes out, which means the band's life coincides with the first blockbuster-movie-star phase of his career. They become a major touring concern—and therefore a big part of Keanu's life, at least timewise—beginning in 1995, right after *Hamlet*. He spends the summer of his *Hamlet* year playing Dogstar shows all over the world, from San Francisco (where they play the five-hundred-capacity club Slim's) to Japan where they're already big enough to sell out much larger halls.

Of course, Dogstar is *Hamlet* all over again. It's Keanu denying—or at least taking a break from—how famous he's become, but he's denying it in a way that wouldn't be possible to do if not for his celebrity. He starts this band and assumes a role in it where he's not the focus, but the band becomes viable as a live act because people want to see Keanu Reeves play in a band. As much as he's risking being laughed out of the room like Bruce Willis singing the blues or Leonard Nimoy singing about hobbits, as much as he's choosing a degree of ignominy by clocking in on the bar-band circuit, as much as what he's doing is about getting back to the basics of making art for fun while banishing all premeditated thoughts of career and image, as much as it's about Keanu seeking the Zen reset of potentially eating shit onstage at the end of the day he's still playing the rock-and-roll video game on "easy" mode. His presence makes Dogstar into something bigger than a regular LA bar band even before they play their first bar. Their first EP *Quattro Formaggi* comes out about two months before *Feeling Minnesota*, a shaggy indie dramedy where Keanu and Cameron Diaz run off together immediately after Diaz is forced to marry Keanu's brother, a small-time hood played by Vincent D'Onofrio. In *Feeling Minnesota* Keanu seems like he's trying to grunge it up by taking a role meant for Ethan Hawke or someone similarly less famous than he is; pretending to be but a humble bass player is another way of hiding out.

They're not Dogstar at first. In the beginning they're Small Faecal Matter, and then they're BFS, which either stands for Big Fucking Sound or Bull Fucking Shit. They need a name because they start doing live shows about six weeks after they first play together. The early gigs are impromptu affairs with little advance promotion, but for obvious reasons they tend to sell out anyway. One night, in March 1992, they book a last-minute show at a club called Raji's on Hollywood Boulevard. When the singer of another, even newer local band cold-calls Raji's that same day looking for a gig, the club owner agrees to put them on the bill that night with Keanu's band. Somehow this band ends up playing last, after Keanu's band, when the Keanu-curious portion of the audience has mostly dissipated into the Hollywood night, so there are only about twenty people in the room at Raji's for what turns out to be Weezer's very first live show.

One of the people who stays behind that night is future Weezer webmaster and archivist Karl Koch, who later writes that Miller and Mailhouse "looked and acted a lot like Joe Piscopo in his *SNL* years. Picture two goofy white guys with big curly afros, aviator shades, and leather bomber jackets freaking out and jumping all over the place like a bar band, and then Keanu in a white T-shirt, standing in the corner quietly playing bass, looking straight down at his feet the whole gig . . . Jason"—Weezer's original guitarist, Jason Cropper—"had a short exchange with Keanu that night, and while the exact words said are lost, the recollection is that Jason felt Keanu was cold to him."

Around 1993 they decide to call themselves Dogstar, a name Mailhouse pulls from Henry Miller's book *Sexus* ("I had long ceased to be interested in her contortions; except for the part of me that was in her I was as cool as a cucumber and remote as the Dog Star."). There's actually another band called Dogstar on the LA scene at the time and they're better than Keanu's band by orders of magnitude. They have two bass players, and a Moog synthesizer, and a singer who wails like Kathleen Hanna from Bikini Kill. Because there can be only one Dogstar, Keanu gets in touch with the band's leader, Bobby Hecksher, and they come to an understanding. "We talked on the phone several times," Hecksher will write years later, "and to my astonishment he was a really cool, sweet guy. He sent me a copy of the book that listed his band name . . . and we talked about music and guitar pedals. Someone like that could have crushed me with lawyers and BS but this guy had a heart of gold." Hecksher's band changes its name to Charles Brown Superstar. They've already pressed copies of their first seven-inch single and paid extra for gold-and-white-swirled vinyl, so they have to put stickers over the old name on the record sleeve. In 2015 a record store in Portland lists it on eBay with the words "RARE Keanu Reeves" in the description; it sells for sixty dollars.

Dogstar's lineup shifts over time—they're joined by Bret Domrose, an actual professional touring musician who's been a member of the venerable San Francisco punk band the Nuns, and eventually Miller leaves. But the bass player sticks around, so things become increasingly absurd. By the end of 1995 Dogstar are opening for David Bowie in Los Angeles and touring New Zealand and Australia with Bon Jovi, whose lead singer, Jon Bon Jovi, happens that same year to be giving the acting thing a try, playing a sexy housepainter who helps grieving widow Elizabeth Perkins get over her dead husband in *Moonlight and Valentino.*

Young women rush the stage at Dogstar's gigs and chase the band's vehicles back to whatever hotel they're staying in. In one press account of a Dogstar show in Washington, DC, some girls slip onto Dogstar's tour bus and swipe an emptyish bottle of beer whose contents they believe have passed through Keanu's actual lips. The bottle-taker tells a reporter, "I took it to drink the backwash." Sting asks Keanu to play bass on a record but he doesn't have time. He still has movies to make.

Keanu sings a song or two with Dogstar, as bass players are often permitted to do. He handles lead vocals on "Isabelle," which he tells people is about his friend's three-year-old daughter, and "Round C," which he tells people is about cheese. Singing onstage feels amazing, he says, because it reminds him of the best parts of being an actor: "When you can feel it, your blood thrills, it's physical, your heart is open." But mostly he keeps his head down and plays the bass. Domrose likes to say that when he's onstage with Dogstar he's always looking out at a sea of left ears, because everyone's eyes are locked on Keanu as he thumps away at stage right.

In 1997, *Spin* sends the writer Benjamin Weissman to follow the band on tour. Denied an interview, Weissman files a "Frank Sinatra Has a Cold"–style write-around that lands on the ostensibly perplexing question of what it is Keanu sees in these doofs he's sharing a bus with. The answer actually seems pretty clear: these doofs afford Keanu the chance to hang out and be a doof as well, to drink beer on a bus while postponing answering the larger and more difficult question of how he's going to make a living as an actor if he no longer feels like making movies like *Chain Reaction* and nobody wants to pay to see him in *Feeling Minnesota*.

What the guys in the band get out of this is obvious. They're in their thirties and have been kicking around the entertainment industry for a while and one imagines that when the offers start coming in, Keanu can't just turn them down unilaterally and forsake commercial advancement to play by Fugazi rules just because he makes $10 million per picture and doesn't need the money. So Dogstar tours before they've even released a record and signs a deal with the major-label-affiliated Zoo Entertainment, and generally ends up sending out mixed signals about how serious a band they're supposed to be. Their debut album, *Our Little Visionary*, is released only in Japan. It sounds a little like a store-brand Foo Fighters and a little like a generic Goo Goo Dolls and a little like any of a thousand other less fortunate postgrunge outfits who managed a hit song or two before tumbling back into the crab-bucket of the midnineties alternative-rock scene, except instead of a hit single Dogstar had Keanu.

This is obviously a double-edged sword for the guys in the band who were not the star of *Speed*. They have access to unbelievable opportunities that only a masochist would take advantage of. Because they're Keanu's band, many people are eager for them to suck, and this is especially true of the big, mixed crowds they play in front of at rock festivals. They get pelted with fruit at Glastonbury and splattered with mud at Milwaukee Metal Fest, where they've somehow been booked as part of a lineup that includes bands like Cannibal Corpse and Deicide, and where they annoy everybody by playing a cover of "New Minglewood Blues" by the Grateful Dead. Another cover song in their repertoire is the Carpenters hit "Superstar," a depressive ballad about a pop singer who abandons the narrator after a one-night stand but continues to haunt her as a voice on the radio. In interviews Keanu denies that there's any particular reason they decide to record this one. It's on their second album, *Happy Ending*, which comes out in 2000. The cover is a simple black-and-white photo of the band standing against a stone wall; Keanu is on the left, eyes downcast, still trying to go unnoticed.

Dogstar played their final US show in July 2001, in Laughlin, Nevada, and—while it's somehow difficult to imagine a band this extremely nineties existing after 9/11—played their final show ever in 2002, at the Ebisu Garden Hall in Tokyo. Mailhouse goes on to play drums in a band called Becky; the singer is his girlfriend, *Real World: Seattle* alumnus Rebecca Lord, and Keanu plays a little bass on their one album, 2006's *Take It on the Chin*. Years later, when the public-facing part of the Dogstar thing is all over, the guys in the band who weren't Keanu will give interviews saying it was hard to know if they were ever really reaching people as a band, or if people would have paid to stand in a small club or a giant arena and watch Keanu do just about anything—card tricks, sock puppetry, mime. They will say this as if they didn't know what the answer was the whole time.

19 | THAT FLORIDA STUD THING

Director Andrew Davis's *Chain Reaction*, released in 1996, basically just plugs Keanu into the template of Davis's 1993 hit *The Fugitive*. That isn't how it's sold to Keanu at first. He speaks to Davis and agrees to do the movie before a script has been written, then goes off to Winnipeg to be unreachably focused on *Hamlet*. "When I got back, it kind of had changed into a different picture," he'll say later. The lesson of the project? "Next time, if I go do a play, I'm going to have a fax machine."

Anyway, *Chain Reaction*: there's this device that generates endlessly renewable energy and there's this CIA-front company that will stop at nothing to suppress this technology, and before long everybody's chasing Keanu all over greater Chicago.

But at first it's a grunge science movie, with Keanu wrapping the energy prototype in duct tape and an old flannel before taking off on his motorcycle. There are parking-garage meetings in the *All the President's Men*/*Three Days of the Condor* tradition, and in that same tradition the movie is a snapshot of what masculine sophistication looked like in its moment—Robert Redford's CIA consultant had tweed sport coats, brass pans, and knit ties, and Keanu has an apartment with a lot of exposed wood and aesthetically pleasing chemistry equipment that looks like it could make you a single perfect cup of coffee very slowly.

Keanu isn't the guy who created the renewable-energy device; he's just the loose-cannon machinist on the team who figures out how to make it work. "This is Eddie—I think, he does," is the way his scientist mentor introduces him. "But he *really* does." This reference to the distinction between thought and action is one of two key moments in the film where somebody describing Keanu's character seems to actually be describing Keanu—the other one is when Morgan Freeman says the thing about Keanu being the poor boy with the frequencies.

Within a few years Keanu will find work in an action movie that really leans into this sense of him as somehow chosen and special and mentally unique, an action movie that bends the template of the form to make it vibrate at Keanu's particular frequency. This one is not it. This one is the action movie that leaves him tired and bored enough to pass on *Speed 2: Cruise Control*, even when the director, Jan de Bont, flies to Chicago to lobby him personally.

"They wanted me to get on the boat," Keanu says in 1997, the year *Speed 2* comes out and flops, because nobody wants to see a *Speed* movie about Sandra Bullock taking a vacation with her new boyfriend Jason Patric instead of Keanu. "But the script wasn't great, and I just wasn't ready to mentally and physically do that picture. I said 'No.' I could afford to say no, because I could pay my rent."

Instead he takes a small role in Stephen Kay's movie *The Last Time I Committed Suicide*, about what Neal Cassady did before going on the road with Jack Kerouac made him famous. Keanu doesn't play Neal Cassady—Thomas Jane does. Keanu plays a made-up character who drinks in bars with Neal Cassady and tries to convince Neal Cassady to ditch his wife and family in favor of the bar life. It's a fun project to prep for in that it gives Keanu an excuse to drink more than usual while he's in Chicago making his stupid renewable-energy movie. Putting on Method bloat is a new kind of transformation and it's probably more fun than getting ripped for *Speed* or dieting into the white zone for Siddhartha. By the time he shoots *Last Time* he weighs around two hundred pounds.

He passes on an $11.5 million payday when he turns down *Speed 2*. He gets that same amount to make Taylor Hackford's *The Devil's Advocate* in 1996. It's another movie that's been floating around. A few years before Hackford signs on, it almost becomes a Joel Schumacher movie with Brad Pitt in the part that eventually goes to Keanu—a hotshot attorney who gets recruited by a high-powered New York law firm and then finds out his new boss is literally Satan. Schumacher bails when he can't find a suitable actor to play the Devil; Hackford reportedly offers the part to Dustin Hoffman, Warren Beatty, Michael Douglas, and Jack Nicholson before Al Pacino agrees to do it.

The Devil's Advocate is an excellently lurid piece of coffee-table camp that now feels eerily predictive of events it could not possibly have predicted. An inside-baseball joke in a party scene about Donald Trump's feud with fellow real-estate mogul Mort Zuckerman gives way to the reveal that Craig T. Nelson's billionaire and accused triple-murderer character lives not just in Trump Tower but in what's instantly identifiable as the future president's own residence—the gold glow bouncing off mirrored marble gives it away before the view does. The sculptor Frederick E. Hart objected to the filmmakers' re-creation of his 1982 bas-relief *Ex Nihilo* in a scene set in Pacino's office; there is no record of Donald Trump objecting to the film's implication that only a real asshole would live in a gold apartment.

It gets weirder: late in the film, catatonic from witnessing unimaginable horrors, Keanu walks out onto the street and runs into Pacino's assistant smoking a cigarette by the door. "Look at you—you're terrified," she says. "Not to worry. He'll take away that fear. You don't ever have to be frightened again." He crosses in front of her, onto an empty, sun-blasted Fifty-Seventh Street, which there is now no way to see as anything but a dream of New York under COVID lockdown. Keanu's long shadow points to the horizon, at the wedge of blue sky in the distance. The camera rises up to show us just how far you can see without seeing anyone outside.

Before that: Keanu is Gainesville's winningest defense attorney; moments after we first see him he's rescuing a guilty client from the gas chamber by destroying a preteen girl (Heather Matarazzo) on cross-examination. His ruthlessness attracts the attention of Pacino's high-powered Manhattan firm, whose prestige derives in part from its dealings in "the Mideast, the Balkans, Central America, West Africa." Until the ludicrous third act, where echoes of John Grisham give way to echoes of *Rosemary's Baby*, the film is an exploration of the seduction of power and privilege, and an atypical Keanu movie because he's drawn into this world by what he wants. There's heat in his eyes when he looks up from the Devil's offer letter.

By casting Keanu in what feels like a Tom Cruise part, *The Devil's Advocate* opens a sliding door into alternate history, and you can see the other career Reeves could have chased, if he'd wanted to—years to come spent jockeying with Cruise and Ben Affleck and Brad Pitt, maybe even Denzel Washington, to play lawyers and doctors and detectives in adult dramas, laying the groundwork for a third act like Harrison Ford's.

Or, for that matter, Al Pacino's, although *The Devil's Advocate* seems to reject that idea as a possibility. At one point in the movie Pacino and Keanu walk the teeming streets of New York, like Pacino's Ratso Rizzo and Jon Voight before them, and Pacino begins telling Keanu in so many words that while he's clearly a gifted attorney, he'll never be what Pacino is, because he's too pretty:

> You've gotta keep yourself small. Innocuous. Be the little guy. You know, the nerd, the leper . . . Look at me. Underestimated from day one. You'd never think I was a master of the universe, would you? That's your only weakness, as far as I can see . . . The look. That Florida stud thing.

It feels less like Satan (whose Earthly name in this one is "John Milton," get it?) talking to Kevin the hotshot lawyer and more like Al Pacino talking to Keanu Reeves—maybe after a long between-setups lunch and a couple of Dunkaccinos—about the all-importance, to a performer, of the element of surprise, of not letting your persona come in the door before you.

Which of course is strange, because by the time he made *The Devil's Advocate*, Al Pacino had largely stopped being the kind of actor people did not see coming, had somewhere between *Scent of a Woman* and *Heat* and this movie become SO BIG AND BOLD AND OFTEN QUITE LOUD a presence you could imagine him not so much taking time off between films as slumbering deep beneath the ocean before his next rampage. *The Devil's Advocate*, suggested the comedian Neal Brennan, "is where Al Pacino finally just said, 'I can't play people. I can play archetypes or weather systems, but I can't play people.'"

Pacino has calmed back down in the ensuing years. But the path forward that John Milton is encouraging for Keanu's character is one that was already essentially closed off to Keanu Reeves as an actor. At the end of the nineties, Keanu can't just disappear into a part any more than he can disappear into the rhythm section of a two-bit grunge band. To paraphrase another emblematic Canadian intellectual of the late nineties, what he's being offered in this scene is some good advice he just can't take. Instead, the work ahead of him will be about taking his own unalterable screen presence and finding ways to leverage and shade and knowingly toy with it.

20

JEAN BAUDRILLARD'S DRAGULA

It's 1998—early September, maybe late August—and Keanu is standing up in the bathtub of a hotel room in Sydney, Australia, shaving off all his hair. Like, *all* his hair. Even his eyebrows. Probably his pubes. An actor prepares.

He's doing this for *The Matrix*, the movie he's been shooting in Australia since February. It's for the scene where Keanu, playing a man who's just discovered his whole reality is actually a vast computer-generated simulation, is extracted from the artificial womb in which he's unknowingly spent his entire life. This happens early in the film but is being shot toward the end of principal photography, for obvious hair-and-makeup reasons.

When Keanu emerges from his growth-pod naked and hairless, it's the first time he's ever been truly physically gross in a movie. (Even Ortiz in *Freaked* had animal magnetism.) After he's finished shooting he will be photographed bald at the airport and play at least one Dogstar show looking like a bass-thumping Voldemort. Having eyebrows, it turns out, was a more important part of Keanu's overall look than anyone imagined.

In less than a year, everyone will know what the deal is with Keanu's Sydney movie, and why Keanu is briefly hairless in it. *The Matrix* enters the cultural conversation the moment it's released and never really leaves, not just a hit movie but an endlessly interpretable and renewable metaphor for almost anything anyone might want it to be about.

"It's cool to get on the computer," Prince will tell the audience at the Yahoo! Internet Life Online Music Awards in the summer of 1999, when the movie's a few months old, "but don't let the computer get on you . . . Y'all saw *The Matrix*. There's a war going on. The battlefield's in the mind. And the prize is the soul."

Everyone understands what he means, to the extent that anyone ever fully understood what Prince was saying. But before *The Matrix* comes out, even the people whose idea the movie was will have a hard time explaining it to anyone else. Will Smith—the first person offered the lead in *The Matrix* and the first person to turn it down, before Leonardo DiCaprio and Brad Pitt did the same—will tell the story of his first and only meeting with the movie's writer-directors, Lana and Lilly Wachowski, whose pitch he says went something like this:

"Dude, we're thinkin', like—like, imagine you're in a fight, and then you, like, jump, but imagine if you could stop jumping, in the middle of the jump . . . but then people could see around you, three-sixty, while you're jumping. While you're stopped jumping. And then we're gonna invent these cameras—and people can see the whole jump, while you're stopped, in the middle of the jump."

And here Smith pauses, to let us imagine ourselves as Will Smith in 1997, fresh off *Independence Day*, with the year's biggest box-office hit, *Men in Black*, already in the can, trying to decide whether to follow up those home runs with this jumping-but-stopping movie he's being pitched.

Then he says, "So I made *Wild Wild West*."

He adds that if the Wachowskis had cast him as Neo, they would probably have gone with a white actor for the part of Morpheus, and that they were leaning toward Val Kilmer: "So, I did y'all a favor."

What the Wachowskis were describing, of course, is "bullet

time," a CGI effect that morphs together multiple still images of a moving object, such as a bullet or Keanu Reeves, to create the illusion that a single camera is observing a split second of action from a gradually shifting angle, moving so quickly the bullet appears to be standing still. Before *The Matrix*, bullet time had been used for a shot or two in movies such as *Lost in Space* and a Smirnoff vodka commercial directed by Michel Gondry; after *The Matrix*, the effect will be duplicated, homaged, and parodied everywhere from Fox Sports' coverage of Super Bowl XXXV to *Shrek* to *My Little Pony: Friendship Is Magic*. When it exists only as an action line in a script ("His GUN BOOMS as we ENTER the liquid space of—BULLET-TIME") it's one of many things about *The Matrix* that people can't quite picture until they see it; afterward, it's an irresistibly cool technique that becomes a cliché almost immediately.

The brief cultural life of bullet time as a trendy effect is the story of *The Matrix* in microcosm. It's a movie that throws out vivid images and equally vivid concepts that others will run with in unpredictable directions. The way the Wachowskis filmed bodies moving through physical space becomes part of the visual grammar of action film and paves the way for the superhero-movie boom. The script's mix of SparkNotes cultural allusion and stoner metaphysics becomes grist for a cottage industry of academic analysis and helps fire up a new class of online pseudocritics who see movies as a puzzle to be decoded, rather than art to be interpreted—within a few years they'll have *Donnie Darko*, *Memento*, and *Inception* to annoy people about, too. And the notion of the "red pill"—a symbolic capsule that allows anyone who takes it to wake up from a dream state imposed by humanity's oppressors—speaks to online misogynists, neo-Nazis, QAnon rabbit-holers, and Elon Musk the way that songs the Beatles wrote in India spoke of race war to Charles Manson.

The temptation is to look at the original *Matrix* as a beginning—the first movie of the twenty-first century arriving slightly ahead of schedule, full of firsts and innovations and ideas destined to sit uncomfortably with troubled people from then on, a groundbreaking work of art and a hairline fracture in the American mind. But as much as it's any of those things, it's also an ending—an everything-must-go farewell to a certain type of blockbuster. There will never be another Keanu movie like it, not even the sequels; there may never be another movie like it, period.

The most-anticipated special-effects movie of 1999 isn't *The Matrix*—it's George Lucas's *Star Wars: Episode I—The Phantom Menace*, the first theatrically released *Star Wars* film in sixteen years, since 1983's *Return of the Jedi*, which everyone assumes will be the watershed nerd-culture event of the latter half of the decade. Lucas's movie looms so large that no one wants to go near it: when principal photography on *The Matrix* is finished, the producer Joel Silver puts up extra money to accelerate the postproduction process and get the Wachowskis' film into theaters by March, so it can live in theaters for a while before *The Phantom Menace* blows every other movie out of the water in May.

Episode I does clear $200 million by the end of its first month in theaters and ends up being far and away the top-grossing movie of 1999, pulling in more than $924 million worldwide. *The Matrix* is only the year's fourth-biggest movie, behind *The Sixth Sense* and *Toy Story 2*. Decades down the road, real-world events have conspired to make Lucas's film play like a prescient warning about how a complacent society's yearning for law and order can abet fascism. And the marketing of *The Phantom Menace* will one day teach studios like Marvel most of what they need to know about leveraging sentimental relationships with legacy IP. But *The Phantom Menace* also leaves a lot of people feeling disappointed and betrayed. Franchise diehards who've spent sixteen years investing their emotional life savings in a children's-entertainment property starring a bunch of Wookies and Smurfs are somehow still taken aback when Episode I turns out to be essentially—and sort of pointedly—a movie for kids, despite George Lucas having said out loud in interviews that this has been his plan all along.

The Phantom Menace is the worst of the three prequels. It's a huge, awkward demo reel for new filmmaking technologies, which Lucas will put to cooler use in *Attack of the Clones* three years later. It's full of images of alien worlds that resemble Windows 95 desktop backgrounds or the landscape on the Claritin box, hilariously stilted dialogue ("Negotiation? We've lost all communication! And where are the Chancellor's ambassadors?"), and performances by ordinarily lively actors such as Samuel L. Jackson and Ewan McGregor who under Lucas's direction seem like they'd have great difficulty fogging a mirror. But it still feels throughout like something that sprang from an individual brain, the way the original *Star Wars* and its two sequels did and almost all post-Lucas *Star Wars* doesn't. No one concerned about extending the life of the *Star Wars* universe as a portfolio of intellectual property would make *The Phantom Menace*. Instead you're watching George Lucas's own best attempt at resolving the question of how to do something new with the fictional universe he created. He'd wrestle with that challenge in two more films before selling Lucasfilm Ltd. to the Walt Disney Company in 2012 for $4 billion.

The highest-grossing film of the 2000s, according to Box Office Mojo's worldwide top fifty list for the decade, is James Cameron's *Avatar*, from 2009; *Attack of the Clones*, the second installment of Lucas's *Star Wars* prequel trilogy, is the thirty-third-highest-grossing movie of that decade, with *Revenge of the Sith* at number seventeen. The twenty-sixth-biggest film of the decade is *The Matrix Reloaded*, narrowly edging out Roland Emmerich's disaster epic *2012*. Further down the list you'll find the superhero satire *Hancock* at number thirty-six and another Emmerich disaster movie, *The Day After Tomorrow*, at number forty-nine. What's striking about this list is that those six films are the only nonanimated movies in the top fifty that aren't adaptations of preexisting media; obviously *Clones* and *Revenge of the Sith* are both prequels to a massive hit movie series from the seventies and eighties, but at least they're original stories. On the equivalent Box Office Mojo list for the 2010s, preexisting IP officially becomes the only game in town; there are no live-action films on the list that aren't reboots, adaptations, or franchise perpetuations by committee unless you count *Furious 7* and *The Fate of the Furious*, the seventh and eighth installments in a series that started out as an original screenplay, not a preexisting set of trademarks.

The Matrix—a pure product of the same go-go age of cultural appropriation that gave us *Odelay* and *Kill Bill*—is obviously as ultra-derivative as any sequel, from its self-consciously mythic structure right down to the part where Laurence Fishburne cracks his neck during a fight scene just like Jet Li does in 1994's *Fist of Legend*. Nearly everything in it is indebted to the way some other work of art wore its hat or sipped its tea. Even the way the story jumps as if by hyper-link from one genre-derived space to the next is a storytelling mode borrowed from comic books, where it's long been standard for an adventure to begin at the Hellfire Club and end thirty-two pages later on the dark side of the moon. But the organizing sensibility behind this profoundly recombinant project is that of Lana and Lilly Wachowski alone, and the project doesn't exist as anything else before it becomes a movie, so even at two decades' remove it feels fresh. In the first *Matrix* the Wachowskis are inventing a specific and specifically cinematic language that lets them mix *Vertigo* with Masamune Shirow and *Mondo 2000* with Frank Miller's *Hard Boiled*—as dumb and overused as it very quickly becomes, "bullet time" is part of that.

But what makes the original *Matrix* greater than the sum of what it borrows is the ideological freight that its pilfered imagery carries. It feels audacious to this day because it's upending and repurposing the traditionally right-wing format of the action movie to celebrate righteous revolutionary violence.

Recall that it starts out as a movie about a hacker seeking out fellow hackers, a detail that falls by the wayside once the story gets going, and disappears from the sequels entirely, but waves a pretty big antiestablishment flag here before it does. Recall also who Keanu is when we meet him in the first film: an alienated young man seeking contact with Morpheus, a cybercriminal so infamous he makes both the English and Arabic newspapers as a "terrorist leader" anytime he's spotted at the airport, as Osama bin Laden might have if he'd been seen buying a mocha and a scone at O'Hare in 2004.

And even though it's maybe the biggest term-paper-bait Easter egg in the history of modern movies, recall that when a group of hipsters come to Keanu's apartment door and wake him from a desk-nap so he can supply them, drug-dealerishly, with hacked software, he pulls it from a hollowed-out copy of Baudrillard's *Simulacra and Simulation*, which opens to "On Nihilism": "Against this hegemony of the system, one can exalt the ruses of desire, practice revolutionary micrology of the quotidian, exalt the molecular drift, or even defend cooking. This does not resolve the imperious necessity of checking the system in broad daylight . . . this, only terrorism can do." Baudrillard, who died in 2007, thought *The Matrix* was pretty dumb, and "hollowed-out Baudrillard with, like, cyber-drugs stuck inside" is a pretty good sick-burn description of *The Matrix* as a movie—but the book is still on-screen because we're supposed to see it and think about what it says.

After the main hipster, an annoying mescaline proponent, clangs a symbolic bell by calling Neo "my savior—my own personal Jesus Christ," he and his pals peer-pressure Keanu into leaving his apartment and joining them at an S&M bar where this unnamed city's most elite hedonists are engaged in transgressive activities like drinking beer and smoking and listening to Rob Zombie's "Dragula." What's great about *The Matrix* is that it's only circumstantially a movie about the future. It's really about the nineties, and its vision of underground cool is very much pinned to its decade. It's an artifact of the last moment in which a certain breed of antiestablishment white hipster could feel like the Internet was theirs to rule. The most off-base thing about the version of cyberspace portrayed in William Gibson's early books—and most cyberpunk literature that predates the ubiquity of the commercial internet—is how hip everybody in cyberspace is. No one anticipated how extremely uncool being extremely online was going to be, how quickly the internet would get malled over, transformed into a luxury Toronto shopping district of the mind.

In a deeper way *The Matrix* captures what the nineties felt like. If you were living on the lucky side of the history that both Francis Fukuyama and Jesus Jones insisted the world was waking up from, it was a moment of peace and theoretical techno-utopian prosperity. At the same time, the booming Clinton-era economy exacerbated income inequality. Lots of people got richer, but the rich really got richer. The seeds of the crises of the 2000s were planted—accounting scandals, a telecom crash, a dot-com crash. And somewhere deep inside the world you knew terrible gears were churning, mashing the poor into fuel for the machine; it was impossible not to know it and necessary to put it out of your mind in order to enjoy *ER* or *Duke Nukem*.

The other visionary action movie of 1999 is *Fight Club*, which comes out in November. In it a tribe of middle managers, service-economy drones, and other misfits led by Edward Norton and Brad Pitt find meaning in ritualized violence, take up residence in a postindustrial wasteland, and eventually turn militant, bombing credit-card-company office buildings to erase consumer debt and bring down capitalism. Twenty years of real-world events have also reframed *Fight Club*, which uses slippery, discomfiting satire to make a number of points about capitalism that now seem not just valid but obvious; I'm pretty sure even *Teen Vogue* is now to the left of Tyler Durden on the issue of blowing up banks. At the time, though, critics mostly saw a hyper-violent sausage party—Yukio Mishima's *Road House*. But like *The Matrix*, *Fight Club* starts with the notion that day-to-day life in the last years of the twentieth century was a palliative falsehood, and they both build to shocking-by-today's-standards depictions of cathartic violence against the architects of that falsehood.

In *The Matrix* what precedes that violent confrontation is an ethical reckoning. At least in its early stages, when Keanu's beginning to understand the true nature of his existence, it's a movie about coming to terms with the hard truth that your comfort and safety are a delusion, and that the upkeep on that delusion often involves outsourcing suffering to other people, and sometimes even the sacrifice of human life at hideous scale, whether that means an overseas war to defend the economic interests of the country in which you get to enjoy a tranquil life, or a situation like the one in the film, where humans dream of unreal jobs and lives while their bodies act as a literal energy source for their cybernetic oppressors.

Later in the film, when Keanu finally wakes up in the nightmarish real world outside the Matrix and looks around and sees all the other pods—miles of them, stretching in every direction, an image off the cover of some industrial-metal band's high-concept triple LP—he's finally facing the true scope of human misery. He's looking at reality for the first time—a world behind the world, where they liquefy the dead to feed the living. So his whole life, he's been nurtured and fed by other people's sorrow, almost literally—that's what the giant tube he pulls out of his throat was for. It's a moment of profound disillusionment and helplessness, and this is the sequence for which Keanu shaves himself—so he'll look more like the baby he is, naked and smooth and helpless and covered in amniotic goo.

First, though, at the S&M club, Keanu hangs back, arms folded, literally the wallflower at the orgy, until Carrie-Anne Moss's Trinity appears out of the shadows, whispering thrilling and terrible truths: *I know why night after night you sit at your computer.* She's playing a character straight out of Philip K. Dick's fiction—the dark-haired girl who shows up out of nowhere to lead you to the truth about reality, which is that it's a dream and a straitjacket. Then suddenly it's morning again, and we see Keanu back at work, sallow to the point of sickly under cubicle-farm light, listening to his boss drone on about the all-importance of conformity while window washers squeegee the glass outside as if wiping suds from our hero's third eye.

And then destiny calls—on a Nokia 8110 cell phone, spring-loaded like a switchblade for cutting holes in false reality, FedExed to Thomas Anderson's desk by Laurence Fishburne's Morpheus, who begins guiding Keanu's trip. The flip phone pins the movie to its decade, too. The world Keanu thinks is reality is actually a re-creation of life on Earth in North America in the last days before artificial intelligence took up arms against its creators and drove humanity underground. We don't see much of *The Matrix*'s simulated nineties or its pop culture; it's fun to wonder if you can walk into a video store in Thomas Anderson's world and rent one of the many other pre-*Matrix* sci-fi thrillers that also used the devices of artificial intelligence and parallel universes and virtual realities to decant some ambient anxiety about a coming ontological crisis—for humanity, for the movies themselves. Could an unawakened Thomas Anderson have gone on, in a few months, to see *Fight Club* without quite knowing why it compelled him?

Keanu is perfect for this story because as a lead actor he's comfortable in stories where his character doesn't drive the story through bold decision making. So many key moments in this film require him to be passive, even placid, as events guide him down a path. Fishburne tells Keanu there are two ways out of the building he's in. He can leave by the window, edging out onto the ledge of a high-rise office tower, or in custody. Keanu checks out the ledge, which is as terrifying as you might imagine, and in the next shot he's being led away in handcuffs by Hugo Weaving and his goons.

When I watched *The Matrix* again in 2019 it had been a few years since I'd last seen the whole thing, and in that interim both of the movie's writer-directors had publicly transitioned. I assumed the movie would play like an obvious-in-retrospect allegory for their experience—the blockbuster as covert coming-out story, metaphorizing trans lives and trans struggle, bodies oppressed, bodies loosed from ontological incarceration. Those themes are there if you're looking for them. The way Hugo Weaving's plummy and despicable Agent Smith keeps addressing Neo as "Mr. Anderson" is a kind of dead-naming. And when Neo gets superpowers inside the Matrix after accepting that reality—just like gender—is a construct, it's at once an allegorical portrayal of self-actualized liberation and an acknowledgment of the way that for some people that kind of liberation can only be found within imaginative spaces. Lilly Wachowski would confirm in 2020 that the movie's apparent gender-transition parallels were deliberate, but that "the corporate world wasn't ready for it"; she confirmed that the character Switch, played in the finished film by Belinda McClory, was originally written as male-presenting in the "real world" and female-presenting in the Matrix.

But by the time we find out any of this about the people who made the film, *The Matrix* has been loose in the culture for years. It becomes an endlessly adaptable metaphor in part because it's explicitly a story about metaphors—just as the trash can on your desktop uses a real-world object as a metaphor for the act of deleting a file, everything in the *Matrix*'s version of day-to-day reality is a metaphor for something. Agent Smith and his crew, who present in-universe as government agents with Secret Service earpieces and shades, are metaphors for the systems that keep the Matrix's plugged-in masses in line. The old landline phones by which people enter and exit the Matrix are metaphors for the actual, more high-tech process by which it's accessed. The spoon—well, you know about the spoon. The movie's own plot, in other words, encourages anyone watching it to assign a hidden meaning to everything on the screen, even props. Its structure is just too potent to stay still; it quickly becomes a song people can pick up and play in their own voice, making it tell whatever story they want it to, like the Simpsons meme whose meaning changes depending on how you label Lisa, her coffee cup, the coffeepot, and Marge.

Eventually Keanu has to choose between the blue pill, which will put him back under the Matrix's spell, and the red pill, which will allow him to perceive the true nature of reality. Morpheus has already alluded to "the world that has been pulled over your eyes to blind you from the truth" and "a prison that you cannot smell or taste or touch—a prison for your mind."

Keanu initially rejects this new reality so hard he barfs up Easter-colored nutritional goop—but soon he's accepted that his life as Thomas Anderson was only a dream and seems relieved to let that identity go. It's hard to imagine thornier actors such as Smith or DiCaprio playing literal selflessness the way Keanu does here; as in *Point Break* Keanu is believable as a character who becomes a vessel for other people's ideas, someone who's still on some level unformed and up for grabs.

One reason *The Matrix* rewards right-wing interpretation is that it's a story about radicalization. Once Keanu's out of the Matrix and Morpheus's gang has restored his body to health, he's programmed, and his programming involves not just weapons and tactics but history and ideology—Why We Fight as well as How To Fight. Part of that involves gun battles with police and other authority figures. Sometimes those authorities are under the control of Agent Smith or his sunglassed associates, but sometimes they're just the Matrix version of regular cops—so presumably they're real people, plugged into the Matrix, dreaming of being police. The movie could have waved this away by establishing all cops inside the Matrix as programs and not people, but it doesn't; instead it's established that they're humans just like Keanu and everybody else, but they're humans whose dependency on and identification with the machine make it necessary to kill them. This is also how terrorists think about collateral murder.

And recall Keanu's jump from building to building in the practice-room version of the Matrix they call the Construct, which is part of a training sequence but also an indoctrination/initiation—Morpheus makes Neo jump because he needs Neo's absolute commitment to the cause, needs him to *believe*. Later, when Morpheus is taken hostage in a building crawling with Agent Smiths and the *Nebuchadnezzar*'s VR operator Tank suggests that trying to rescue him is suicide, Keanu—who's now playing this video game in "fanatic mode"—says, "I know that's what it looks like, but it's not."

The most powerful sequence in the first movie is the one that feels the most unthinkable now. Keanu and Carrie-Anne load up on guns—lots of guns—and enter the building where Morpheus is being held. When they're stopped in the lobby at a security checkpoint—a site that was about to become one of the most politically charged spaces in American life, a universalizing point of interaction with state power—they kill everyone who tries to stop them from getting upstairs, beginning with the security guards and ending with a team of guys in helmets with rifles who may be SWAT or military. You're watching the heroes of the film commit a mass shooting in cool, seductive slow motion.

In the coming years, the original *Matrix* would be mentioned as a possible inspiration for the Columbine massacre, largely because the perpetrators, Eric Harris and Dylan Klebold, wore trench coats, like Keanu does in this scene; attorneys pleading insanity on behalf of other shooting suspects, including the so-called Beltway Sniper John Lee Malvo, will invoke the film's influence on their clients so often the tactic becomes known as the "*Matrix* defense." The after-the-fact conversation about *The Matrix*'s lobby-shooting scene will play out the same way nearly every debate about the influence of violent entertainment on real-world violence does—First Amendment partisans will argue that depiction is not endorsement and Second Amendment partisans will argue that gun movies play a larger role in gun violence than gun availability does. What no one really discusses is what *The Matrix* is actually advocating. It's a movie about the necessity of violent revolution, written from a leftist, antiauthoritarian perspective; the cops in *The Matrix* are metaphorical, but they might be metaphors for the actual cops.

Despite all this, troubled souls drawn to the authoritarian politics of leaders like Donald Trump—or to the even stranger and lonelier ideological position that Elon Musk is cool—continue to declare themselves "red-pilled." In 2018, during Kanye West's impromptu lecture tour of the offices of important media outlets such as TMZ and *The Fader*, West praised Trump and the conspiracist broadcaster Alex Jones as "Matrix-breakers." Over twenty years later, *The Matrix* continues to hide in plain sight, which is probably for the best. In 1999, the world would not have been ready for a heroic sci-fi story that was explicitly and openly about a glorious uprising against the police and the government by trans folk and their POC allies. It's barely ready for one now.

***

Keanu later tells an interviewer that he enjoyed hairlessness as an experience.

"It's so odd to look in a mirror and to feel the same on the inside yet all semblance of your physical outward self is removed," he says. "I noticed people would shy away from me and I'd start wondering: What did I say? What did I do? It's interesting to learn what your own relationship really is to the outside!"

Neo lives in a false identity imposed on him by external forces; this is among other things what a movie star's life is like. When *The Matrix* comes to him Keanu's lost in a muddled moment of being Keanu Reeves, reluctant action hero and celebrity, the way Neo is lost in Thomas Anderson.

The Matrix makes use of his movie-star persona. It metaphorizes Keanu's own life as a reluctant action hero and reluctant celebrity, perpetually at the mercy of external forces. Being Neo is exactly like being a movie star. Everyone he meets knows who he is; everyone has an opinion about him and whether he's really all he's made out to be. And everybody wants to see him do kung-fu—when Morpheus fights Neo in the simulation program, the other members of the *Nebuchadnezzar*'s crew rush to a monitor to watch it happen, surrogates for our own excitement about seeing Fishburne and Keanu throw down on-screen.

For years Keanu has been searching for some kind of creative fulfillment and self-discovery through work that *Chain Reaction* and its ilk are never going to provide. *The Matrix* is an action movie where the "mission" and the hero's need to understand himself and his place in the universe are one and the same. It imagines a world where you don't have to transition from making *Little Buddha* to making *Speed*, where you can tell both of these kinds of stories at once.

EXPRESS
NYC
T

PART THREE
WHOLESOME GOD

16

21 | SAFE HOUSE

Even after *The Matrix* leaves theaters, the *Matrix* phenomenon keeps growing. When it comes out on DVD in September 1999, it will outsell *Titanic* three to one. In the meantime, in July, news breaks that Keanu has signed a $30 million deal to play Neo again in two *Matrix* sequels, which the Wachowskis hope to shoot back-to-back beginning in 2000.

Also in July, the E! Online gossip columnist Ted Casablanca reports that Keanu is feeling disenchanted with *The Replacements*, a football comedy he's been shooting in Baltimore that summer. It was an ensemble piece when he signed on and is starting to feel more and more like a Keanu Reeves movie. Same as it ever was. Nobody really pays attention to this news, though, because in the same column, Casablanca writes, "Busy little bees inside Keanu's honeycomb tell me his pregnant girlfriend is none too happy right now, only because Keanu is none too happy himself about his impending papa-hood." The following week, Keanu's reps confirm the pregnancy story but deny reports that Keanu isn't stoked about the baby or *The Replacements*.

The baby's mother is Jennifer Syme. She works in the music industry and before that she was the director David Lynch's assistant; she has a small part in Lynch's *Lost Highway*. She meets Keanu at an industry party for Dogstar sometime in the late nineties. When she gets pregnant they don't move in together but according to the gossip columns Keanu buys her a safe house somewhere outside Los Angeles, which he only visits after dark.

They lose the baby at the end of 1999, on Christmas Eve. This is part of the story of Keanu's work in that it deepens the perception of Keanu as someone who's endured unfair and unfathomable loss—first River and now this—which in turn will shape his latter-day screen persona in large and small ways. It affects how he's cast and how his work is received and interpreted; it's a big part of the reason he will seem so right as the grieving John Wick a decade later.

It becomes another thing we know about him that Keanu himself will almost never talk about.

***

The Replacements, the first Keanu movie of the twenty-first century, arrives in theaters in August 2000 with the shelf dust of 1988 all over it. The story is *Major League* pastiched in pigskin: When the players in a pro football organization that is for presumably legal reasons identified as not being the NFL go on strike, a coach is given carte blanche by an owner to recruit a scab team. He decides to get creative, bringing in a sumo wrestler to block passes and a lager-swilling Welsh footballer to kick, and when it's time to choose a quarterback he looks up Keanu's character, Shane "Footsteps" Falco, who washed out of college ball after a disastrous Sugar Bowl loss a few years back and now lives on a boat, which if you're a person in a movie is how you tell the world it can get fucked for what it's done to you. Keanu wears a wet suit, just like in *Point Break*, but he wears it to dive below the harbor water to scrape barnacles off other people's hulls, and he looks a little puffy in it.

Falco's first step toward shaking his self-perception as a loser and a has-been involves crossing a picket line, a plot point whose ethical implications the movie smooths over by making all the striking players into preening overpaid jerks who show up in the stadium parking lot to personally bully the scabs. Never has a sports movie been this eager to win the hearts of people who keep lists of their favorite sports movies; Jack Warden from *Rocky* plays the owner of the team and Gene Hackman from *Hoosiers* plays the coach and Jon Favreau from *Rudy* plays a rageful linebacker and John Madden and Pat Summerall from televised sports immemorial play John Madden and Pat Summerall. Keanu's playing the squarish guy thrust reluctantly into a world of eccentric characters, which isn't his most fruitful zone as an actor—yes, that's also roughly the plot of *The Matrix*, but at least in *The Matrix* he never has to say "That's gonna leave a mark" when someone gets knocked down.

The soundtrack keeps insisting that something is happening when it clearly isn't—in one game sequence alone we hear "Rock and Roll Part 2," "Takin' Care of Business," and "You Got Me Rockin'" by the Rolling Stones, one of three songs from the 1994 Rolling Stones album *Voodoo Lounge* that for some reason appear on the soundtrack of this movie from the year 2000. There's also a choreographed dance sequence set to "I Will Survive"—it breaks out in the drunk tank after the scabs get arrested for brawling in a bar with the striking players, and you can see Keanu wants no part of it, that he slinks around the edges of the shot and eventually disappears entirely, like he's just danced out the door and straight to his trailer.

Keanu falls for the team's head cheerleader, played by Brooke Langton, who doesn't date football players. Langton was on *Melrose Place*, and had a few scenes in *Swingers* as the woman whose answering machine Jon Favreau fills up with neurotic messages, and went on to play the Sandra Bullock part in the TV version of *The Net*, which makes her another of the most nineties actors who has ever lived. In *The Replacements*, after fighting their desire to kiss for almost an entire movie, she and Keanu exchange wordless love-looks for what feels like seventeen minutes of screen time while "Every Breath You Take" plays, and when they finally make out it feels like television—specifically, like the season finale of a basic-cable drama.

In this moment *The Replacements* gives us at least one valuable thing—a glimpse of a parallel-universe vision of Keanu, a Keanu who never made it quite as big, who rattled around on TV for years, sometimes as a series regular mentoring young doctors or profiling serial killers with the help of sassy ghosts, but more often a guest star, a murderer on *CSI* or a small-town sheriff on *Supernatural*. This is the career Keanu might have had if he'd agreed to be Chuck Spadina—the comfortable life of a familiar face. In this world he's not rich but he's always a welcome presence on the small screen. He's divorced and remarried. Lives half the year in Studio City and the other half in Toronto, possibly on a houseboat.

***

In *The Watcher*, which opens a few months later, Keanu is a serial killer and James Spader is the haunted cop who almost caught him and won't let him get away again, so before it even starts the movie feels like a Freaky Friday joke about Keanu and Spader switching roles. If there's anybody in this equation who should be donning latex gloves and planting goodbye kisses on his victims' duct-taped mouths, it's Spader, one of cinema's most natural-born creeps, and if there's anybody who should be playing the detective risking it all to rid the world of a monster, it's Keanu, our hero.

Instead it's Spader we see wearing a fleece vest to department-mandated therapy sessions with Dr. Marisa Tomei and coming home after work to a textbook haunted-cop shithole of an apartment—newspapers piled in the corner, no lid on the trash can, nothing in the fridge but salad dressing and an orange—where he gulps prescription pills by the fistful to numb the part of his brain that throbs because of the case he can't solve. And it's Keanu who's shown hunting women for sport; you know it's a serial-killer movie shot in the late nineties because Keanu covertly photographs his future victims with a Kodak Advantix while the Sneaker Pimps' trip-hop hit "6 Underground" sets a tone of inappropriately sexy foreboding.

The Watcher is released on September 8, 2000, and it ends up being the number one movie in America during its second weekend in theaters. This is sort of a misleading statistic, though, because the weekend of September 15, 2000, also happens to be a record low point for domestic box-office revenue in the 2000s. That record will stand until mid-March of 2020, when a majority of American moviegoers decide not to risk contracting the novel coronavirus COVID-19 just to see *Bloodshot*, *The Hunt*, or *I Still Believe* on the big screen.

Weirdly, this is not the most ignominious extracinematic fact about *The Watcher.* The director of *The Watcher* is a guy named Joe Charbanic, who prior to *The Watcher* was best known as a producer and director of music videos and an associate of Keanu's band, Dogstar. "I was hanging out with them, helping them with their gear, just to go to parties and meet girls," he told *Billboard* in 1996, in a story about the enhanced-CD release of the band's EP *Quattro Formaggi*, whose bonus features included behind-the-scenes video footage shot by Charbanic. After *The Watcher*, Charbanic becomes best known as the guy who allegedly tricked Keanu Reeves into being in *The Watcher*.

"I never found the script interesting," Keanu will admit to the *Calgary Sun* once enough time has passed, "but a friend of mine forged my signature on the agreement. I couldn't prove he did and I didn't want to get sued, so I had no other choice but to do the film."

He then watched as a role he'd been told was a cameo ballooned into a colead in what turns out to be one of the very worst films he's ever been in. The material appears to have been tailored to him in a way that makes it way worse: Keanu's serial killer in *The Watcher* turns out to be the kind of serial killer who likes to make his victims feel special first, which is a very Keanuish way to approach serial killing as a pastime. He coaxes one victim into striking sexy pouty poses for his camera. When a young punk panhandler catches his eye, he waltzes with her in the street. Then, as the movie builds to its climax, Keanu dances to a Rob Zombie song in a room full of candles and gasoline. Will Spader get there in time to stop this sinister tribute to the Police's "Wrapped Around Your Finger" video from turning deadly?

You could come away from *The Watcher* convinced that real evil and authentic darkness are notes Keanu can't quite hit. But within a few months, he'll turn up as one of the bad guys in another, far less embarrassing movie, doing genuinely frightening work that erases everything he's done before, and—at least while you're watching it—forecloses anything he might do afterward, leaving us to wonder how Keanu got there and how he managed to come back.

22 WOLF AT THE DOOR

The lesson of *The Watcher* is that it's not enough to give Keanu some bad things to do. You have to remove his Keanuosity from the equation entirely. In Sam Raimi's *The Gift*, also from 2000, he's a Georgia redneck who comes to Cate Blanchett's house in the middle of the night to threaten her and her family. Raimi doesn't even let us see him at first; he plays the first part of the scene through a chained door with a curtained window. Blanchett plays a widowed small-town psychic who does readings at her kitchen table, Hilary Swank is a client who's recently come to Blanchett with a black eye, and Keanu is Donnie, the abusive husband who gave it to her.

Donnie is the scariest Keanu's ever been on film. Keanu doesn't do a showy, mannered crazy-guy performance in this part. But there is a showy, mannered crazy-guy performance in *The Gift*; it's by Giovanni Ribisi, as another Blanchett client, a sad, doomed, mentally unstable garage mechanic who wants to kill his abusive father. Keanu as Donnie is just cold and mean, like he's conserving his energy so he only has to hit you once. Donnie drives a pickup with the Confederate stars-and-bars on it and his jaw is loose like a snake's. Donnie is Keanu purged of anything recognizably Keanu.

When he comes to the door Blanchett's two sons are in bed. A wolf howls on the soundtrack. The screen door creaks like a coffin lid. Donnie knocks hard. Blanchett comes to the door. She talks to him through the curtain. He speaks to her politely in a southern drawl with a touch of menace and a drop of Elvis—*Ma'am, I promise I'll just take a minute.* The voice comes out of a faceless Keanu—Raimi shows us the back of his head in a trucker cap, then his outline through the curtain, then a single Keanu eye in the gap between the chained door and the doorframe. When she lets him in he pushes straight past her into the house and steps on a painting one of Blanchett's kids left on the floor. He'll do what he wants in this house.

A full sixty seconds passes between the knock at the door and the first time the camera catches Keanu's whole face, and when he turns to look at Blanchett we no longer recognize him—it's like someone else is driving. Keanu drops the polite-good-old-boy act, starts laying into Blanchett, who he's convinced has been feeding his wife ideas. Keanu says Blanchett's fortune-telling is voodoo. Keanu says she's either a Satan worshipper or a con artist. Keanu says Blanchett "ain't no better than a Jew or a [N-word]," except he says the actual word. It rolls off his tongue with discomfiting ease, and that's the exact moment Raimi shows us Blanchett's two kids watching and listening, half-hidden behind their bedroom door.

When Keanu notices the kids Blanchett moves to stand in front of them and starts shouting, "Get your ass out of my house," and seeing that he's rattled her, Keanu smiles a little. She tells him to get out before she has him thrown in jail and opens the front door. He starts to walk out and she goes to close it behind him, and he whirls around and slams it back open with one big hand and knocks Blanchett into the wall as he leaves. But having violated Blanchett's space once, he knows he can haunt it forever.

In the very next scene Swank shows up at Blanchett's place to beg her for another reading, and before Blanchett can turn her away, Keanu reappears, wearing the same hunting jacket and cap from the night before, but without a shirt underneath. He bursts into the house, and the house seems to close in on everyone in it. What happens next between Blanchett and Keanu doesn't play like two actors acting. It feels scary, unsafe. Keanu throws Blanchett to the ground. He picks up a chair and hurls it at the wall. He grabs Swank by her hair, spits, "Get your ass in the truck," and shoves her so hard toward the kitchen door she actually seems to hit her head on the camera.

In interviews promoting the movie he'll talk about how he and Swank and Raimi rehearsed for their scenes together. He'll talk about improvising in a trailer with Swank and Raimi, calling Swank a liar over and over while pushing her against the wall and pulling her pants down. In one interview he'll talk about the research he's done for the movie and what he's learned about domestic violence and sex between abusers and the abused. He'll say, "There's a kind of submission that goes on in the female and dominance in the male, which is a turn-on. They call it the circle of violence and there's something the female likes about it."

It's not the most out-there thing anybody's ever said about the dynamics of abusive relationships, but at least one British tabloid decides to nail him for it, and turns for comment to Carolyn Hill of the National Organization for Women. Hill says, "Big movie star or not, this man needs to take a course in female sensitivity and if he doesn't have time for that, tune in to Mel Gibson's movie *What Women Want*," a zinger destined to age poorly for non-Keanu-related reasons.

Not to spoil *The Gift*, but Donnie is so obviously and objectively the shittiest character in the movie that there's no way he'll turn out to be the actual killer everybody's trying to catch. He does end up standing trial for murder, though. He sits in the docket in an awkward courtroom suit, his hair immaculately blow-dried. He looks like a celebrity defendant from the nineties who'd field marriage proposals in jail, or a soap-opera character destined to die in a boat explosion and return as his vengeful, eye-patched twin.

Having pulled a performance out of Keanu unlike anything

in Keanu's filmography, Sam Raimi then goes off and makes three *Spider-Man* movies in a row and never works with Keanu again. Keanu spends the next few years filming the second and third *Matrix* films concurrently and does nothing remotely like *The Gift* for quite a few years. And even when he plays a string of darker roles in the 2010s, in films including *The Neon Demon* and *The Bad Batch*, those performances still feel like they're contained within the imaginative space of "Keanu Reeves" as a concept. They're bold choices from a professional standpoint, expressions of Keanu's willingness to play a guy who isn't a hero, but even in their worst moments these characters will lack Donnie's harsh edge.

The risk involved in playing Donnie might have been personal as well as professional. Keanu starts filming *The Gift* in the spring of 2000; it's the movie he's making when it's announced that he and Jennifer Syme have split up, in tabloid stories that mention the loss of their child as the cause of the breakup. Whatever he's working through around that time is what he brings with him onto that set; it's possible what we're seeing when we look at Donnie is Keanu lashing out against the whole world. *The Gift* opens to mixed reviews and good-not-great box office, suggesting that nobody wants to watch Keanu hurt people, at least not like this.

Early in the morning on April 2, 2001, Jennifer Syme dies in a car accident. According to a wrongful-death suit filed in Los Angeles Superior Court in 2002, Syme had spent that night at a party at the home of Marilyn Manson, where she consumed "various quantities of an illegal controlled substance" before getting a ride home from a designated driver. Syme then got behind the wheel herself, apparently intending to return to Manson's house, before striking three parked cars and flipping the vehicle.

Syme had reportedly struggled with depression since the end of her pregnancy. A woman identified as Syme's roommate tells a tabloid that Syme and Keanu had been in contact since their breakup, but had recently stopped talking.

A few months later, David Lynch's *Mulholland Dr.* opens in

theaters. It's a movie that portrays the Hollywood casting process as a malevolent and possibly interdimensional conspiracy to torment an actor, and it begins with a car accident. Lynch, Syme's former boss, dedicates the movie to her memory.

23 | KEANU REEVES SINGS CHET BAKER

The number one movie in America the weekend after the September 11 attacks is *Hardball*, starring Keanu as a degenerate gambler who is forced to coach a baseball team of scrappy youngsters from Chicago's Cabrini Green housing projects, and is thereby redeemed. A shattered nation yearning to think about something other than terrorism probably deserves a more creative *Bad News Bears* rip-off than this one, but it's not like you can plan these things.

Keanu spends most of 2001 in Australia and the San Francisco Bay Area making two highly anticipated sequels to *The Matrix*, a movie that—like *Speed*—posited Keanu as a new and nontraditionally masculine alternative to the more stereotypically butch action heroes of the past. So the two Keanu movies that drop in 2001 are weird, because they both play like attempts to reframe Keanu as a bro, not a postgender future messiah in sci-fi sackcloth.

The year 2001 is a bro-y moment in the culture. *Maxim* is outselling every men's magazine on the newsstand except *Playboy*, Jimmy Kimmel and Adam Carolla's semi-ironic rumpus-room fantasia *The Man Show* is pulling in 1.3 million viewers a week on Comedy Central, and a former DKE frat boy is president of the United States. It's as good a time as any for Keanu to experiment with playing a brash, feelings-suppressing, guy's-guy type of guy.

Hardball is at least a slightly better Keanu sports movie than *The Replacements*, because *Hardball* has a young and already undeniably magnetic Michael B. Jordan playing one of the kids in Keanu's care. Plus there's a scene where Keanu and his even-more-degenerate gambler pal John Hawkes walk into a bar rapping the Notorious B.I.G.'s "Big Poppa" like they learned the lyrics phonetically. This can't save the movie, but Hawkes and Keanu, reunited for the first time since *Freaked*, have amazing dirtbag chemistry. In every scene they share, they seem like they're about to run out and mount a production of *True West* together, as soon as they finish the dead-end job they're doing here.

The best bro-Keanu movie of 2001 is *Sweet November*, which comes out first—in February, the optimum month to release a movie with "November" in the title. It drops Keanu and Charlize Theron into an uptight-dude-falls-for-free-spirited-lady structure that's worked in films from *Bringing Up Baby* to *Something Wild*, not to mention the original *Sweet November*, a 1968 movie starring Anthony Newley, who'd go on, coincidentally enough, to cowrite the bad songs Keanu sings with Drew Barrymore in the 1986 version of *Babes in Toyland*.

Anyway—the screenplay for this version of *Sweet November* is really something else:

> OPENING CREDITS and MUSIC play as dawn breaks over the city by the bay. Sounds of intense SEXUAL EXERTION fade up.
>
> INT. NELSON'S APARTMENT—BEDROOM—DAY
>
> In what is more workout than lovemaking, NELSON MOSS (36) thrusts vigorously into ANGELICA (32), lying spread-eagled on her back. An ALARM goes off, and on cue, Nelson climaxes. OPENING CREDITS and MUSIC FADE OUT.

Keanu doesn't have time to linger with poor Angelica. He has televisions to watch. Keanu has a whole wall of televisions in his apartment, like the TVs David Bowie rots his alien brain with in *The*

Man Who Fell to Earth. Keanu is an advertising guy who thinks only of being an advertising guy and he needs to get media into his face as efficiently and overwhelmingly as possible, so he can beat the other advertising guys.

He's pitching a hot-dog campaign this week. "Doctor Diggity," he says. "It's practically an American institution." He's the kind of guy who says things like this. He's the kind of guy who says things like "Worrying about losing keeps you winning." He's the kind of ad-agency guy who has a state-of-the-art-for-2000 vertical-loading CD player in his ad-agency office. He has motorcycle memorabilia and scrawled notes and sketches pinned to the walls. His job at the ad agency is apparently to walk around looking at design mock-ups laid out on a table, barking instructions like "More cleavage, more legs" and circling things with bold, confident strokes of a Sharpie.

But on the day we meet him he has to leave the world where he's in total control and go down among normal people—people who probably don't even own more than one television—to renew his license at the DMV, where he meets Theron, a kooky cactus flower whose whole kooky life spills out of her tote bag at Keanu's feet. He has to hand her back her salami. When he tries to cheat off her during the written test it's Theron who gets caught and loses her license. He agrees to drive her from San Francisco to Oakland, where she surprises him by breaking into a science lab—but it turns out she just wants to rescue some dogs from a place that does animal testing.

Theron has just met Keanu and this is crazy but she wants him to move in with her—for thirty-one days. It turns out Theron treats men like rescue dogs. She fosters them, trains them to see the world differently, then sends them on their way after one month. She's seen guys like Keanu come and go. "You live in a box," she says. "I could open the lid, let some light in." She asks him to be brave enough to do it. Keanu is not interested. He says he'll call the cops if she doesn't leave him alone.

Keanu loses his cool and rips the client a new one during the Dr. Diggity pitch. Keanu's boss tells him he can either take a leave of absence or be fired, and Keanu laughs mirthlessly, like a Satanist in a Jack Chick comic—*Haw! Haw! Haw!*—and says "You can't afford to lose me! I'm two Clios ahead of the game, Roy!" So he gets fired. Now he's at home with his stuff. His ad agency awards. His David Hockney coffee table books. What good are they? He smashes his awards and bleeds. Then he goes to Charlize Theron's house, where she's Jazzercising to Robbie Williams's "Rock DJ" in her camisole and Doc Martens. When Keanu shows up she takes his shirt off and goes to wash it. He is suddenly vulnerable in the camera's presence, holding his body awkwardly, bashfully. One of his motorcycle-accident scars is very visible here.

They embrace on the couch. He makes a move to escalate things, to get on with some of his trademark aerobic lovemaking. Charlize tells him, "Go slow." Keanu gets mad at this and says, "To hell with the whole goddamn thing." He doesn't do slow. Eventually he storms out of the room, spewing angry-guy clichés: "This has been the day from hell!" But later she comes to him, shows him what slow feels like. He's sitting, she's standing. She remains taller than him with her head higher than his as she pushes him down onto the bed, and once again Keanu is made love to on-screen.

Eventually Keanu agrees to give Charlize the month of November so she can free his mind. From the moment he watches her dance at the beach with some dogs, turning cartwheels, laughing into the camera like she's in a perfume commercial where the camera is her boyfriend, it's clear Keanu's going to fall for her and find himself in the process. Casting Keanu as the uptight guy—Mr. Jones from the straight world, a kind of yuppie Spock—never stops feeling awkward, though. He doesn't seem fully at home in the part until the story turns and Charlize Theron's character strips him of his defenses, finding someone gentle and wounded and Keanulike underneath.

Charlize helps Keanu loosen up. Charlize and Keanu take a bubble bath and she gives Keanu an Ed Grimley hair-horn with the soap. Keanu starts telling her things. His father used to shut himself in the TV room after dinner and listen to 45s of Frank Sinatra and Tony Bennett. For years Keanu wanted to be a singer because of this—not because it would have connected him with his father, but because Frank Sinatra and Tony Bennett seemed like men who had it together.

Charlize turns out to be a dot-com founder who walked away when her site got big, thereby missing out on the payday when it got really big. This is quietly an emblematic "Generation X values" movie—Charlize as the free spirit ambivalent about money, Keanu as the guy who's determined to outdo his father by deploying edgy imagery to sell dumb crap and hates himself for it.

Charlize is also secretly dying of cancer, a thing we discover before Keanu does. So this is another Keanu movie where Keanu has to accept a new reality. With Charlize's help he discovers the beauty of the world, becoming the kind of guy who can pause to appreciate a little girl dancing to her Walkman, a Che Guevara poster in a store window. But when he finds the locked cabinet full of empty cancer-medicine bottles that Charlize keeps around like a secret art installation, he also discovers the reality of disease, of sweat and puke and unignorable human impermanence. Show me death.

Keanu doesn't care that she's sick. He wants to stay with her past the November deadline. He throws his phone and his watch in a sink full of dirty dishwater to signify his commitment to the possibility of a love that transcends time. But she doesn't want him to remember her as a sick woman dying. She makes him leave. He walks on the beach, missing her. The song that plays over this scene is by Enya, because this is not the kind of movie that takes chances with your feelings.

They do not get back together. She leaves him alone on a bridge on a blue morning, blindfolding him so he can't watch her go. But before that he tries to convince her to reconsider, because he's still a pitchman even though his heart is open. He tries to sell her a dream of romance transcending everything else. He fills her apartment with calendars all open to the month of November and promises that it can be November forever for them. He gets her to meet him at a jazz club, and when she gets there he comes out, in a white tuxedo against blue velvet curtains, backed by a little jazz trio, and when he starts to sing what comes out is "Time After Time"—not the Cyndi Lauper hit but the jazz standard by Sammy Cahn and Jule Styne.

The best version of this "Time After Time" is the one on Chet Baker's 1954 album *Chet Baker Sings*, where Baker's narrow range and pillow-creased vibrato tell the story of the song, about a guy who's found a girl who makes him feel "so young, so new," and who still can't quite believe she's chosen somebody like him. That's how Keanu sings it—like Chet Baker, but in his own narrow, uncertain register, and it turns out to be a perfect song for Keanu to sing, not just an ode to romantic love but an ode to romantic gratitude, and for as long as it takes him to sing the song the rest of the movie falls away outside the spotlight, and there is only Keanu trying to sing a song, his careful awkwardness indistinguishable from grace.

24 | IN EVERY IMMACULATE NANCY MEYERS DREAM KITCHEN A CARDIAC EPISODE

People respond to Nancy Meyers movies because there are practically no mainstream movies that love a Diane Keaton–aged protagonist this much. The entirety of *Something's Gotta Give* as a story—everything about it: Jack Nicholson as the recalcitrant lothario, and Amanda Peet, and the subway tile in Diane Keaton's dream kitchen, and the sea, and Keanu—functions as a giant concave mirror beaming love and light at Diane Keaton. In *Something's Gotta Give* Amanda Peet plays Diane Keaton's daughter and Jack Nicholson plays Amanda Peet's boyfriend, who only dates younger women as a matter of policy. Jack Nicholson takes Viagra before going to bed with Peet in Diane Keaton's successful-playwright house in the Hamptons, and when he has a heart attack, Keanu is the physician at the hospital who says Jack Nicholson has to stay in Diane Keaton's Hamptons house until he's well enough to travel.

This gives Jack Nicholson time to fall in love with Diane Keaton and come to terms with the unpleasant truths he's tried to avoid by chasing younger women. But it also means Keanu Reeves has to come around with his blood-pressure cuff to check on Jack Nicholson, which gives him time to fall in love with Diane Keaton, too. This

does not seem to have been a hard thing for Keanu to act. “He was incredibly excited to meet Diane Keaton,” Nancy Meyers said later, in a *Premiere* story about Keanu. “I had met other actors for the part, and they would say things like ‘Do you think it’s believable that a guy my age falls for a woman that age?’ He didn’t have these hang-ups.”

He’s *never* had them. It’s hard to think of another actor who’s been paired so often with older women—or, later, age-appropriate women—without playing it for comedy *or* “Maggie May” tragedy, from *The Prince of Pennsylvania* in 1988—when Amy Madigan, then thirty-seven, asks him for poetry, Keanu, twenty-three, kisses his way up her leg, saying “I think that I shall never see a poem as lovely as your knee, or a pie as tasty as your thigh”—all the way through *The Private Lives of Pippa Lee* twenty-one years later, in which Robin Wright, born two years after Keanu, dreams of a lion on a leash, sleepwalks into the convenience store where Keanu’s character works, and winds up in the back of his van with his hands down her pants; he watches her get off, silent and dutiful, her experience his only concern on Earth. In Jon Amiel’s *Tune in Tomorrow*, from 1990, he’s in trouble right away—the story transplants Mario Vargas Llosa’s *Aunt Julia and the Scriptwriter* from 1950s Lima to New Orleans, and Keanu’s New Orleans accent turns out to sound like somebody workshopping a Jimmy Carter impression while also trying not to swallow gum—but you absolutely believe he’s falling for Barbara Hershey when it happens. She’s his father’s brother’s wife’s sister, so it’s not unheard-of that he pursues her, but it’s untoward; when she makes an issue of their age gap he says, cheerfully, “I’m twenty-one and I lost my cherry five years ago.” His face is wide-open and eager, like his horniness is real and forefront-present in his mind but doesn’t torment him—it just tickles. The way he comes on to her is a kind of earnestness about his own desires. In a *Tracey Ullman Show* sketch from 1989, Ullman’s a landscape architect who gets too drunk at a client’s party and wakes up naked in the bedroom of the client’s Truffaut-loving teenage son, played by Keanu, the joke is in the gulf between Ullman’s dawning dread and shame and Keanu’s grinning wide-openness—this may be the worst thing that’s ever happened to her, but it’s the best thing that’s ever happened to him. "You saw yourself the way I see you," he tells her, "and it was the greatest feeling you've ever had," and then he kisses her up against his *Day for Night* poster.

Jack Nicholson's process of falling in love with Diane Keaton takes a whole movie to work itself out—we're supposed to root for it to happen, and against things working out with Keanu, whom Jack Nicholson describes in the movie as "nonthreatening," and who's supposed to represent the absolutely perfect catch of a guy whom Keaton nonetheless throws over for the cynical, elusive, complicated Jack Nicholson—whereas Keanu has to literally perform "falling in love with Diane Keaton" as a believable human action in a single scene.

Like every important thing that happens in a Nancy Meyers movie, this happens in a clean, white, light-flooded Nancy Meyers kitchen. You can see it on Keanu's face right away—he can't believe his good fortune, how lucky he is to be here, doing this scene with Diane Keaton, watching her pour a cup of tea. He asks her how she's "holding up," she hears the words, gets flustered, tugs at the hem of her sweater, crosses her arms, says she's *fine, fine, fine,* and Keanu, fake-stern, says one more "fine" and he won't believe her, and she does an *Oh, you* thing with her hands. The phone rings and he passes her the receiver. She answers, and he turns away, puts his hands on the counter, gives her the privacy he can give her without leaving the room—but as she talks he turns back to sneak a look at her, blinks, and Meyers eases the camera imperceptibly closer to him.

Then we see Diane Keaton the way Keanu Reeves sees Diane Keaton, bathed in Hamptons light, a light that is flattering but not dishonest, and in a subtle slow motion she laughs and shakes her head glamorously, and he laughs a little and looks down at the counter, tightening up, suppressing a smile, and then Diane Keaton tells the person on the other end of the phone, "Part of the play takes place in Paris, so I've been listening to French music, trying to get inspired," and he looks at her again and before he writes HAVE DINNER WITH ME TONIGHT on his prescription pad and slides it in front of Diane Keaton, we see him take a breath, working up the nerve to do it.

25
GIVING THE ARCHITECT THE FINGER

In the second and third *Matrix* movies the trilogy implodes. The original film ends with Keanu emerging from a phone booth like Superman and flying up and away while Rage Against the Machine bellows a badass song about COINTELPRO; the end of the third film dumps us back into real life with a tenuous happy ending that slaps a literal rainbow on a depiction of good and evil at a stalemate. Released months apart in 2003, these movies do the kind of business they're expected to at the box office but no one quite loves them. It isn't only because emotional returns almost always diminish over the course of a movie trilogy, and it isn't only because you can only watch a CGI Keanu bowl a CGI Hugo Weaving at a bunch of other CGI Hugo Weavings so many times before it stops being cool. It's because all the brilliantly choreographed action set pieces—a kung-fu fight that breaks out on top of a freeway chase, old soldiers strapping into robot battle-suits one last time to hold the fort down for humankind—serve a story that withholds the easy satisfactions of the traditional blockbuster in favor of a message that calls the meaning of the whole story into question.

Maybe this was bound to happen. The first *Matrix*, driven by antiauthoritarian hacker politics of distinctly nineties vintage, was

pre-9/11 art. The sequels were already written and in production when the towers fell, but they're post-9/11 art in crucial ways, and you can still feel them sidestepping a lot of what was provocative about the original. The sequels downplay any equation of state power with machine mind control, pitting Neo and his crew against nonuniformed, traditionally villain-coded henchman types and robot squids instead of the cops. In *Revolutions*, the primary antagonist in the real world is a giant drill, and there's no one left to fight in the Matrix except an army of copied-and-pasted Agent Smiths.

Now fully unbound by physical laws, Keanu and his equally unbound nemesis Weaving bounce off each other over and over in a sky full of lightning, their I'm-rubber-you're-also-rubber clash inadvertently (or advertently) illustrating the meaninglessness of scenes like the one we're watching. Eventually Keanu realizes the only way to defeat Smith is to stop fighting, so he lets himself die, a sacrifice that brings about a fragile peace between man and bot while propping open the door for more sequels. Production on a fourth *Matrix*, directed by Lana Wachowski, was nearly complete when world-altering disaster struck again; it's set for release in December 2021.

At the end of *The Matrix Reloaded*, Keanu encounters the Architect, a distinguished white-bearded elder who claims to have built the Matrix and tells Keanu that the appearance of "the One"—the humanity-saving messiah Keanu has come to believe himself to be—is actually just a recurring systemic anomaly within the vast programmed reality of the simulation. The Architect says the Matrix is older than Keanu knows, and that this is the sixth time they've faced each other. All this has happened before, and all of it will happen again. Visually and symbolically, the scene is about Keanu as a prisoner of his own image—struggling to understand who he actually is within a system of deception and control, trying to stay true to himself and the needs of the people around him amid the machinations of forces beyond his imagining.

When the Architect drops this bomb on Keanu they're in a room full of round-edged tube-TV-style monitor screens depicting the ways the previous iterations of Neo handled the news of their cosmic insignificance. They curse, shake their fists, insist on their own agency, flip the bird, and tell the Architect he's fucking dead. The Keanu in the room stays cool, which suggests that he's an anomaly among anomalies—the one who's actually the One. But it's also entirely possible that behind each of those Neos there's another wall of Neos, and a wall of Neos behind each of those. If we take into account what we already know about the nature of the Matrix simulation—that it's the way it is because the pod-people didn't accept the false reality as real until the machines programmed it to include the illusion of struggle and suffering—it opens up the question of whether the Architect is telling the whole truth. It could be a hundred years from the false nineties where Neo lived as Thomas Anderson; it could also be the year 3000, or the year 30000.

The coldest idea in the *Matrix* trilogy, the harshest toke in its catalog of late-night dorm-lounge bong-sesh what-ifs, the notion that ruins the whole party if you think it through for half a second, is this one, that everything that happens in these movies—from Neo's arrival on the scene to the final semidecisive clash between humanity and machinery, but also the rest of the whole deal, including the alluded-to backstory of somebody waking a small group of minds and unplugging those people's bodies and forming a civilization in a cave and calling it Zion and believing in a prophecy and waiting around for a Neo to show up—has happened before, not in some mythically cyclical Gilgameshian a-hero-will-rise way, but countless times, as part of the orderly functioning of a world the Matrix itself still totally controls. The unsettling idea that lurks around the edges of the whole story—Morpheus teaching Neo how to fight, Joe Pantoliano selling everybody out for access to virtual steak, the Architect and the Oracle, the battle-bots and the drill, even Neo mysteriously developing the ability to zap the squids in the "real world"—a detail that by the way makes a lot more sense if you assume it's because Keanu has moved up one level of lucidity in what's still a layered *Inception* dream—is the possibility that none of it matters, that this is all essentially just a jet of steam that blows out of the roof of a factory at five o'clock, a planned release of pressure within an all-encompassing and all-powerful system that actually enables that system to persist, a thing that happens because the Matrix or some governing force above and outside the Matrix that keeps tabs on what's doing within the Matrix allows it to happen, because that force has run the numbers on this and determined that hope is a more effective sleep aid for the copper-tops than despair.

Writing after *Reloaded* but before *Revolutions*, Slavoj Žižek compares the first two *Matrix* movies to "the proverbial painting of God that seems always to stare directly at you from wherever you look at it; practically every orientation seems to recognize itself in it." He was writing about how his "Lacanian friends" saw Lacan in these films, how Frankfurt Schoolers of his acquaintance saw "kulturindustrie, directly taken over," how New Agers saw Plato's Cave. Žižek posits any attempt to divine these movies' actual philosophical leanings as "a trap to be avoided"—a bold statement from a contributor to the cottage-industry-inaugurating anthology *The Matrix and Philosophy*, in stores before the first sequel dropped. He suggests we're better off reading them as "rendering, in their very inconsistencies, the antagonisms of our ideological and social predicament" and "the complications and confusions of the politics of liberation." The Architect tells Neo that when previous Neos have attempted to liberate humanity, it's caused the destruction of Zion; he intimates that this, too, is part of the Matrix's plan. "If part one was dominated by the impetus to exit the Matrix, to liberate oneself from its hold, part two makes it clear that the battle has to be won within the Matrix, that one has to return to it," Žižek writes.

Before Neo takes flight at the end of the first *Matrix*, we hear him leaving what sounds like a threatening voicemail message for the world's enslavers. "I'm going to show these people what you don't want them to see," he says. "A world without rules and controls. Without borders or boundaries. A world where anything is possible." His speech sums up the romantic nineties notion of cyberspace as a swashbuckler's paradise and anticipates the communiqués of the real-life hacker group Anonymous, who'd soon turn the Guy Fawkes mask worn by the anarchist hero of 2005's *V for Vendetta* (adapted from Alan

Moore's comics and produced by the Wachowskis) into their trademark. But according to the *Matrix* movies' own rules, in order to be a cool leather-clad quasi-superhero who bends or breaks physical laws like Neo, Morpheus, or Trinity, you have to remain within the Matrix; Keanu can fly because unlike the plugged-in masses he's aware that he's inside the Matrix, but he's still inside.

By the same token, what the *Matrix* movies can't really give Keanu is liberation from the need to participate in the blockbuster-production cycle of the business he's chosen. All they are is a way to participate in it that feels a little more conscious and meaningful, a little more Baudrillard-y. He remains at the mercy of the industry; he can assert some free will over the specifics of the kinds of movies he's pushed to make, just like when he had Jack Traven's one-liners stripped out of *Speed*. But he can't do away with the perceived demand for a certain type of Keanu Reeves movie, the audience's addiction to pure adrenaline and easy answers. He will spend the years after the *Matrix* sequels looking for another project that lets him split the difference between what he wants and what everyone else wants. The trailer for *The Matrix Resurrections* makes it look as though Keanu and Lana Wachowski's return to the franchise will be partly a riff on this exact dilemma. It works its way up to the money shots—glowing doorways, magic mirrors, rabbits to chase and hallway walls to run up and bullets to dodge in the rain. There's even a dojo fight with Yahya Abdul-Mateen II, as a younger Morpheus; "You don't know me," Keanu tells him, before throwing a slow-motion sucker punch. But before that we see Keanu trying in vain to make a go of it in the so-called real world—popping blue pills, going to therapy, and crying in the bathtub. You can't be Neo forever, but once you know it's possible, it's tough to go back to being Thomas Anderson.

26| A BIBLE WRITTEN IN HELL

Keanu Reeves smokes, but like all smokers, there was a time when he didn't. Unlike most smokers, he picked up the habit late—when he was thirty, shooting *Feeling Minnesota*, not even one of the ones people liked—and couldn't put it down. How this happened I'm not sure, since it's standard practice to supply actors with herbal cigarettes to smoke on-screen, but maybe Keanu felt his character would know the difference, and built his performance from the lungs out. The Method tastes good like a cigarette should, and the false self wants what it wants. He's cursed Sir Walter Raleigh in interviews ever since, claiming he'd like to quit but can't. But being an actor who actually smokes does have cinematic advantages. You can always spot a nonsmoking actor playing a smoker; they smoke without rhythm. They don't really know what it is to be that intimate with fire and formaldehyde. In *Constantine*, supernatural pulp-noir from 2005, Keanu plays a freelance exorcist who learns he's dying of lung cancer but continues to light up, because he's caught up in a proxy war between Heaven and Hell, and that's a lot of pressure. Every time he smokes in the movie—a numerologically ominous thirteen times, according to people who've counted—you believe he's been looking forward to it, even though it's

making him sicker. This is something nonsmoking actors will never understand. The best cigarette of the day is always the next one.

Constantine is a DC Comics antihero from the eighties, introduced by Alan Moore in the pages of *Saga of the Swamp Thing*, a series that formed the rootstock of DC's mature-Goths-only Vertigo universe, whose core titles included *Constantine*'s solo spin-off *Hellblazer*. Moore soon fell out with DC over the rights to the characters he created in his monumentally and sometimes detrimentally influential twilight-of-the-superheroes series *Watchmen*, and has spent the past few decades studying magic and cursing corporate comics from a modest three-bedroom in Northampton. The credits of *Constantine*—like those of previous Moore adaptations such as Zack Snyder's *Watchmen* and the James McTeigue-Wachowski-Wachowski film of *V For Vendetta*—never mention Moore's name, at the request of the magus himself, who wants nothing to do with them. The Snyder and McTeigue films, for whatever it was or wasn't worth to Alan Moore, are pretty faithful to their four-color sources, whereas no jury in the world would convict *Constantine* director Francis Lawrence of having spent more than a few minutes in a room with the early-nineties Garth Ennis/Will Simpson *Hellblazer* issues where Constantine battled cancer. Lawrence's film predates 2008's *Iron Man* and the dawn of the more literal-minded, franchise-furthering Marvel age of superhero movies. In the comics, Constantine is canonically a blond bloke from Liverpool—a working-class magician in an old trench coat, Merlin or Mandrake as conceived by Mike Leigh—rather than a cool LA private-eye type in a black suit, so casting Keanu is the first and biggest liberty Lawrence takes with the original text. Fan-men groused—but when the artist Stephen Bissette first drew John Constantine in a *Swamp Thing* comic, he looked exactly like Sting. As with the Bible and the Constitution, a strict constructionist take is not always the move.

Constantine is dying because thirty cigarettes a day for decades will do that to you. But he's bound for Hell because once, as a young man tortured by demon-spotting abilities he couldn't yet control, he attempted suicide; now he does God's wet work in a vain attempt to change his destiny. By the end of the movie, he's looking right in the camera and growling his case to the Most High: "I know I'm not one of your favorites. I'm not welcome in your house. But I could use a little attention." Critics outside comics fandom looked at this story and wrote it off as a murky *Matrix* retread painted with a thin coat of theology. "I will leave the issue of blasphemy to the experts," wrote David Denby. "But maybe some of the audience should wonder if they aren't doing the Devil's work by sitting so quietly through movies that turn wonders into garbage."

But *Constantine* also turns garbage into wonder. Lawrence made his name directing videos for *Total Request Live* megahits by the Backstreet Boys, Destiny's Child, and Justin Timberlake, and his first feature has a music video's throw-it-at-the-wall, this-might-look-cool, don't-overthink-it visual energy and a similarly loose approach to tone. It has sinewy, shrieky CGI demons, a sorrowful Rachel Weisz as a cop investigating her twin sister's suicide, Pruitt Taylor Vince asphyxiating like a spilled goldfish as an alcoholic priest cursed with endless thirst, Bush frontman Gavin Rossdale as a power-suited succubus, and subplots involving a Bible written in Hell ("It takes a different view of Revelation") and a spear stained with Christ's blood and smuggled into Mexico by the Nazis, presumably after it slipped through Indiana Jones's fingers.

By the third act, Keanu's running around with a gold Gatling gun shaped like a crucifix. All this sets the table for the appearance, as Satan, of Peter Stormare, who just about eats the table. Pillsbury-pale and pink-eyed, he lisps and giggles and sucks his teeth and generally suggests Klaus Kinski if someone had cast him as Hannibal Lecter and then told him to feel free to "go a little bigger with it." No other actor in the film seems as confident about what kind of movie they're in and what kind of performance they're supposed to be giving, except Keanu, who walks a fine line perfectly, delivering every absurd tough-guy zinger ("God's a kid with an ant farm, lady—he's not planning anything") with just enough doom in his throat and arch in his eyebrows to let the camp properly decant, honoring the script's pseudoprofundities while releasing us from the obligation to take them all that seriously. Whether he's coughing up blood in a doctor's sink, vibing ominously to Dave Brubeck's "Take Five" in his downtown loft, or giving an all-powerful cosmic entity the middle finger as he slips from one dimension to the next, he'll rarely wear a dramatic role this lightly again.

The opening seconds of *The Matrix* turned the Warner Bros. production logo black and green, teasingly indicting the movie itself as part of a system of control; *Constantine* starts with the Warner Bros., Village Roadshow, and DC Vertigo logos burning to ash as if swept away by a nuclear blast. In *Constantine* Hell is a nightmare Los Angeles where it's always Judgment Day; Keanu visits through a side door, via a ritual that requires him to hypnotize a cat. But the movie's Los Angeles is a nightmare Los Angeles, too—perpetually dark and wet, like they shot the whole thing in the cabinet under a sink. As with *John Wick*'s New York, *Constantine*'s LA conceals a shadow city with its own protocols and bylaws, its own norms and jargon, its own legends and celebrities—including Tilda Swinton as an androgynous angel Gabriel in immaculately tailored men's suiting—and password-protected underground nightclubs where its demonic elite can lounge like interdimensional Eurotrash. To keep the expository world-building coming at speed and save Keanu from having to provide all of it personally, Lawrence gives Constantine an informal support staff—Shia LaBeouf as his taxi-driving chauffeur and magician's assistant, plus a bespectacled archivist to whom Keanu can say things like "Check the scrolls anyway—see if there's any precedent," plus Djimon Hounsou as a voodoo priest and nightclub proprietor who runs his joint as neutral ground, like the Continental Hotel in *John Wick*. "Demons stay in Hell, angels in Heaven," Hounsou says. "The great detente of the original superpowers."

Constantine is the first Keanu film that really tries to reflect the bleak post-9/11 era its audience was waking up to. LA has been left to rust and crumble by effete, rule-bound angels immune to mortal suffering and a God who can't be bothered. The feeling of existential abandonment *Constantine* captures was the mood of 2005, even before Hurricane Katrina hit New Orleans that fall and the most avowedly Christian US president since William McKinley left thousands to drown. *The Matrix* saw through the ahistorical fog of the complacent late nineties to the millennial anxieties behind it, but *Constantine* is the first Keanu movie that really attempts to process the sense that—as citizens of a republic—we'd be left to face the consequences of the twentieth century more or less on our own.

Grim times demand new fantasies, escapism that doesn't deny what it's an escape from. *Constantine*, a movie about human powerlessness in the face of uncaring forces, brings out a darker Keanu than we've seen before, a Keanu for a more jaded world. He might have gotten here anyway; after being rudely awakened to the true nature of reality in three *Matrix* films, playing innocent again was probably no longer an option. Instead he's a Raymond Chandler mystic, a wised-up and unsentimental navigator of the mean streets. John Constantine is a bridge from the Keanu of the nineties to the Keanu of right now; you don't get from Neo to John Wick without him. Lawrence, who went on to make three *Hunger Games* movies in a row, has talked about wanting to revisit the character, and so has Keanu, but this probably won't happen. As of February 2021, director J.J. Abrams was reportedly seeking a "diverse lead" for a new HBO Max *Constantine* series, which will be set in London.

Of course, the fact that Keanu's *Constantine* is destined to stay a weird one-off makes it cooler. It's hard to imagine a more responsibly synergetic hunk of franchise entertainment finding room to equate the plight of sinners forsaken by God and the feeling of dying under late capitalism the way this *Constantine* does in the space of a single brief sequence. It's early in the film; Keanu walks out of a gas station with a big NEVER FORGET 9/11 sign on the door, having just purchased a bottle of cough syrup to chug down in the rain. A crow flaps past him, unnervingly close to the ground—more unnerving, in its total visual wrongness, than any of this movie's more obviously gnarly demons. As Keanu turns to follow the crow with his eyes, he sees a billboard that reads YOUR TIME IS RUNNING OUT . . . TO BUY A NEW CHEVY. Then he fights a guy whose body is made of bugs.

27 | PHILIP K. DICK ENERGY

A Scanner Darkly is Keanu's first experience making a movie on digital video, a medium that allows a director (Richard Linklater, in this case) to let a take play out indefinitely. This way of doing things takes some getting used to, if you've learned to act in movies according to the rhythm imposed on the process by the capacity of a film-camera magazine. "I was just, like, can we please stop?" Keanu says to Danny Boyle a few years later, in a documentary about digital filmmaking called *Side by Side*. Boyle, answering in the voice of a diabolical director, cackles, "No! We don't have to!" and Keanu says, "But I *want* to." This is actually the perfect way for an actor to feel while making a movie like *Scanner*, which is about a man forced to give a continuous performance that begins to consume him, costing him his health and his sanity and eventually even his ability to remember who he was before the performance started.

You often see *A Scanner Darkly*, based on Philip K. Dick's 1977 novel, recommended to people in the mood for something "trippy," a taxonomical error I imagine has led to harshed mellows for more than a few trippers. *Scanner*—a movie about some users of an instantly addictive drug called Substance D—paints CGI over live footage to

mimic the way psychedelics can lend a hallucinatory beauty to the everyday. A jumbo bottle of Tapatío hot sauce, the purple UV glow of a closet pot farm, the Muppet-fur pink of fiberglass insulation, the specific quality of light in a room where some thin hippie scarf has been pressed into service as a curtain. As in Linklater's earlier quasi-animated feature *Waking Life*, human outlines waver and everyone's hair moves like undersea grass stirred by the current.

So we see cool visuals, but we never see the characters seeing cool visuals. Substance D has no transcendent effects that anyone talks about; all it seems to do is take away the feeling of not having taken it. Then it eats you alive from the brain on down. Twenty percent of the population is hooked; *Scanner*'s near-future Anaheim, California, is a case study of a country in the midst of a low-key epidemic. This is still a Linklater movie, built to fit loose, but it's darkest-timeline Linklater; old comic-relief characters reappear in dire psychic straits. In *Dazed and Confused*, Rory Cochrane was Slater, the bakedest potatohead in the ensemble and the one with the most conspiracy theories: George Washington was in a cult, and the cult was into aliens, man. In *Scanner*, Cochrane is Charles Freck, a twitchy and far-gone addict whose skin is crawling with imaginary aphids. Linklater's take on Dick is a weird crossbred bird, a stoner movie about speed.

Keanu is Bob Arctor, another Substance D user on the downslope to deterioration, which is a problem, because Arctor is really Fred, a deep-cover narcotics cop working for the sheriff's department. At the office, Fred wears a "scramble suit" that obscures his appearance with an ever-shifting mosaic of strangers' faces, so even his superiors don't know his street identity. When they order him to focus his investigation on Bob Arctor, they're really telling him to keep tabs on himself.

Again: it sounds trippier than it is. The way the movie delivers information sometimes mirrors Keanu's mental slippage, but this isn't really as much of a what-is-reality movie as it's cracked up to be. We know pretty much right away that Keanu is both Bob and Fred, and then we watch both Bob and Fred crumble mentally. Parts of the movie are improbably funny, especially when Robert Downey Jr. and Woody Harrelson are on-screen as Arctor's bickering flop-housemates and the story becomes a bleak nineties sitcom about roomies with terminal brain fog—"Two Guys, a Girl, and a Guy Who Is Mentally Two Different Guys," maybe, or a grim *Seinfeld* reboot with Keanu as the Jerry whose place everyone hangs out at, Winona Ryder as Elaine, Downey as a scheming Kramer, and Harrelson as George.

It's also a drug movie starring a bunch of actors who've experienced drug prohibition's effects up close, from Ryder (charged with possession of illegally procured prescription pills after her shoplifting arrest) to Downey (repeat nonviolent drug offender whose path to superhero-movie redemption involved jail time as well as rehab) to Harrelson (arrested in 1996 for planting four hemp seeds in Beattyville, Kentucky as an act of protest). And Keanu, the guy playing the narc playing the addict, was River Phoenix's friend and the son of a man who went to jail after a drug bust. The casting may be a coincidence, but no self-respecting paranoid would accept it as such.

***

A Scanner Darkly was one of Dick's most conventionally autobiographical books, a fictionalized account of one of the darkest stretches of Dick's life. In 1970, when Dick was forty-two and his dependency on amphetamines had grown dire, Dick's then-wife Nancy left with their three-year-old daughter Issa.

"I had to be with people," he says in an interview in 1974. "I flooded the house with people. Anybody was welcome. Because the sound of their voices, the sound of their activity, the din in the hall, anything, it kept me alive. I literally was unable to kill myself then, 'cause there was too much going on."

Dick's Marin County home soon develops a reputation and Phil finds himself surrounded by a rotating cast of freaks and burnouts half his age and embroiled in the increasingly hard-edged counterculture of the early seventies Bay Area.

He stops writing but still takes over a thousand tablets of methedrine per week. Then in the fall of 1971 his house is broken into and his file cabinets are ransacked and some of his personal items are stolen—a gun, the good stereo. The break-in will preoccupy Dick for years. His list of likely suspects includes narcs, religious fanatics, the John Birch Society, the Black Panthers, neo-Nazis, government agents, or agents of something bigger than the government.

In early 1972, he accepts an invitation to speak at a science-fiction convention in Vancouver, abruptly decides to relocate to Canada full-time, then survives a suicide attempt, which leads to his weaning himself off amphetamines for the first time in decades. *Scanner*, the first book he completed without speed in his system, is a document of the end of the golden age of drugs in America, dedicated to a list of users of Dick's acquaintance who wound up dead or incapacitated, including "Phil" (described as having suffered "permanent pancreatic damage").

"Everything in *A Scanner Darkly* I actually saw," Dick told an interviewer when the book was published in 1977. "I mean I saw even worse things than I put in *A Scanner Darkly*. I saw people who were reduced to a point where they couldn't complete a sentence, they really couldn't state a sentence. And this was permanent, this was for the rest of their lives. Young people. These were people maybe 18 and 19, and I just saw, you know, it was like a vision of Hell."

When Ridley Scott's *Blade Runner*—based very loosely on Dick's novel *Do Androids Dream of Electric Sheep?*—is released in theaters in June 1982, Dick has been dead since March. He never gets to see the film before he dies. Nor does he get to see his deepest paranoid preoccupations enter mainstream public consciousness through the side door of the multiplex—in *Total Recall*, in Steven Spielberg's *Minority Report*, in Amazon's prestige-TV expansion of *The Man in the High Castle*. He never gets to see a certain Keanu Reeves blockbuster whose portrayal of the "real world" as a simulacrum masking an all-encompassing prison would undoubtedly have struck him as familiar. ("I think he would've loved it," Dick's fifth wife, Tessa Dick, said of *The Matrix*, "and would've sued them.") On the plus side, he escapes this plane of reality without ever having to hear the Weeknd sing "She like my futuristic sounds in the new spaceship / Futuristic sex, give her Philip K. Dick" in 2020, which makes him luckier than us.

Dick is the perfect sci-fi writer celebrity for the sixties—a guy who becomes convinced that vast and sinister and possibly ancient conspiracies are responsible for stealing his stash and his stereo. But his work has never felt pinned to one decade; to open Dick's books now is to find uncanny descriptions of your own time staring back at you. By the time Linklater made *A Scanner Darkly*, the electronic-surveillance aspects of the story barely seemed futuristic anymore—it was five years after 9/11, boom years for warrantless wiretapping. *Scanner*'s vision of America as a pharmaceutically addled community under the boot of a police state feels like Linklater conjuring the spirit of 2020 in the middle of the Bush II years. The movie turns transparent and you can see the future through it; there's even an unsettling cameo by future Sandy Hook conspiracy theorist Alex Jones, as a ranting street preacher who gets dragged off in a van by government thugs.

But as much as it's about Dick's own story or a dystopian future that was approaching faster than Linklater could have anticipated, *Scanner* is also about Keanu—or at least it's another movie in which Keanu, by his presence, burns a Keanu-shaped hole in the material.

Keanu is good in movies that attempt to explain him to us and maybe to him, movies that provide a fictional explanation for his inner mysteries, the way he always seems to be processing reality at half speed. He's great in movies like this and *The Matrix* and *Johnny Mnemonic*, where some part of his brain is inaccessible, where his whole life is an attempt to work around a black hole, where he plays a character with a patched-together self.

In his very first scene he's speaking to a lodge full of community leaders about the scourge of illegal drugs. Keanu starts to lose his place, forgets what he's supposed to say next—or doesn't *want* to say what he's supposed to say next, despite the supervisor's voice in his ear telling him—*directing him*—to just say the shit and get it over with.

The camera—it's animation, so there's no actual "camera" making this camera movement, but the image replicates a zoom—passes through the digital skin of the suit and finds Keanu's dismayed face underneath it, murmuring, "This is terrible."

To the voice in his ear back at headquarters, he mutters, "I think I have a mental block against this shit." The scene becomes about an actor being pushed to give a performance he won't give.

The voice in his ear feeds him lines: "Retribution will swiftly follow. I would not for the life of me want to be in their shoes." He won't say them.

Instead he starts talking honestly, about the "slow death from the head down" that every Substance D user eventually faces, which we'll soon learn includes him, too. He gives what's actually a far more heartfelt antidrug speech, full of sadness and loss and regret, of experience. The language—"D is for dumbness and despair, desertion, desertion of your friends from you, you from your friends, everyone from anyone. Desolation. Loneliness. Pitying and suspecting each other"—is straight from Dick's book, an antidrug book born of firsthand knowledge.

Whatever else it is it's a movie about an actor. "Arctor" even sounds like "actor," and in Dick's book, as Fred scrutinizes surveillance footage of his drug friends and himself lost in the schizophrenia of performance, the connection becomes explicit: "In the script being filmed, he would at all times have to be the star actor. Actor, Arctor, he thought. Bob the Actor who is being hunted; he who is the El Primo huntee."

Fred had a life before this—a wife and a family and a house. He remembers only that it bored him. He has a sense memory of hitting his head on a cabinet, drawing blood, a sharp epiphany: "I realized I didn't hate the cabinet door. I hated my life."

The family never reappears. He's left them, or they've left him, and he's thrown himself into the work. Over the course of the story he forgets them more and more; he doesn't remember that the house he shares with his drug buddies was his house once, that a family lived there, that it was *his* family.

After a while the life of an actor is all a star actor has to draw on. The movie becomes a metaphor for Keanu's life, and maybe for his loneliness: "Now in the dark world where I dwell," he says in voice-over, "ugly things and surprising things, and sometimes little wondrous things spill out at me constantly, and I can count on nothing."

28

KEANU REEVES IS AN ARCHITECT WHO SAYS "COME TO PAPA" TO A BOWL OF SOUP AND SANDRA BULLOCK DOESN'T KNOW HOW TO PRONOUNCE "DOSTOEVSKY" AND WITHOUT EVEN TOUCHING THEY FALL IN LOVE

Constantine and *A Scanner Darkly* came out in 2005 and 2006, respectively, so they're the first non-*Matrix* sci-fi/fantasy Keanu films that postdate 9/11 and respond in some way to the reality created by that day—an event that still feels like the beginning of "today," like everything since then has been one long decade. But there's a case to be made for *The Lake House*, also from 2006, with Keanu and Sandra Bullock as residents of the same waterfront property in 2004 and 2006 who fall in paradoxical love by exchanging letters transtemporally via the house's magic mailbox, as the secret third movie in this category—an attempt to process, within the safe space of a fantasy-tinged romantic drama, our renewed sense of time's passage as volatile and disorienting, of history as a thing you can't take your eye off for even a minute.

In *Speed*, Keanu and Bullock play people who get together under intense circumstances, but we never actually see them *together* together, because of those circumstances. *The Lake House* keeps them even further apart. Separated by the space-time continuum, they share very little screen time, so what they have is *most chaste*. Once the conceit of their being able to communicate by writing each other letters is established, they begin having conversations in voice-over, as in *You've*

Got Mail; sometimes Keanu or Bullock says one line of dialogue and then the other person responds, which implies that they're exchanging dozens of one-sentence letters at a time, like instant messages that aren't very instant.

But at one point Keanu asks Sandra Bullock, "What is 2006 like?" and it's strange that it doesn't sound more strange—the notion of the two-year interval between Keanu's time and Sandra Bullock's being some kind of vast historical gap feels like the product of a post-9/11 conception of time. Anything could have happened, between his and her *now*.

29 TRANSLUCENT PLACENTAL BLUBBER

The *Speed 2* decision makes Keanu persona non grata at 20th Century Fox for years, until 2008, when he works with the studio again on Scott Derrickson's remake of *The Day the Earth Stood Still*. It ends up being both a $233 million worldwide box-office hit and a creative low point—Keanu's last blockbuster before a long wilderness period that won't really end until *John Wick*. The original movie is a science-fiction landmark that's been reduced, in the popular consciousness, to a single scene—the alien Klaatu landing a flying saucer on the Washington Mall. In Derrickson's movie the alien craft is a brilliant ball of light that touches down in Central Park, and the alien is a blob that sheds a few pounds of translucent placental blubber on the operating table and over the course of a few hours begins to look like Keanu Reeves.

A plodding cross-country chase movie ensues, featuring Jennifer Connelly as an astrobiologist, Jon Hamm as an anxious unshaven government agent, John Cleese as a Nobel Prize–winning scientist enlisted to help convince Keanu not to carry out his mission of eradicating Earth's human population in order to prevent further environmental destruction, Kyle Chandler as a gruff government official who can't believe what he's seeing, and Jaden Smith as a pain-in-the-ass kid. Derrickson works the Jesus analogies even harder than the original did: when the army's gunships catch up to Keanu, the red dots of their targeting lasers illuminate his palms like stigmata. But if you count Siddhartha as well as Neo, Klaatu is the third-least-interesting movie Jesus that Keanu's ever played. Or the fourth-least, if you count martyr and stomach-wound survivor John Wick. Supposedly Keanu wanted to do this one because he loved the original; supposedly it was his insistence that got the alien's catchphrase "Klaatu barada nikto" added to the script of the remake. He seems authentically nonhuman in his interactions with the rest of the cast. He also seems really bored. In every close-up you can practically see him wondering if this is all there is, if alien affectlessness is all the movies will ever want from him, if the job will always feel this much like a job.

Despite all that, *Earth Stood Still* goes down in film history on December 12, 2008, as the first movie ever transmitted into deep space. Per a Fox press release: "As millions of Earthbound movie fans get their first look at THE DAY THE EARTH STOOD STILL . . . the film will be zipping through space at 186,000 miles per second to a heretofore untapped possible consumer base orbiting the three star system, Alpha Centauri . . . Industry watchers and film historians will note that due to the distance between our solar system and the Alpha Centauri system, it will take over eight years (accounting for a roundtrip communication) to receive any Alpha Centauri reviews. The transmission is not a single beam aimed at just the Alpha Centauri system, but can be received by any advanced technologically capable civilization along the way to Alpha Centauri, and beyond." As of 2022, six years after *The Day the Earth Stood Still* was set to open in the all-important Alpha Centauri market, there has been no response, which either means we're alone in the universe or that the aliens are just being polite.

Movies lost in space: For a while after 2008 that's how it is for Keanu. He doesn't stop being famous, because there's no way for that to happen, but for a good five years he lives in a kind of self-imposed movie jail, throwing up airball after airball, zagging away once again from the orderly progression of a movie-star career. No one sees *The Private Lives of Pippa Lee*, no one sees *Generation Um...*, no one sees *47 Ronin*, no one sees *Man of Tai Chi*, and no one sees *Henry's Crime*—and yet in almost every one of these, even in the bad ones, there's a moment that stops you in your tracks, where Keanu finds the ground in a movie that seems to have no shape, does something you can imagine no one else doing.

In *Henry's Crime*, directed by Malcolm Venville, Keanu is a Buffalo toll collector who gets suckered into driving a getaway car for some bank robbers and goes to prison. When he gets out he decides to try the same bank job again, on purpose this time. The bank adjoins an old theater where Peter Stormare is directing Vera Farmiga and a troupe of local actors in a production of Chekhov's *The Cherry Orchard*. Specifically: the old service tunnel connecting the bank to the theater is bricked up behind the wall of a dressing room. So Keanu steals the role of Lopakhin out from under the actor whose dressing room it is. Which creates complications because by then Keanu has met and started falling in love with Vera Farmiga. The movie pits the higher goals of acting—human connection, expression, truth-telling, activating your subconscious in the service of art, everything the movie shows us Stormare yelling at his actors about—against the survival instinct, in the form of Keanu's need to take the money and run.

As Lopakhin he wears an absurd pompadour, an absurd goatee. He looks a little bit like certain portraits of Anton Chekhov and a little bit like Beastie Boy Adam Yauch's alter ego Nathaniel Hornblower. In the movie's climax Keanu will have to run from the tunnel under the bank to the stage in order to make a moment happen up there with Farmiga, because the stage is a place where truth is possible, even if the circumstances—the fact that Keanu is robbing a nearby bank—render the emotion false, corrupted. There is money in the bank and acting is the most efficient way to get it, but there may also be some other purpose that acting can serve, for Keanu, in this situation. Sometimes Keanu, by his presence, brings into a story a bubble of self-referential metaphor so big it can swallow a movie that isn't ready for it.

In *Henry's Crime* that moment happens after Farmiga takes Keanu on a spur-of-the-moment drive to Niagara Falls. Now they're back at her apartment eating ice cream. She starts to talk.

"I want to dance and clap my hands," she says. "I think I must be dreaming."

At first it sounds like normal speech, thrown away—he thinks they're still having a conversation—but the words turn into non sequiturs as Farmiga gets up from her chair.

"God knows I love my country," she says. "I love it deeply. I couldn't see out the train window, I was crying so much."

It's *The Cherry Orchard*. She's found her way into the part from inside herself like Stormare has been yelling at her to do, making the lines her own. She asks Keanu if he'll read Lopakhin in the script on the table.

"I have to go to Kharkov on the five o'clock train," he reads, with no inflection, running the words together like they're instructions for the proper assembly of a bookshelf. "Such a bother. I wanted to stay and look at you and talk to you. You're as wonderful as ever. Even more beautiful and dressed like a Parisian you could blow me down."

Farmiga wants more from him—she needs more, in order to get wherever she's trying to go. She asks, "Can you say it like you feel it? Like it's real?"

And it's at this point that we get to watch Keanu act the act of acting, which means he says the lines about "dressed as a Parisian" again, but says them this time like *Keanu Reeves* would say them, like he's flipped the switch that turns him into Keanu. There's a deep note in his voice, some ragged emotion, because in saying these words he's also admitting that he's fallen in love with Vera Farmiga, and it almost hurts to admit it.

"That's what I'm for," the actor-director Randolph Driblette says in Thomas Pynchon's *The Crying of Lot 49*. "To give the spirit flesh. The words, who cares? They're rote noises to hold line bashes with, to get past the bone barriers around an actor's memory, right? But the reality is in this head. Mine. I'm the projector at the planetarium, all the closed little universe visible in the circle of that stage is coming out of my mouth, eyes, sometimes other orifices also."

It's not about Chekhov's words or what they mean; all there is in the scene is Keanu's need to reach for Vera Farmiga, which is so big he can only be humble in the face of it, blown down. The play itself falls away, along with the question of whether he'll rob the bank. He does, but that's not the point.

30
AND FEATURING KEANU REEVES AS "KEANU REEVES"

A 1974 article in the Hawaiian Journal of History draws a line from a woman named Sarah Momilani Victor all the way back to a Chinese immigrant "sugar master" who moved to the island of Kaua'i in the early nineteenth century to grow cane in Waimea. Sarah Momilani Victor was Keanu's paternal grandmother. According to a 2019 Reddit post summarizing this study's Keanu-relevant content for the readers of the subreddit "r/KeanuBeingAwesome," this makes Keanu "9/16 British, 7/32 Native Hawaiian, 1/16 Irish, 1/16 Australian, 1/16 Portuguese, and 1/32 Chinese. But in terms of culture and historical roots, it's fairly accurate to say that his father's side is Chinese-Hawaiian (as is ethnically still the case for most of his relatives), with the occasional foreigner marrying into the family."

I'm not sure this information is accurate and I haven't checked that those fractions add up. Also, even including these specifics in this book makes me feel a little weird. There's only one kind of person who needs a definitive answer about what percent white somebody else is, and it's not a good kind of person. And it feels particularly weird to make an issue of Keanu's race, because Keanu never has.

There was a time when people did it for him, of course. When Keanu first starts doing interviews, many reporters take note in print of his "exotic" appearance, sometimes even his "exotic features," because it was the eighties, when it wasn't considered quite as racist—or even as weird or rude—to size up a human face in terms more applicable to rare plants, animals, or tropical fruit. The word was a way of asserting Keanu's ethnicity as an aesthetic positive while avoiding a definitive statement about his race. After a while, it stops being a thing writers mention at all.

Keanu has never had much to say about this aspect of his background, either. He's talked about taking after his British mother's manners and referred disparagingly to his hippie father, but he's made few definitive statements about how he identifies ethnically. He's famously private and unpindownable about his sexuality, too, but he's been asked about that subject way more often. Even when he tells Jimmy Fallon about his agents urging him to change his name, he immediately pivots away from the anecdote's deeper implications. "They didn't think 'Keanu Reeves' was hirable?" Fallon asks. Keanu hesitates for half a second, then says, "I'm not gonna talk about that," and keeps the story moving, briskly and breezily, to the punch line, which is "Chuck Spadina." It's possible that as a person of only (okay, fine, I'll do the math) approximately 25 percent non-European ancestry, he didn't feel comfortable categorizing himself as the victim of Hollywood racism, even in a tangential way. And it's not as if Hollywood didn't give pretty much the same advice to Thomas Mapother and Archie Leach.

For years, the movies didn't bring it up, either. Not counting films in which his character happens to have an ethnically specific surname (such as "Marshetta" or "Kasalivich") or his performance in *Even Cowgirls Get the Blues* as Julian Gitche (who in Tom Robbins's novel says "I am a Mohawk Indian in the same sense that Spiro Agnew is a Greek—a descendant, nothing more") or John Wick (who's established as canonically Romani as of *Chapter 3—Parabellum*), he's played few characters whose race is even mentioned, let alone relevant to the plot of a movie.

One pretty bizarre exception is the 2008 crime drama *Street Kings*. Keanu is an undercover cop who's also an alcoholic, the kind of peace officer who helps himself to a long slug from a suspect's King Cobra tallboy before tuning up that suspect with a Yellow Pages on his own plastic-covered living-room couch. On the force, they call him "Phone Book Tom." *Street Kings* credits a decades-old James Ellroy screenplay called "The Night Watchman" as source material, but that nickname—an echo of *L.A. Confidential,* where Guy Pearce's character becomes known as "Shotgun Ed"—feels like almost all that's left, in the finished movie, of Ellroy's voice—that, and the story's obsession with race and racists.

Keanu's character is referred to in the film as "LA's deadliest white boy"; Keanu says that when he and his African-American ex-partner shared a squad car, they were "black and white in a black-and-white, back when that meant something." When he's accused of racially profiling after gunning down two suspects who turn out to be guilty of human trafficking, his response is that if blowing away lowlifes who deserve it makes him a racist, then he's a racist.

This is a movie about how sometimes only a bad cop can stop really bad cops, and it wants us to see Keanu's character's political incorrectness as emblematic of a broader willingness to bend or break the rules of policing in the single-minded pursuit of justice. "He's like a guided missile," says Keanu's supervisor, played by Forest Whitaker. "He just locks on."

In the movie's opening sequence, Keanu wakes up at sundown fully clothed, brushes his teeth and pukes, hits the liquor store for a few airplane bottles, heads out to look for trouble on the street, and promptly finds it, in the form of a Korean dude who wants to buy an illegal machine gun. Keanu says "Konichiwa" to the dude. The dude—identified in the credits as "Thug Kim"—responds that this is "insultin' to Koreans." Keanu replies, "You got eyes like apostrophes, you dress white, talk black, and drive Jew. So how am I supposed to know what kind of zipperhead dog-munching dink you are if you don't?"

Here's the old Ellroy razzle-dazzle, this burst of painstakingly curated midcentury-vintage racist invective—but in context, it's discombobulating. Obviously there's no rule that says Keanu can't play a white racist. But you keep expecting the movie to account for or justify the disconnect, and it never does, even though the idea of an Asian-American cop whose identification with the job supersedes his connection to his own ethnic identity might have made for a better film. Instead the movie presents and discards a bunch of other half-hearted motivations (dead partner, dead wife, a forced team-up with a rookie played by a young Chris Evans, etc.) to keep Keanu moving from one violent episode to the next. Shall I compare thee to a guided missile?

Then there's *47 Ronin*, an expensive would-be-blockbuster that became a $170 million write-down on Universal Pictures' 2013 balance sheet and reportedly led to Keanu parting ways with longtime manager Erwin Stoff. The story—forty-seven leaderless eighteenth-century samurai avenge the death of their lord—is based on a real historical event from the 1700s, which has inspired countless movies, plays, ballets and TV productions in Japan, but this version adds a new character, a half-Japanese outsider played by Keanu. He's the product of "the love of one night" between an English sailor and a peasant girl, who left him to die in the woods as a baby; his mixed heritage is the reason he can never be a full-fledged samurai or marry the daimyō's daughter, played by Ko Shibasaki, who sees tenderly to his battle scars.

It's the first time he's played a character who's the subject of racial prejudice or discrimination. But it's also a bad movie, its quieter moments drowned out by tedious CGI monster-action scenes, many of them reportedly insisted upon by studio execs meddling in the editing room; its release is pushed from 2012 to the same Christmas weekend as *The Wolf of Wall Street*, *Anchorman 2*, *American Hustle*, and the second Hobbit film, and on that weekend it dies an ignoble death.

***

The comedian and actor Ali Wong wrote *Always Be My Maybe* with her costar Randall Park and another screenwriter, Michael Golamco. They imagined it as an Asian American *When Harry Met Sally*—a comedy about a platonic friendship that takes years to turn romantic. In *Always Be My Maybe*, Wong and Park are Sasha and Marcus, who grow up as neighbors in San Francisco, part for sixteen years after a single regrettable episode of precollege sex, then reunite. Sasha, now a celebrity chef, has just broken up with her restaurant-developer fiancé, played by *Lost* alum and cheekbone god Daniel Dae Kim, whom Sasha calls "a sexy handsome statue of a Korean Arab from *The Little Mermaid*"; Marcus, who's still living at home with his dad while pursuing a half-assed career as a rapper, begins to realize that she's the one who got away. The story needs a complication to keep them apart, so before Marcus can make his move, Sasha shows up with a hickey she tells Marcus is from a night of "insane, freaky-ass sex" with her new boyfriend, who turns out to be Keanu Reeves, playing himself as an eccentric and belligerent blowhard.

A lot of the most interesting casting what-ifs in Keanu's career involve comedies he didn't end up making. He's been offered intriguing, self-referential parts like the one he plays in *Always Be My Maybe* before, and he's always turned them down. According to producer Brian Grazer, the dual lead role in Steve Martin's original script for *Bowfinger*—a neurotic movie star and his schlub lookalike—"was written for Keanu Reeves, literally" before Grazer suggested Eddie Murphy. Ben Stiller wrote *Tropic Thunder* thinking Keanu would play the movie star Tugg Speedman but ended up playing the role himself.

So there was a backup list for Keanu's part in *Always Be My Maybe*—if he'd passed, the role might have gone to longtime Wong Kar-Wai leading man Tony Leung, the mixed martial artist and *John Wick: Chapter 3* antagonist Mark Dacascos, or even the director M. Night Shyamalan. Jokes were made about casting Paul Giamatti, but Wong says she vetoed that idea. "It was very important to me that it be someone who was Asian-American who would also be Marcus's worst nightmare," she told *Vulture*. "It's got to be even worse than [Daniel Dae Kim]. So it's got to be someone who's internationally iconic, and someone who fits those two Venn diagrams is basically Keanu Reeves."

By situating Chinese-American and Korean-American characters in a straight-down-the-middle romantic comedy, *Always Be My Maybe* makes the obvious-but-still-necessary argument that the genre's formulas can work just fine even if the leads aren't white—and that a movie built around those formulas can also portray the specificities of nonwhite characters' cultural backgrounds without sacrificing any of its universality. But by claiming Keanu for the Asian-American team, it's also making a bolder statement about one of the most famous actors alive—one that Keanu's never really made for himself.

"Since I first watched *Speed*, I was very aware that Keanu was Asian American because my family and community wouldn't shut up about it," Wong said. "Maybe other people didn't know but I never forgot that."

Always Be My Maybe never mentions Keanu's race either, but that's the point. What's quietly revolutionary about the movie is that it's an extremely conventional romcom whose leads happen to be Asian, and Keanu's casting lets the film introduce the complication of a rival for Park who's a huge movie star without breaking that particular spell. So it's Keanu's first great identifiably Asian-American role—but even as it claims him as a racial subject in a way few Keanu movies ever have before, it grants him back his unpindownability. From the moment he makes his slow-motion entrance, blowing kisses to Wong across the dining room at a surreally pretentious San Francisco restaurant, he's doing an impression of a self-important celebrity actor—wearing lensless eyeglasses as research for a part, asking a waiter if there are any dishes on the menu "that play with time? The *concept* of time," confessing during a Truth or Dare game that his childhood crush was Mother Teresa, and eventually breaking a vase over his own head in a macho outburst.

Finally Park's character sucker punches Keanu in the mouth, and Keanu puts him in a sleeper hold, and having seen this version of Keanu for the jerk he is, Wong ends up leaving Keanu's hotel suite with Park. The lovers we've spent the movie rooting for are finally brought together thanks to a context created by Keanu. Park even writes a rap song about punching Keanu Reeves: "It was better than any scene you could see in *Speed*." The part fixes Keanu in an identity and then complicates that identity by imagining him as a complete weirdo warped beyond all relatability by absurd privilege. It turns out to be very easy to see Keanu as Asian-American on-screen; thinking of him as a normal person is much harder.

31 | GOOD, CLEAN FUN

In the spring of 2010, a celebrity photographer named Ron Asadorian takes a picture of Keanu on a bench in Manhattan, in front of what appears to be a construction site, eating a sandwich. In the picture Keanu is wearing jeans and a gray blazer. There's a to-go cup of something that may be coffee or tea by his right boot and there are some plastic grocery bags on the bench beside him. A brown pigeon is walking by in the foreground.

Asadorian actually took a sequence of photos of Keanu in this moment, capturing him in successive phases of sandwich consumption. There's an image of Keanu looking down at the sandwich and one where it looks like he's picking a little piece of the sandwich from between his teeth. But the first picture is the one that becomes iconic. Keanu has his mouth full. His posture is a little slumped, a little dejected.

His posture suggests something about the kind of store-bought sandwich he's eating. It's the kind of sandwich that's better than being hungry, but not by much, the kind whose chief selling point is that it's there and *pret* for you to *manger* immediately. It probably came in a triangular clamshell container made of paper, or of nonbiodegradable plastic that will still be on this planet long after Keanu himself is dead.

On May 23, 2010, someone notices the Asadorian photo and posts it to green-ovale.net, a now-defunct 4Chan-style imageboard. The first reply is from an anonymous user, because everyone on a board like this is anonymous by design. The anonymous poster writes, "Classic keanu, what will he do next!" This is the first appearance in meme-culture discourse of the image that quickly becomes known across the Internet as Sad Keanu, and within hours of the picture's first appearance, Sad Keanu is being woven into Keanu's larger mythology, related to the Keanu Extended Universe, connected with his tragic backstory.

"cheer up Keanu," somebody writes.

"I dont like keanu reeves as an actor," someone else says, "but my god you have to applaud him for how much shit he's had happen to him, and still pulling off that hobo look like a boss."

Someone asks "like what," and another user writes, "His girlfriend died along with his stillborn baby."

"Immortals live long enough to see all of their loved ones die," someone writes, and someone else posts a picture of River hugging Keanu in response.

"The way he sits there and stares empty into the ground looks really sad man. I know a single picture is prone to be taken out of context, but he looks like an empty shell. Forcing himself to live on for the sake of the ones he has lost."

"I really hope the man finds someone to truly love again. It's sad to see a man that broken."

The Sad Keanu photo propagates virally out through the meme-o-sphere, from 4Chan to Tumblr to Urlesque to BuzzFeed. Reddit users flex their Photoshop skills, creating images where Sad Keanu is holding the pigeon instead of the sandwich, or eating his sandwich in the sky above a monochrome Manhattan with the rest of the ironworkers in Charles Ebbets's iconic 1932 photo of the construction of the RCA building. In February 2020 that last image accidentally makes it into a Ukrainian textbook for world-history students; Ukraine's minister of education and science, Hanna Novosad, releases a statement expressing her dismay.

In the Reddit images Sad Keanu rides a dolphin and a tiny bicycle. He shares his bench with an equally dejected-looking panda, with a down-in-the-dumps Donald Trump, with Vladimir Putin and Barack Obama, with Bill and Ted, with a sad Jack White and a sad Kanye West. Reddit covers him with smaller Sad Keanus, like Gulliver in Lilliput. Reddit puts him on a flying carpet with Aladdin, in the *Watchmen* panel of Dr. Manhattan meditating on the moon, in a teeming *Where's Waldo?* beach scene, and in US Air Force Lieutenant General Brad Webb's seat in the famous picture of President Obama and his staff waiting for word on the death of Osama bin Laden.

A picture of Keanu in a motorcycle helmet holding a bottle of juice becomes its own spin-off meme, and soon enough there are Photoshops of Sad Keanu and Helmet Keanu hanging out together. Someone does an illustration of the photo of Sad Keanu and someone else turns that drawing into the cover of a hip-hop-style mixtape called *For Aeons I Have Lived and I Have Lost More Than Man Can Remember.*

It's only been two years since *The Day the Earth Stood Still*, and Keanu's career-jump-starting debut as John Wick is still four years away, but this is where and how the Keanaissance really begins—with the Internet inventing a new way to appreciate Keanu while also having fun with the idea of him.

A Sad Keanu meme with an out-of-context Keanu quote attached ("I really enjoy acting . . . because when I act I'm no longer me") inspires a Reddit thread full of positive stories, mostly about Keanu's generosity to below-the-line coworkers on movie shoots. The time Keanu wrote a twenty-thousand-dollar check to a set carpenter so the carpenter could give his family a Christmas. The time Keanu gave a crew member on *Chain Reaction* a ride when the crew member's car was in the shop. In the aggregate these stories of selflessness turn Sad Keanu into a story about Keanu being sadder than such a good guy deserves to be.

On June 17, 2010, Splash News, the photo agency that represents Asadorian and controls the rights to his photo of Sad Keanu, orders the blog Sadkeanu.com to cease and desist. But by then the photo and the ideas attached to the photo are everywhere.

Keanu is asked about it in 2011, in an interview with the BBC.

"There's this sort of mythology that surrounds you . . . that you're sad. That you're someone who carries a lot of burdens around with you," the interviewer says.

"Well, that started with a, uh, *paparazzo* picture," Keanu says, drolly overenunciating the Italian word.

He describes the photo's viral afterlife as "good, clean fun" but adds, "Do I wish that I didn't get my picture taken when I was eating a sandwich on the streets of New York? Yeah."

He is of a generation of actor who can recall a time before the Internet and camera phones and can't quite bring himself to embrace this phenomenon spawned by a paparazzo picture, rooted as it is in an invasion of his privacy. He's never been the type to take a swing at the paps, like Kanye, Shia, or Sean Penn. (In 2007 he was sued for bumping a pap with his Porsche in Palos Verdes; a court ruled in his favor.) But he's always seemed determined to live the way he'd live if guys with cameras were not watching his every move, and living this way is a kind of defiance of them. To be too excited about the popularity of Sad Keanu would be to validate someone's decision to sell for publication a photo of him eating a sandwich while looking vulnerable and dejected.

In 2011, one year after Sad Keanu goes viral, he does write the text for *Ode to Happiness*, a book of drawings by the artist Alexandra Grant, a friend of Keanu's who is not yet known for being Keanu's *special* friend, although it's been suggested they were already dating by this point.

"I draw a hot sorrow bath," Keanu's text begins,

> in my despair room
> with a misery candle burning
> I wash my hair with regret shampoo
> After cleaning myself with pain soap
> I dry myself with my gorgeous white
> one hundred percent and it will never change towel

. . . and it goes on like that. The German art-book press Steidl prints four thousand copies of this book; a used one will run you four figures on Amazon or eBay if you can find one at all.

But he never capitalizes on his memeability by, say, playing himself in a Super Bowl commercial where a tuna footlong from Subway turns Sad Keanu's frown upside down. He just lets people have their good, clean fun with Sad Keanu. Sad Keanu makes Keanu a part of meme culture, spawning its own subgenres and takeoffs and cross-references. Keanu becomes an Internet celebrity without having to do anything embarrassing to make that happen.

The Sad Keanu phenomenon comes along when Keanu's career has stalled a little. When it starts moving again, Sad Keanu has reframed his public image. He may not be a sadder man, but in the popular imagination he's a sadder celebrity. The theme of loss and hardship becomes a part of his story. He's no longer just the goofball from San Dimas who grew up to be the One. He's now the guy who's endured so much—years of professional frustration, the absent father, the loss of River Phoenix, the loss of a child and that child's mother—without going nuts or turning cynical.

This idea of him starts to manifest in his work, a metatextual weight he carries into movies. In Marti Noxon's *To the Bone*, from 2017, Lily Collins is a college student struggling with anorexia whose autobiographical drawings have made her a celebrity in Tumblr's "thinspo" community, and Keanu is the therapist who helps her recover after her art inspires a woman she's never met to take her own life. As Dr. Beckham, he's a fantasy therapist in the tradition of movie shrinks from *Ordinary People*'s Judd Hirsch to *Good Will Hunting*'s Robin Williams, sensitive and selfless and bearlike.

He uses the words "fuck" and "shit show" in session, makes Collins and the other patients read Anne Sexton's "Courage" aloud, and takes them to the Rain Room at the LA County Museum of Art so they can relearn how to enjoy having a body and taking up the space they're meant to take up in the world. He's the only one who has nonjudgmental things to say about Collins's art and the only one who can see the depth of Collins's pain—the bruises on her back from endless sit-ups, the symptomatic hair growth on her arms—and the only one willing to tell her she's full of shit about the things she's full of shit about.

His eyes are careworn and crow-footed, his voice is a low and comforting ashtray rumble, you can practically smell the coffee dregs drying unnoticed in his WORLD'S OKAYEST DOCTOR mug. He's a dream of a clinician but also a dream of quiet, forbearing masculinity. When a family therapy session devolves into bickering after Collins's father fails to show up, Keanu takes control with firm but empathetic authority, acknowledging everyone's individual struggles without judgment. In this room he is a redeeming representative of manhood itself. He is everyone's father and yet he's no one's father and this is his tragedy.

We find out Dr. Beckham has given everything to the job. You have to let the kids hit bottom to do what he does, and a lot of the time that hurts. He has no wife—"Women like to spend time with the people they date," he observes—and no children. He's allowed this symbolic father-work to consume him. "If your buddy saved you," Sexton wrote, "and died himself in so doing, / then his courage was not courage, / it was love; love as simple as shaving soap."

Noxon's film leverages for dramatic effect the air of deep tiredness that's crept into Keanu's screen persona, but so does the 2014 movie that makes Keanu the star of a hot action franchise again. *John Wick* starts out as a script about a hit man in his seventies. Derek Kolstad, whose previous credits include two different Dolph Lundgren movies, imagines Paul Newman playing the role, but Keanu sees something for himself in it. The choice says something about Keanu's instincts; while Tom Cruise (for example) denies time's passage by hanging out of airplanes in his fifties, Keanu skips past this awkward stage to age down a part he's too young for, reinvigorating himself as a star by slipping into midlife like a hot sorrow bath.

I can imagine Keanu Reeves making *John Wick* movies until he's actually seventy, maybe until he dies. I can imagine other people making them after that happens. I imagine at some point they will get dumber and cheaper and pass through a Roger Moore–in–*A View to a Kill* twilight zone, and I will continue to watch them anyway. But nothing will ever have quite the same weight as the first half hour or so of the original *John Wick*, which is both the least representative passage of the whole *John Wick* saga and the most crucial. It's the frame that makes the picture make sense; it turns everything that follows it into a story of loss compounded and compounded.

It's there in the wordless scene between Keanu's John Wick and his wife, played by Bridget Moynahan, as she's dying of an unspecified movie illness. The careful way Keanu plants a last kiss on her forehead, and the way his body seems to crumple as he gives her a last kiss, all the resolve going out of him. "There's no rhyme or reason to this life. It's days like today scattered among the rest," Willem Dafoe tells him at her funeral. Dafoe, like Keanu, plays a hit man—in this case, an ambassador of condolence from the world Keanu left behind when he took up with Moynahan and stopped killing men for money. That world is a world without meaning, a world that offers the comfort of nothing mattering and the freedom that comes with that.

Moynahan arranged one last gift for Keanu before she died—a puppy named Daisy, who's meant to anchor Keanu in the real world the way having a wife presumably did. This movie is a perfect use of Keanu not because Keanu looks cool doing tactical-firearms stuff or close-quarters knife fighting, but because you need to believe that somewhere inside John Wick is the capacity to be a softboi for real—he has to be played by someone who can melt believably in the presence of this puppy. Up until now this could be a Hallmark Channel movie where Daisy the dog helps Keanu meet cute with somebody new at the dog park, and Keanu learns to love again. Instead he goes and aggressively drifts his Mustang on an airfield where he and the security guy have an understanding, and afterward gets into a beef with a couple of Russian mob guys at a gas station, and later they break into Keanu's house, beat him unconscious, and leave with his car after killing the dog in front of him.

This is where we find out who John Wick used to be. When he takes a sledgehammer to the concrete floor of his garage he's busting open a buried part of his consciousness. Soon enough we'll see him in the shower covered in mysterious tattoos and watch him putting on a black suit. From then on it's a movie where the folkloric Keyser

Söze from *The Usual Suspects* is the protagonist instead of the unseen mystery villain. He will move through a shadow New York where everyone is an assassin or at least adjacent to the murder-for-hire industry, from the staff of the Continental Hotel (assassins-only luxury, with bellmen in white gloves and red coats with brass buttons and a strict no-murder policy on the premises) to the secret room where murder contracts in the Wickverse are administered, staffed by a team of old-fashioned switchboard operators whose prim fifties blouses are sleeveless to show off that they're all inked like longshoremen. Aesthetically John Wick's whole world feels a little bit stuck in the nineties, like a rum commercial directed by David Fincher—but leave it to people whose aesthetic headspace is stuck in the nineties to really understand how to use Keanu properly. This is a moral universe where no one is innocent, where everyone John Wick encounters can be killed because everyone he encounters is probably another murderer, where nothing matters, where it's even cool for Marilyn Manson to sing about guns again.

"The one thing that I was really moved by was the protocol of it," Keanu's *Johnny Mnemonic* collaborator Robert Longo told me a few years ago. "How nobody innocent died, outside of those spheres. They weren't random people on the street getting shot—it was this hermetic world, and it was within that world that all this horrible shit happened. It enabled the whole fantasy to be that much more real. I really appreciated that. And I thought the choreographed violence—I thought it was really exciting. It looked great, and it moved really fast. It was really quick, really intense. But the protocol part was really important to me. It had this world it existed in and that in itself made it really powerful.

"With John Wick—there's this kind of character that started with Clint Eastwood, and *The Road Warrior*," Longo said. "These guys that you're not quite sure if they're good guys or bad guys. Their hearts seem to be almost dead, but at the same time you realize how passionate they really are through their technique. And how well they shoot people and how they're always shooting the right people. It's not a heart that's dead—it's a heart that's been redirected somehow."

The *John Wick* movies live on the line between kung-fu solemnity and high camp, and Keanu walks that line perfectly, never more so than in the "I'm thinking I'm back" speech, where his voice seems to be coming from someplace impossibly deep inside his body, as if John Wick could kill you with his diaphragm if he felt the need.

But the most important part of *John Wick*—the part that requires an actor like Keanu, rather than almost any other actor who could put on a suit and learn the moves—is the part at the beginning, with Bridget Moynahan and the dog, where we're made to understand that John was capable of love, and that another life was still possible for him. Instead, for four movies and counting, he'll lose his soul by degrees. What did Bridget Moynahan know about John Wick and when did she know it? Was he already a regular guy by the time they met? Did they talk about what he'd once done for a living? Did they talk about it as her death approached? Did he make her a promise to stop doing this kind of thing, and is he breaking that promise to her at every turn? A movie about John Wick's life before he went back to being John Wick would be the saddest movie Keanu's ever made. The most interesting character in *John Wick* is the guy cradling his dead puppy. Then there's a hard cut to the dog's grave, and that guy has been replaced by the guy in the black suit, who has nothing left except a job he can never quit.

32 | ROOM 214

John Wick reminds people that they've always loved Keanu. The Keanaissance is afoot—but as his comeback is taking shape, he begins showing up in movies that feel designed to undercut it, nightmare-Keanu movies that twist and distort everything innocent and benevolent about his public image.

The Nightmare Keanu cycle really starts in 2013, with *Man of Tai Chi*, to date the only movie Keanu has ever directed. It opens and closes quietly, in one week, about a month before *47 Ronin*. It stars Tiger Chen—a member of Woo-Ping Yuen's stunt team on the first *Matrix*—as a martial artist forced to take part in bloodsport, and Keanu himself as the mysterious businessman Donaka Mark, who's bent on making Chen betray his principles. When Keanu sees Tiger winning a match on video, he presses pause on a close-up of Chen's face, points to it, and says, "Innocent." He decides that the corruption of Tiger Chen will make for great television, and lures him in with the promise of big money, which Chen needs to save his master's Tai Chi temple. The rest of the movie is about Chen struggling to stick to his principles while Keanu—a malevolent force forever manipulating events from behind a two-way mirror or a video screen when he's not

mixing it up on the floor in a black leather Destro mask—works to mold him into a murderer.

Keanu pushes Tiger to use Tai Chi in fighting competitions, even though this is a violation of the rules of Tai Chi, and then goads him to new heights of brutality; before long Tiger falls out with his master and gets banned from the aboveground martial-arts circuit for beating his opponents too severely. All of this is captured on film by Keanu's henchmen, and this footage winds up in a sizzle reel to entice rich creeps to pay to watch the big fight in which Tiger will finally take a life. His fall from grace becomes a story line, a part of the sales pitch.

"Anyone can watch a fight, Tiger," Keanu growls in his ear. "But to watch a person's life evolve and change—that is what I offer. This was never about the fighting—this was about you, your life. Because we want to see the loss of innocence. We want to see a pure-hearted, good-natured man of Tai Chi become a killer."

There's never a moment in which the end seems in doubt—sooner or later, Tiger Chen will have to fight Keanu and make a choice about how to end that fight without compromising his principles. But in Keanu's hands this grave-to-the-point-of-silliness genre exercise is also an allegory for the way the entertainment industry and the media feed on the suffering of movie stars. Early on, when Chen finds out that his training sessions have been streaming online, he asks Keanu if the fans are always watching. Keanu, contemptuously, replies, "Does it matter?" and hands him a box full of cash. It's another one of those moments in which Keanu seems to be speaking directly to us: He knows better than most people that exploitation begins when you can't choose who's looking at you, and that a paycheck is never the end of it.

***

In *Knock Knock*, from 2015, Keanu is Evan, a husband and a father and a well-off LA architect with a beard and a chambray shirt and a cute dog. It's a rainy night and his wife is away with the kids for the weekend and Keanu's catching up on work. He's designing what looks like a museum and he's got a glass of wine and a cardigan and he's blasting "Detroit Rock City" on vinyl and he's about to pack a bowl for what you somehow intuitively know is old times' sake—a once-in-a-great-while bowl full of dry pot from deep in a drawer. But then there's someone at the door. Two young women who've gotten lost in the rain while looking for a party and are in need of a mobile device to call an Uber. Ana de Armas is Bel and Lorena Izzo is Genesis and before this night is over they will have seduced him into a threesome, and before the weekend is over they will destroy his whole life.

Directed by the torture-horror maestro Eli Roth, *Knock Knock* blipped on and off the cultural radar at the last moment before its premise—sadistic women have a consensual sexual encounter with a decent guy, then ruin his life just for kicks, while threatening to lie to the cops and tell them the sex was assault—might have rendered it unreleasably problematic. It's actually a remake of a little-seen 1977 exploitation film called *Death Game*, which starred the John Cassavetes mainstay and human *Wind in the Willows* character Seymour Cassel as the family man and Sondra Locke and Colleen Camp as his tormentors. But as decanted by Roth into a *Funny Games*–shaped container, it plays like a predictive articulation of male fears extremely specific to the age of #MeToo. Its *Penthouse Forum* setup gives way to an EC Comics–worthy denouement involving a reputational dismemberment that unfolds bloodlessly and in real time on a Facebook comment thread, but feels as brutal as any torture-murder in Roth's *Hostel* films. You can imagine any number of canceled men watching it a few years later and nodding along, thinking, *Yes, that's exactly how it happens.*

On paper it seems like a strange choice for Keanu but it's really a stroke-of-genius use of Keanu. Our sympathies are with him at first, because he's Keanu Reeves, and because he seems guilty of nothing except an ill-advised infidelity. But over the course of the movie we're pushed to interrogate the reasons we sympathize with him, and what that might mean about us, and whom we extend the benefit of the doubt to and why. Roth and Keanu thread an impossible needle, introducing a pair of wildly over-the-top monster-women in order to turn around and tell a story that's actually about men—their insecurity, their sublimation, their overriding presumption of their own innocence, and the durability of their belief that they're the Keanu Reeves of their story. The movie only seems irresponsible; it's actually diabolical.

Keanu and his family live in a house that is white and cold and modern but warmed up significantly by big goofy family portraits and his artist wife's drippy and colorful Gaudí-inspired sculptures. In the first act it's early morning on Father's Day; Keanu and his wife are in bed. She bends his arm the wrong way, as a joke, and he cries out; she needles him about how he should cut his hair. They're about to have morning sex when the kids rush in. As always when sex is interrupted in a movie it becomes a gun on the table; sooner or later, somebody is going to have to have sex with Keanu.

Keanu's never fully convincing as a husband and dad here, but that's often the case with actors who aren't parents. When they have to act opposite their movie kids it's like watching someone make small talk with their nieces and nephews on Thanksgiving. They always seem to be waiting to do some big, physical funny-dad action that shifts the moment away from real intimacy. In this case Keanu does a monster voice and chases his fake kids down the hall. Afterward he tries to reinitiate sex but his wife has already shifted gears, moving into the flow of the day. Keanu does the monster voice again, using it as a cutesy, avoidant way of expressing frustration: "Monster sad. Monster's been waiting three weeks."

Once you've heard him do the monster voice in this movie his actual speaking voice begins to sound strange—deep and booming in a way that feels like overcompensation. When de Armas and Izzo show up at the door, he's thrown at first, but when he takes control of the situation, switching back into big-man mode—"Hang on, I'll get you an iPad and some towels"—he puts the fake-Keanu voice on again. He's Keanu doing a Keanu Reeves impression, Keanu wearing the person we think of as Keanu like a mask.

Knock Knock starts with a series of establishing shots of wealthy Los Angeles—Malibu cul-de-sacs, mansions on rolling plots of grass, drought-conscious cactus gardens. But the very first shot of that sequence is a drone's-eye view of the Hollywood sign, which suggests we're meant to think about this as not just an LA story but a *Hollywood* story, which means something different.

Two years after *Knock Knock* comes out, another Hollywood story—the revelations concerning Miramax cofounder and longtime film-business kingpin Harvey Weinstein's decades of sexual harassment and assault, a reign of terror that also turns out to have been an open secret—will help inspire a national reckoning with the issue of sexual predation by powerful men. Weinstein won't be the first high-profile entertainment-industry man to be accused of repellent sexual misconduct; by the time the Weinstein story breaks in the *New York Times*, Bill Cosby will have been accused of rape by nearly twenty women, the first of sixty who'll come forward with similar accusations before Cosby goes to jail in 2018. The Weinstein story is bound up with national politics, too—it unfolds almost exactly one year after a man is heard blithely bragging on a hot mic about committing sexual assault and getting away with it. This development somehow fails to stop that man from becoming president of the United States—not only escaping consequences of his actions but escaping into the highest office in the land. After that, everything else starts to change. Countless famous men are revealed as loathsome; others are revealed as having been craven in the face of great wickedness by others.

Around this time—for reasons that are largely but not entirely unrelated—everyone gets really into Keanu Reeves again. The Keanaissance happens thanks to *John Wick* and about five years' worth of Keanu-related memes reaching critical mass online. But it also happens because as dozens of previously well-liked famous people are outed as creeps—as it begins to seem like male-celebrity creepdom is the rule, not the exception—Keanu fandom feels more and more like a safe space.

A viral tweet from 2019 consisted of four images of Keanu posing for snapshots with women: some female fans, two smiling models at a tactical-shooting range, and his mom's old client Dolly Parton. They're completely normal celebrity-meets-a-fan photos, except that in each one, he's very clearly not actually touching the people he's posing with. You can always see his hands; they're always hovering just above what would be their natural point of contact with the body of the person he's posing with. He's Keanu Reeves, and—aside from Parton—all these women are presumably Keanu Reeves enthusiasts who've asked him to pose, and would (again, presumably) not object to some nonintrusive physical contact with Keanu, because he's not just some guy—he's *Keanu.* And yet even Keanu doesn't presume the right to transgress their physical boundaries, even in a friendly way, even for a second; as far as he's concerned, their personal space is an invisible force field. Of course it's possible that these photos are just proof that he's a germophobe—but they make him seem like a Gallant in a business of sleazy Goofuses, and one of the few stars of twentieth-century vintage whose legacy could be held unproblematically to the new behavioral standards of the twenty-first.

Keanu's never been the kind of actor who makes a sideshow of his own rectitude, and he's never seemed particularly interested in making films in which his acting can double as advocacy. But *Knock Knock* is part of a loose trilogy of Keanu films from the early to mid-2010s in which he plays hard against type, a hero turning heel like Henry Fonda in *Once Upon a Time in the West* or Gregory Peck as Josef Mengele in *The Boys from Brazil.* In these films Keanu isn't just playing bad guys—he's playing a specific type of bad guy, a bad guy who takes advantage, an exploiter, an abuser. To some extent this darkening of his screen image is just the long shadow of John Wick, who despite his tragic biography and longing for redemption is a more merciless and violent character than we're used to seeing Keanu play. But the Evil Keanu films also play like prescient explorations of sexual coercion as a grim constant in Keanu's industry. Of course Keanu never seems to go into any project with a sense of how it might speak to the zeitgeist, and usually seems reluctant to consider the zeitgeisty qualities of a piece of work even after the fact. One of the reasons we love him is that he never seems to realize how ready the world is for a particular kind of Keanu movie; instead he makes his own path to a moment, and seems surprised to find us waiting for him there.

But there's also another movie inside *Knock Knock*, and it's about getting older, maybe becoming a little less cool and a little more boring and maybe feeling insecure about it. Evan tells the girls to be careful with his record player because it's old. "Everything's online now," he says, "but I love the sound of vinyl." From the way he says it you know he knows it sounds pathetic, that this turntable is obviously a symbol of everything he's holding on to, a piece of a former self. It turns out Evan used to be a DJ. De Armas pretends to be impressed: "You're like Major Lazer!"

They keep on flattering him, telling him they can't believe he's forty-three, feeling his muscles, saying things like "You must work out." Keanu has never made an out-and-out Blake Edwards–style sex comedy and he's never made a film noir where he's the sap who gets played like a fiddle, but in this passage *Knock Knock* comes delightfully close to being both of these things. De Armas chews Bubble Tape and kisses the sugar off her fingers. Keanu, beginning to warm up, says, "DJing is like mixing a drink. You find the right ingredients, then you find the blend," which is exactly the kind of thing a DJ-turned-architect would say while playing you records in his fancy house.

Before long they're singsonging "*Happy Father's Daaaaay*" while all but forcing him to receive oral sex, and from there everything escalates—to a furious threesome shot through fogged shower glass, and eventually to Izzo and de Armas refusing to leave. When Keanu threatens to call the cops, de Armas says she'll tell them she's underage and makes a joke about *To Catch a Predator*. The idea that these women may have been victims of past sexual abuse is floated as an extenuating circumstance; the idea that they're just fucking crazy is also strongly implied. Either way, nothing the movie reveals about them lets Keanu off the hook.

He may not have deserved this, but he's absolutely brought it on himself, and the rage that comes out once these women have torn through his house and his life is toxic enough to recast even his initial participation in the threesome as an expression of bottled-up resentment. What de Armas and Izzo are really tormenting him with the knowledge that when he gets angry—finally screaming "cunt" and "whore"—that's who he really is, deep down. He begs them not to do what they're doing, protests that he's a good father, but that's what they all say. In spitting his denial he confirms the accusation's broader truth.

***

John Wick opens in 2014, changing Keanu's luck for the better. It quadruples its modest $20 million production budget; a sequel, *John Wick: Chapter 2* will open in 2017, ten days after Donald Trump is sworn in. In the meantime, Keanu continues making Nightmare Keanu movies. *Knock Knock* opens in October 2015, a few weeks after the second *John Wick* starts shooting in New York. In the spring of the following year, another Evil Keanu movie premieres—to the chorus of boos it's a hundred percent designed to elicit in this context—at the Cannes Film Festival.

Nicolas Winding Refn's *The Neon Demon* suggests an alternate timeline where Keanu got as far as, say, *Point Break*, then lost the plot entirely—started believing his own hype, squandered money and opportunities and goodwill, maybe had trouble with alcohol or heavy drugs, and slipped through a crack in the world for a while. Now imagine that version of Keanu coming back years later, showing up out of nowhere in a movie, wearing all that lost time on his face and his shoulders. Keanu as Mickey Rourke in *The Wrestler*, Keanu as Jan-Michael Vincent in *Buffalo 66*. A Keanu long since fallen from grace, a Keanu who looks like Nick Nolte's mug shot feels, a Keanu whose best-case scenario Keanaissance might take place at airport-hotel autograph collectors' conventions if it happened at all. That's how Refn uses him in *The Neon Demon*—like a superfan resurrecting a faded movie star he's never stopped loving.

The Neon Demon stars Elle Fanning as a sixteen-year-old model whose youth and beauty are so profound and self-evident that casting agents are moved to tears when she shows up on a go-see. She's new to Los Angeles and by the end of the movie she's been psychically and then literally chewed up by the beauty industry, as personified by a coven of well-connected witches led by Jena Malone. The movie talks back to 2016's other lushly colored Los Angeles show-business fantasia, *La La Land*, except *The Neon Demon* is about how the city's cult of beauty teaches newcomers cruelty and narcissism before devouring them, and at the end of it there's nothing left of Fanning but a dismembered eyeball and a bloodstain to be hosed off the pool deck, which is not how *La La Land* ends.

Refn's previous films *Drive* and *Only God Forgives* were hyperstylish crime dramas centered on taciturn, violent antiheroes played by the deceptively sweet-faced Ryan Gosling. In *Drive*, Gosling even gets his own theme song. "A real human being, and a real hero," sang Electric Youth's Bronwyn Griffin, sounding utterly unconvinced that either descriptor actually applied to Gosling's character, an emotionally blank, hammer-swinging spirit of vengeance in a shiny satin jacket. *The Neon Demon* is Refn trying for the first time to make a movie about women, and specifically the way a culture hung up on youth and surface dehumanizes them. But because Refn's a fetishist at heart, *The Neon Demon* is also an excuse for Refn to look at women in states of pop-arty duress and make us look at them, too—women bathed and splattered in fake blood, women getting smeared with glittery gold paint, women posing in colored light or the glare of a strobe, women pleasuring themselves by humping corpses on the autopsy table, women tearing up the Pacific Coast Highway in fast cars, women performing pagan rituals under the full moon. His movie about exploitation is also an exploitation movie, full of images of ethically reprehensible violence so beautifully rendered we can't help but respond to it aesthetically, which is one of the ways Refn is like Martin Scorsese.

One of the ways Refn is not like Scorsese is that the women in this movie say things to each other like "Are you food or are you sex?" and "I hear your parents are dead—that must be really hard for you," lines that technically pass the Bechdel Test despite not being things real women would ever say. *The Neon Demon* is as brutal in its assessment of Hollywood and humanity in general—and as indulgently deliberate in its pacing and as airtight in its visual aesthetic—as *Too Old to Die Young*, the gonzo 754-minute miniseries Refn made for Amazon in 2019, but *Die Young*'s nearly thirteen hours actually seem to fly by faster than *Demon*, a two-hour creepy-crawl to a foregone conclusion.

The other big difference is that *The Neon Demon* features Keanu Reeves—and features him the way a bad dream might feature him.

The Neon Demon is about an ingenue who comes to town and plunges into the darkness of LA, and every person Elle Fanning meets seems to be part of a plot to bring about her debasement and destruction. This includes Keanu, as the manager of the preternaturally underlit apartment complex where Fanning rents a room. At first, like in *The Gift*, Keanu is just a shadow on the other side of a metal screen door, grunting, "Yeah?" after he's been rudely awakened. Fanning's just come home to find what she thinks is a prowler in her room; when she rouses Keanu he immediately assumes she's on something, and doesn't even open the door until she says she's going to call the police. "Whoa, whoa, whoa, whoa," he says, telling her to relax, like whatever this has come to, it hasn't come to that.

He opens the door and we get a look at Refn's idea of Keanu—sweaty in a blousy rayon shirt, a little weight on him, stooped posture, his voice a hollow carton-a-day bark. They head up to her room. Keanu has his buddy kick Fanning's door down. The room is trashed and there's no sign of how it happened, not right away. Keanu gets mad, tells Fanning she's going to pay for the damage, shoves her against the railing of the motel balcony, grabs her by the arm. Like most of the men in this movie, he feels he can do whatever he wants to her. Then his friend spots something moving in the dark. He pulls out a flashlight, and a mountain lion jumps down off the dresser and onto the bed.

In another movie—a more traditionally Keanuesque kind of Keanu movie—this introduction might set up Keanu's emergence as Fanning's gruff and reluctant protector, the deep-down decent woodsman in this fairy tale. This being Nicolas Refn's Keanu movie, that's not in the cards—Keanu's more like the mountain lion, a creature of the same night Fanning's lost in. Refn's deliberately abusing our trust in Keanu, our sense that his presence means things are going to be okay. It's implied that his character is pimping out the young Hollywood hopefuls who rent from him; when Fanning's hopelessly devoted boyfriend, played by Karl Glusman, comes looking for her, Keanu urges him to visit Room 214 for a good time. "Rented this week to a girl from Sandusky, Ohio," he says. "Runaway. Thirteen years old. Real Lolita shit." Then he adds a line Keanu supposedly ad-libbed: "Room two-fourteen—gotta be seen."

The last time we see Keanu it's night at the motel again. Fanning, who's quickly become a successful model, comes home a little drunk after an evening out with some of her new fashion-business friends. Her personality is starting to change. Glusman shows up. They argue, and she sends him away. Keanu, in a dirty Adidas jacket, steps outside to smoke. Fanning turns on the light in her room, just down the hall from 214. She zones out on the bed with her high heels still on. Outside, the camera moves down the darkened walkway to her door, a slasher-movie POV shot. We hear muffled footsteps, the sound of someone walking carefully.

Inside Fanning's room the lights are off and Fanning's asleep in bed. Someone unlocks the door and walks in. It's Keanu. He makes his way to the bed and looks Fanning over. Then—over the course of what might be the longest-feeling seventy seconds in any Keanu Reeves movie ever—he takes out a folding knife and maneuvers the blade inside her sleeping mouth. When she wakes up and gasps, realizing what's happening, he chuckles and says, "Wider. *Wider.*" Then—cut—Fanning wakes up on the floor. The lights in her room are still on. Keanu's not there. So maybe it was all a dream. But then Fanning looks up. The doorknob is moving. Someone's outside, trying to get in. They start banging on the door and she runs to throw the deadbolt. After a second, she hears a woman crying and pleading in the room next door, which might be 214. It sounds like a sexual assault, but the movie never shows or tells us what's happening in the room, or if it's Keanu in there doing something awful. We never see Keanu in the movie again.

The first time I watched this movie to write about it I could have sworn there was a shot, right before Fanning's dream sequence, that established the presence of a prowler at the motel, a guy we never see too clearly, whose presence suggested that maybe it's not Keanu in the room next to Fanning's. When I went back to watch the scene again I realized there's no prowler in it—the guy I thought was a new character lurking in the shadows of the apartment building is just Glusman, leaving after the argument with Fanning, presumably walking to his car, which is when Keanu steps out and lights up. It's strongly implied that Keanu notices Glusman leaving and realizes Fanning is alone. My brain supplied an alibi for Keanu's character that the film hadn't actually shown me; this is the power of an actor's image, even when he's this game to do work that cuts against it.

***

In Ana Lily Amirpour's dystopian-future love story *The Bad Batch*—released in 2017, a few months after *John Wick: Chapter 2*—Suki Waterhouse plays a young woman expelled from the United States as a genetic undesirable, and Keanu plays the Dream, a charismatic cult leader who rules a desert settlement called Comfort. When he's not preaching to a flock of eugenic refugees like Waterhouse—America's sick, her deformed, her poor, her mentally ill cast out by a country that's become a genetic apartheid state—the Dream hangs out in a house where it's always night, lounging in Hefnerian silk dressing gowns and a gut-baring Speedo. He keeps a harem of continually pregnant concubines who wear T-shirts that read THE DREAM IS INSIDE ME over their baby bumps; the signs at the border of Comfort read YOU CAN'T ENTER THE DREAM UNLESS THE DREAM ENTERS YOU.

The Dream is a drug kingpin, a kidnapper, and a symbol of patriarchal and quasi-religious sexual oppression. When he first shows up on-screen—emerging from a door in the side of a rolling, mobile-home-size boom box at a wasteland rave—Keanu's almost unrecognizable under doughy makeup and a fake mustache. He's wearing a white silk shirt and his nipples protrude. He looks like a one-man pantheon of the odious—Jim Jones, Pablo Escobar, Tony Clifton, with just a dash of American Apparel founder and sex criminal Dov Charney for hipster cred. Of course, as soon as he begins to speak in a TV preacher's voice the spell of the look is broken—we recognize Keanu because the southern accent is, as always, a bridge too far.

The best thing about *The Bad Batch*, apart from the Road Warrior-goes–to–Burning Man world it builds, is Waterhouse's close-to-the-vest performance, a portrait of internalized trauma that avoids easy revenge-movie catharsis. She keeps you guessing as to where her character's going until the movie finally lands there. Keanu by comparison sometimes seems like he's playing the character from the outside in, letting the makeup do the work. *Knock Knock* is the most effective Bad Keanu movie since *The Gift* because it gives us what feels like a glimpse of the real Keanu and then uses our idea of him to manipulate the audience. *The Bad Batch* has far more to say about the actions of characters motivated by trauma, but it lets Keanu get away with a performance that doesn't put his image at risk; instead of a true villain all we get is the opposite of a great guy.

33 | FLAWLESSLY TAILORED KEVLAR HAIR SHIRT

It's exhausting, being John Wick. The third film in the series will find him bruised and battered and still seeping blood from untreated stab wounds sustained at the end of the second one, when John fights one hired assassin after another but the movie blurs the attacks together, so they seem to be happening all at once, which is how you'd remember them if you'd gotten into multiple knife fights per day. This is an action franchise about what it is to be tired and unable to rest. They're some of the best movies ever made about the increasingly universal condition of being a freelancer without the wherewithal to stop working. They may also be about Keanu, whose resurgence as a latter-day icon after years off the map depends as much on his willingness to keep making *John Wick* movies (or at least *John Wick*–esque movies) as it does on the quasi-ironic adulation of the Internet. The sequels are movies about a guy whose life is one long series of fights, and they are also movies about being a performer whose life is a long series of fights. They are about a job and a guy's ambivalence about coming back to resume doing a thing he's really good at but doesn't love doing.

In *John Wick: Chapter 2* Keanu puts his guns back in the hole in the floor of his garage and covers the hole up with fresh concrete, and

then as soon as that happens a mob boss played by Riccardo Scamarcio comes to the door to talk to Keanu about another job that needs doing. Scamarcio recounts the history of the marker that obligates John to do his bidding, and once again we get the sense of John having lived a whole life that we haven't seen—that this could be the twelfth *John Wick* movie as easily as the second.

The franchise will eventually give in to the modern instinct to spackle exposition into every gap in its story; in *Chapter 3*, we find out that John was a Byelorussian orphan who learned the craft of killing while being raised by a Romani crime syndicate in New York, and his name is Jardani Jovonovich. But the first two *Wick* films' refusal to give us anything but fragmentary backstory on John is admirable, a throwback to James Bond, whose pre-007 existence was rarely acknowledged in the Bond films until the Daniel Craig era.

The *John Wick* movies are also like the James Bond movies because they're fantasies of expertise and seamless access. John Wick knows the right words to say to everyone to get the results he needs. When John Wick goes to Rome he knows which antiquarian bookshop keeps maps to the city's old sewers in the back room, and how to order firearms from a sommelier who talks up each Italian shotgun and Austrian Glock like a fine Gewürztraminer, and which sweatshop is a front for a secret tactical-clothing atelier. John Wick likes his trousers tapered and his jacket linings bulletproof.

In accordance with the laws of sequelization, the second *John Wick* movie cranks the volume on the first one's pulp-decadent tone. Phrases like "DEATH'S VERY EMISSARY" and "GET HIM!" flash on-screen in comic-book lettering as they're spoken. All the hit men's haircuts make them look like elite Vegas mixologists. And nothing is impossible—when John arrives in Rome, the manager of the local branch of the Continental asks him, with concern, "Are you here for the Pope?"

But *John Wick: Chapter 2* also amps up the sense that all this methodical, thrillingly choreographed violence is a tragedy, for John as well as the countless poor bastards he mows down. The thing about John is that he never *wanted* to be back; letting this part of himself out of the box again takes an immense psychic toll, and Keanu shows us that, too. In *Chapter 2* when John has to go back into action he puts on a black Steve McQueen turtleneck and then the camera waits in the hallway while we hear him let out a primal *yaaaargh* of frustration and sorrow. The essence of John Wick is that he can hold on to nothing except the black-suit life and the reputation that comes with it. In the first movie he loses the wife he tried to start a new life with and then the dog he tried to start another one with; in this one even that nice Italian shotgun is just another weapon he will throw down empty in some catacomb he's just painted black with the blood of a half dozen ineffectual henchmen.

Sometimes Keanu imbues John with a Keanulike gentleness that takes you by surprise. When the Italian countess he's been ordered to terminate in Rome slits her wrists in a massive marble bath before he can shoot her, Keanu takes her hands and holds them as she dies, a very Keanu way for a moment like this one to play out—he's granting her one last moment of intimacy with another human being. *Then* he shoots her, just to make sure, because the job is the job. Once he kills the countess he's chased by her bodyguards—led by an old Wick acquaintance named Cassian, played by Common—onto the stage at an outdoor concert, where Keanu shoots one of the henchmen in the head and the crowd goes wild, like this is what they really came to see.

Common follows Keanu back to New York, where *John Wick: Chapter 2* pays off the long-running David Geffen subplot in Keanu's public life by having John and Cassian exchange gunshots through the cascading fountains in front of the Lincoln Center concert hall that now bears Geffen's name. Keanu can't escape his history any more than John Wick can, though—after the Lincoln Center fight, Keanu and Common discreetly pepper each other with silencer-ed bullets in a crowded subway station. But when they make it to the platform, they politely board the train that arrives and stare hard at each other across the crowded car, a beat that counts as a knowing *Matrix* reference by virtue of how studiously it avoids reprising Neo's train-tracks fight with Agent Smith.

By the end of the film, as every assassin in the city lines up for a shot at John, the fights begin to overlap in time. We see him moving on to the next challenger before he's finished off the last one; here again is the freelancer's lot, the feeling of work piling up, assignments blurring together. The kills from three separate fights happen in quick succession. Then Keanu and a mute killer played by Ruby Rose and John's nemesis Santino and a few more disposable henchdudes stalk each other through a mirror-walled digital-art installation called *Reflections of the Soul*, while Santino taunts John by stating the superobvious: "You know what I think? I think you are addicted to it. To the vengeance! No wife. No life. No home. Vengeance—it's all you have." Uh, *no duh*, dude.

A recorded female voice, ostensibly describing the art, says more about what we're actually looking at in this sequence: "Within this exhibition, the interplay of light and the nature of self-images coalesce to provide an experience which will highlight the fragility of our perception of space, and our place within it." These rooms reimagine the hall-of-mirrors sequence from *The Lady from Shanghai* as a kaleidoscope and a shooting gallery; the mirrors rotate, duplicating images of Keanu and his assailants on the floor and the ceiling, quilting them across the screen. It's another moment in which the story of the movie falls away and we're given the pure uncut experience of Keanu-watching: Keanu with a gun, moving against an ever-shifting backdrop of digital abstraction, a wall of light and color that makes him the realest thing in the picture, the only real thing. Keanu fights through a maze of images that include his own, destroying his enemies along with his false selves, the focal point in confusion once again.

***

Once he's lost everything, the secret world of high-end international contract murder is the closest thing John Wick has to a home. But his former life as an assassin is also a big part of the *reason* he's lost everything. At the end of *John Wick: Chapter 2,* when he violates one of that community's cardinal rules by offing someone on the premises of the Continental Hotel, it's not just a rash act—it's an act of vengeance against the only world that he's welcome to, against the Continental and all the bullshit D&D-rulebook lore and Magic Castle rules of assassin-land in general. *John Wick: Chapter 3—Parabellum* begins where 2 left off, with John Wick's official excommunication from his professional community. So now he's running through Times Square past billboards for American Eagle and T-Mobile, bleeding in the rain like a schnook in a city that's suddenly full of regular people.

Soon he's shot and stabbed and hit by two cars within ten seconds. Of course he'll be fine. He will ride a horse through New York City and live to wander into the Moroccan desert for a reckoning with the Elder, a mystery man who heads the secret government of the assassins' underground and offers John a chance at redemption if he's willing to sacrifice another part of himself. He has to cut off a finger and of course it's the finger he wore his wedding ring on, and of course there's already a new black suit somehow waiting for him on a hanger in the next room, an elegant torture device to amplify John's pain.

John Wick is the great tired action hero of our time. He's tired the way Harrison Ford's Indiana Jones could seem tired sometimes, tired like Steve McQueen at the end of *The Getaway*, a movie Sam Peckinpah shot in sequence so as to maximize the dramatic effect of Steve McQueen and Ali MacGraw's tiredness. That's the elite tier of action-hero tiredness John reaches here. He has had it with this world, despite the fact that he's a celebrity in it. The first *John Wick* derives some of its elemental power from our perception of Keanu as someone who's known real sorrow and loss, but the sequels become riffs on Keanu's fame, and the inherently burdensome aspect of a reputation that precedes you, and maybe on the idea of a guy who keeps being offered a type of work he no longer derives satisfaction from. Even hired assassins whose mission brief is to kill John Wick before he kills them say things to him like "It's good to have you back" and "We're both masters of death" and "It's an honor to fight with you," helping him to his feet before another round begins (and presumably friend-requesting him on LinkedIn immediately afterward). The fact that they're on the clock doesn't mean they aren't excited to meet him; they're even excited to meet his dog.

34 | DIGITAL GHOST

In 2019 Keanu stars in a movie called *Replicas*, in which he's a brilliant scientist who breaks most of the important science rules by reanimating his dead wife and children in cloned bodies. Shot—but only half-heartedly set—in Puerto Rico, *Replicas* was brought to life by Company Films and Entertainment Studios Motion Pictures, two suspiciously unmarked-white-van-ish corporate handles that turn out to be, respectively, Keanu's own production company and the movie-distribution arm of a media conglomerate that was founded by Byron Allen and also owns the Weather Channel. Everything about *Replicas* suggests a direct-to-Redbox joint, but it actually opens in theaters—almost 2,400 of them. In its opening weekend it pulls in just $2.5 million, the lowest wide-release opening of Keanu's career. A few months later, *John Wick: Chapter 3—Parabellum* will open and make over $171 million in the United States and Canada and $326 million worldwide. For at least this moment it's as if Keanu exists in two parallel and contradictory states at once, enjoying the *Wick*-abetted cultural-icon Keanaissance phase of his career while also saying yes to paycheck gigs like this one, the kind of abject film Nicolas Cage knocks out four or five times a year to cover the upkeep on his pyramid.

In *Replicas* Keanu has developed the technology to digitally map an entire human consciousness, which is an important step toward his project's long-term goal—copying and pasting human minds into living cloned bodies. Keanu's colleague Thomas Middleditch has already perfected the human-cloning part, but Keanu's mind-transplant technology is still in the beta stage. We see Keanu in his lab, a thoroughly modern Prometheus moving three-dimensional images of data around with his hands like he's in a Super Bowl commercial for Google or Accenture, and speaking in torrents of most excellent technobabble gobbledygook: "Stasis modality exceptional. And—translate. Finalize. Confirm. All states go. All functions go . . . Margaret, energize the body."

Keanu finalizes the translation and Margaret energizes the body, and the robot he's just imbued with human consciousness wakes up and immediately starts freaking the fuck out.

"You've transitioned into a synthetic body," Keanu says. "Try to relax. You're coming online."

The robot—whose brain belonged to a soldier who's pretty sure he remembers having died—is horrified and ontologically shattered. It rips off its own faceplate and tries to beat itself to death before Keanu and his fellow scientists pull the plug.

This is a deeply unsettling setup that could have benefitted from the chilly yet unerring bedside manner of a young David Cronenberg. In the hands of this movie's actual director and screenwriter, Jeffrey Nachmanoff and Chad St. John, it makes for a ludicrous movie full of lines Ed Wood might have been inappropriately proud of writing for stupid humans to say, like when Alice Eve, as Keanu's wife, says to him, "You can't just keep bringing people back from the dead until you work this stuff out."

And yet: there are serious concerns being explored here, concerns that feel Keanuesque, questions he's been pondering in his work all along. What are the ethics of making exact copies of people? Is the self just a bundle of neurochemical reactions and electrical signals constituting the recorded sum total of our experience? Would the ability to create indistinguishable simulacra ultimately cheapen human life, removing death from the equation and with it the context that gives life meaning? What does it mean to create a false self that lives independently of you? If those two selves, the real and the simulacrum, become indistinguishable from one another, does that erode the realness of the real?

On the way to a vacation that Keanu has barely had time to think about because he's been too preoccupied with his robots, Keanu and his family get into a horrific car wreck, and a traumatized Keanu, as the only survivor, has to carry the lifeless bodies of Alice Eve and their three children to shore. It gets worse from there, because while we already know what Keanu's grief and despair will motivate him to do, Thomas Middleditch can only bring him three clone-pods, not four, which means Keanu has to choose which of his dead family members to not resurrect.

The next stretch of the movie is both stressful and heartbreaking. As the new bodies he's growing for his wife and two of his three kids gestate in the basement, he goes around the house, carefully and delicately gathering up all traces of his youngest daughter's life and throwing them in the garbage. It's a crushingly sad sequence despite being entirely borrowed from *Eternal Sunshine of the Spotless Mind* and born of an insane horror-movie plot. It also makes no sense—assuming his revived family members are somehow able to return to their normal lives like nothing has happened to them, how does he expect to keep other people from asking his revived family members what happened to little Zoe, the third kid they used to have?

Middleditch has the thankless job of playing the character who keeps a movie about children dying in a car crash from being too much of a bummer by saying things like "Hey, man, let's pump the brakes on the crazy train, all right?" when Keanu starts raving like Seth Brundle. But as wobbly a movie as it is, *Replicas* is also a showcase once again for the most important thing Keanu does as an actor—his ability to both identify and profoundly commit himself to the emotional truth of a ludicrous scene, like when Alice Eve is asking him why he erased her memories of her child and Keanu has to tell her, in a voice full of grave guilt, "*There weren't enough pods.*"

In 2016, when word reaches Keanu that the comedy duo Keegan-

Michael Key and Jordan Peele and the director Peter Atencio are making a movie where hijinks ensue after Key and Peele's characters find a lost kitten and name it Keanu, he agrees toward the last minute of production to provide the voice of the cat for a *Matrix*-referencing dream sequence. In the dream Keanu the kitten wears a do-rag and identifies itself to Keegan-Michael Key as "Keanu Reeves" and reminds Key, "People can't be excellent to you unless you're being excellent to *yourself.*" Keanu—the real Keanu—described the project as 'wacky' in an interview. "Which is interesting," Key told *ET Canada,* "because it's a word I feel like he's never said before."

Keanu is not the kind of guy who can throw himself all the way into "wacky" as a tone; he approaches it bemusedly, with some distance, as if smiling through a talk show where the jokes are in a language he doesn't speak. But Keanu has also existed long enough to see the specific job requirements of stardom change in significant ways. We are now a culture that wants to see its famous people be wacky, particularly when they're promoting something. Peter O'Toole or Oliver Reed would not have let puppies lick them in a BuzzFeed video, but Keanu did. When he has to say "I'm here with BuzzFeed to play with some puppies and answer some questions," you can see him sort of wince at each word in the sentence, but he answers the questions thoughtfully, and seems to genuinely enjoy the puppies when they lick his face, because he's not made of stone.

Keanu still does as little as possible to feed the growth of Keanu memes, and yet Keanu memes proliferate anyway, because memes are the ideal medium of expression for the odd mix of we're-not-worthy reverence and affectionate mockery that latter-day Keanu engenders on the Internet, and because the world likes an excuse to look at Keanu. Hence social-media phenomena like Keanu Reeves Walking to Music, a Twitter account that began setting Keanu's protracted slow-motion entrance from 2019's *Always Be My Maybe*—the part where he's crossing the dining room of some unbearably trendy foodie hotspot blowing kisses to Ali Wong—to a variety of pop hits, from the K-pop boy band GOT7's "Teenager" to the Notorious B.I.G.'s "Hypnotize."

Sometimes Keanu's walk matched the beat of the song and

sometimes it didn't. Sometimes the song choices—such as Bill Medley and Jennifer Warnes's "(I've Had) The Time of My Life," from *Dirty Dancing*—were about placing Keanu in the context of classic movie romance. Some of them (a lot of them) were topically about Keanu and what it's like to drink him with one's eyeballs—"Forever Young," "Whatta Man," "Just Like Heaven," "Can't Take My Eyes Off You," "Take My Breath Away." Between the time I started writing this chapter and the time I finished it, the Keanu Reeves Walking to Music account was suspended for violating Twitter's terms of service; it's unclear what happened, although uploading the same unlicensed movie clip about once a day with a different piece of unlicensed music attached might have had something to do with it.

2019 is a pivotal year for Keanu virality. In March his flight to Los Angeles is forced to land in Bakersfield due to mechanical trouble, and when Keanu and his fellow passengers have to ride the rest of the way to LA in rented vans, he entertains his fellow passengers by reading facts about Bakersfield from his phone. Then in June, Keanu makes a surprise appearance at the video-game trade show E3. He's there to announce his until-then-undisclosed voice-acting role in *Cyberpunk 2077*, a sprawling new open-world game set in a dystopian early William Gibson–esque future, produced by the Polish game-development studio CD Projekt Red, creators of the hit *Witcher* games franchise. In videos of his appearance, Keanu strides onstage in a carpet of dry-ice vapor. A tidal wave of screams drowns out his walk-on music.

He touches both hands to his heart and opens his arms, as if returning to the audience the love they are feeding him in scream form.

"How's it goin'?" he asks. "Hello, Los Angeles!"

He talks about meeting the game's creators, how they talked about creating "this vast open world with a branching story line. How you'd be able to customize your character through in-game choices."

"I'm always drawn to fascinating stories," he continues, reading the teleprompter with a hint of a grimace that functions in Keanu's menu of facial delivery options like a raised eyebrow. This story, he says, "is set in a metropolis of the future where body modification has become an obsession. You play as an outlaw, an enhanced mercenary working in the sleazy underbelly of the city."

Some sleazy-underbelly fan far off in the cheap seats hollers at this. Keanu chuckles at his enthusiasm, resumes the spiel.

"Lemme tell you—the feeling of being there, of walking the streets of the future, is really going to be breathtaking."

Another voice from the audience, this one audibly masculine: "*You're* breathtaking!"

Keanu laughs, points at the crowd, says, "You're breathtaking! You're *all* breathtaking!" Cheers.

With that, he directs everyone's attention to the big screen above his head, where a trailer featuring visuals from the game starts to play.

In the game, Keanu plays Johnny Silverhand—a military veteran with a cybernetic arm, a deserter from a dirty US action in Central America who becomes a rock star as the politically outspoken front man of the rock band Samurai, then dies. He exists in the game as a "digital ghost," guiding the protagonist through the story and commenting on the action, although he may not actually be dead.

It's a game that aspires to be movielike; its main story line takes thirty to forty hours to complete, although it can run up to a hundred hours if you go down the rabbit hole of each side-quest mission. The script is reportedly a hundred-million words long, and when the localization manager in charge of translating all of those words into Japanese posts a picture of a full hard copy of the script on Reddit, it consists of four two-foot-high stacks of paper, like the tax code. This is a strange way to tell a story, but Keanu takes to it. He's said to have asked that his role in the game be expanded after seeing what the studio had planned.

When Keanu tells the E3 audience that they're breathtaking, the game is not yet finished, and at the time no one except the people working on it knows just how unfinished it is. The trailer announces a release date in April 2020; that date is later amended to September, and when that date comes and goes, news breaks that Projekt Red has mandated "crunch"—six-day workweeks for employees working on the game—so that lingering bugs can be addressed in time for the game's new release date, which is now November 19. When it's released—on December 10, 2020—it's still so bug-filled and crash-prone that Sony takes the unusual step of removing the title from the official PlayStation store, and both Sony and Microsoft give refunds to disgruntled early buyers. Oh, and: by January, fans have figured out that the game's customization options can be tweaked to make *Cyberpunk*'s in-game sex workers, known as JoyToys, look like other *Cyberpunk* characters, and Projekt Red is forced to release a statement politely requesting that players please not make the in-game choice to engage in simulated sex with Keanu. People do it anyway, but even in this artificial context, Keanu remains a sexual enigma; for a hundred dollars the JoyToy version of Johnny Silverhand will take you in the back room, but his face gets glitchy and his pants stay on.

By the time all this happens, the E3 presentation has spun off into a weird life of its own. "You're breathtaking!" becomes a moderately successful meme format—turned into an image macro with Keanu pointing at various breathtaking things, like a screencapped headline about a guy who built a train for puppies to ride on, or a boy in the Philippines who sheltered a mother cat in a typhoon so she could give birth.

Cheezburger.com runs a blog post headlined "12 'Breathtaking' Memes That Celebrate Keanu Reeves, Our New Wholesome God," positing that Keanu "should be inducted into the wholesome hall of fame that included Steve Irwin, Mr. Rogers and Bob Ross." Curiously, all those guys are dead; only Keanu gets this honor without dying.

"Wholesome" is a strange attribute to see someone praised for in the twenty-first century; until recently, it was a code word that belonged to conservatism. "Wholesome" was what Pat Boone represented as opposed to Elvis, what *Full House* stood for that *The Simpsons* supposedly didn't.

In a 2019 essay for *Vox*, Constance Grady traced the shifting place of the word "wholesome" in pop-cultural discourse—how it shook its connection to the retrograde moralism and purity culture of the American evangelical movement. Pointing to phenomena like BuzzFeed's "Wholesome" vertical—collecting heartwarming good-news stories about human kindness and interspecies friendship between cute animals—Grady posits the "wholesome" revival as a response to the increasing toxicity of Internet culture after the rise of GamerGate, the alt-right, and Donald Trump. She even uses Google Trends to chart how "wholesome" as a search term "began to gain traction in the cultural vocabulary around the same time that the vocabulary of the alt-right was at its peak." One of Grady's search words for alt-right language was "cuck"; another phrase was "red pill." Both trended downward in 2017 after Trump's first year in office, as "wholesome" began to grow.

The polarity of the culture was shifting. In the eighties, "wholesome" belonged to the right, to Reaganism and Christianity and the Moral Majority; snark, sarcasm, and irony were the weapons the left used to attack the hypocrisies of those movements. Then the alt-right movement stole irony, using it to mask real racism, misogyny, and anti-Semitism behind a joking veneer. Among other things, the Keanaissance is about a world that longs for a respite from irony and turns to Keanu, in whose body there is not one ironic bone.

"Breathtaking" isn't the only meme that comes out of Keanu's E3 appearance. Just hours after it happens, a Twitter user going by @KojiMads tweets a screengrabbed image of Keanu onstage—standing with his arms hanging stiffly at his sides, like he's not sure what to do with them, while an apeshit crowd raises cell phones to photograph him—and writes, "he really just stood like this and everyone went nuts." Later that day another Twitter user, @JT_0907, alters the image for comic effect; Keanu's head is the same size but he looks like he's walking past one of those convex fun-house mirrors that make you look shorter and wider. This is Mini Keanu, who's like a pocket Keanu Reeves you'd get out of a gumball machine.

Sometimes Mini Keanu is depicted standing next to a regular-size Keanu, and the size differential between them is part of the joke; sometimes he's alone, and the joke is how strange Keanu's normal way of holding his body like a poseable action figure at rest looks when Mini Keanu does it. But every single Mini Keanu meme is funny. Some Mini Keanu memes imagine Mini Keanu as a little brother or a son to his larger counterpart, like the one where the large Keanu is labeled "My dad working on his car" and Mini Keanu is labeled "8 [year old] me passing him tools." Because Mini Keanu's facial expression is a look of vague discomfort that implies he's waiting for something, he's often portrayed as an awkward child struggling heroically with his own impatience, in memes with captions like "8 Year Old Me waiting for my Mom to stop talking on the phone so I can tell her my Bulbasaur evolved" or "Me telling the other kids that the teacher said I get to be line leader." Sometimes the joke plays off the proportion between regular and Mini Keanu in other, more conceptual ways. A large Keanu labeled "All the other months" stands next to a Mini Keanu labeled "February." Eight Mini Keanus labeled with the names of the planets orbit a large-Keanu sun. "What I think I'll say" stands tall above "what I actually say."

By the time Mini Keanu catches on, Sad Keanu has been a part of meme culture for a decade. But Mini Keanu has nothing to do with the story of Keanu. He has nothing to do with the story of *Cyberpunk 2077*, or *John Wick*, or any other movie. You do not need to know that Ted "Theodore" Logan is a simpleton the way you do with Conspiracy Keanu. To appreciate Mini Keanu you don't even need to know Keanu's full name, the way you do with Keanu Leaves (a leaf pile with Keanu's face). Mini Keanu is where the signifier fully parts ways with the signified, where Keanu's meme-self takes its leave of Keanu and embarks on a solo career.

It's possible Keanu does not even know Mini Keanu exists, which is the other brilliant thing about Mini Keanu; Mini Keanu is a Keanu that goes about its business on the Internet while the real Keanu roams free and unexamined.

In *Replicas*, Keanu has to put his consciousness into the robot from the beginning of the movie in order to save his job at the lab and prevent his employers from finding out that he's doing illegal human cloning on the side, and in the end—after the robot commits a few necessary but also cathartic acts of violence—there are two Keanus in play, a human and a machine, and the machine goes to work in the clone lab while the human Keanu goes off to be with his family. So it is with Mini Keanu. In the post-Keanaissance age of Keanu, the public persona becomes a dream-self he can send to work in his stead, a sacrifice to our amusement, while going about his real business in private, whatever it might be.

Originally the above paragraph that began "By the time Mini Keanu catches on" ended with the following joke: "If Keanu's journey through meme culture is the Stargate sequence from *2001: A Space Odyssey*, Mini Keanu is the Starchild reborn on the other side." But the thing about meme culture is that it's constantly changing, making it really frustrating to attempt to address memes in the pages of a printed book about Keanu Reeves whose text will be at least a year old by the time you read it.

Nonetheless, as of summer 2021, the most obvious indication that meme culture has adopted Keanu as a kind of spiritual leader was the existence of a blockchain cryptocurrency called Keanu Inu. Like Dogecoin—a cryptocurrency based on the enduring Shiba Inu–based meme known as Doge, whose price surged when Elon Musk convinced some of the dumbest Americans alive to get in on the action—it's a peer-to-peer cryptocurrency whose brand identity includes a picture of a cute dog. A white paper on the Keanu Inu website described the dog thing as an attempt to build on "the extreme hype for dogs, particularly surrounding [the] Japanese dog breed: Inu." But it's also pretty transparently an attempt to distinguish Keanu Inu from every other Bitcoin successor in the ether by trading on the evergreen hype surrounding Keanu Reeves, who the white paper suggests is "broadly referenced" in the project.

This is putting it mildly. There's a picture of a dog on the cover of the white paper, but the background is unmistakably the vertically cascading green code of *The Matrix*, and the back cover reads JOIN THE JOURNEY! KEANU IS THE ONE. An early Medium post by Keanu Inu's developers features an animated image of Neo with a Keanu Inu coin for a head, beating up Agent Smiths representing other dog-based cryptocurrencies. Although Keanu Inu's creators promised to donate 0.2% of eligible transactions to charity, the coin does not seem to be catching on; when I last checked one site listed its dollar value as $0.00000000067. Keanu Inu is the kind of project you might embark upon if your real goal in life is to meet a process server working for

Keanu's lawyers, but its existence illustrates one of the hard truths of Keanu's life. Even if you create an autonomous meme-self that belongs to the world, there will always be someone out there, trying to own you.

CONCLUSION
THE ESSENCE OF THE FOREST

"I think each movie is a part of your life, even if you don't want it to be, because while you're living you're working and through your work you're expressing yourself . . .

"But with Little Buddha *this was even more true. The night before you shoot you review the script for the next day. It's not just a scene of some people fighting or a car chase or a love sequence. You read the script to* Little Buddha *and you say, 'Okay, tomorrow we're shooting the birth of Siddhartha,' or 'Tomorrow we're shooting the enlightenment,' or 'Tomorrow the lama who is dying will witness his own death through deep meditation.' So you wake up the next day and you're coming to terms with what you will do to complete the scene, and to do that you must confront the major questions that exist in your own life.*

"Do you know what I mean? You are constantly aware, at any single moment, in any single frame, of the meaning of your own life, the meaning of mortality, the meaning of hope, the meaning of love and compassion, the meaning of the past and the future, the meaning of your journey."

—VITTORIO STORARO, 1995

In *Bill & Ted Face the Music*, which ends up being one of the few high-profile movies released in theaters in 2020, Keanu again plays Ted "Theodore" Logan and Alex Winter plays Bill S. Preston. They've known for around thirty years that it's their destiny to someday write a song that will align the planets and usher in an age of global unity, but they've spent thirty years trying to write that song and it hasn't happened yet. So right away the third *Bill & Ted* is about things the first two movies weren't really concerned with the actual process of making art, and ambition, and how being told at a young age that you're destined for greatness can paralyze or frustrate or otherwise undo you in life, and how it may be impossible to make something brilliant and world-changing on purpose.

The movie starts with a montage that mimics the visual grammar and the exact ironic-to-sentimental ratio of hey-remember-these-guys documentaries about cult musicians, as if Wyld Stallyns were a real one-hit-wonder hard-rock band who had a brush with legit fame in the early nineties and then spent the ensuing years sliding deeper and deeper into bargain-bin ignominy, which is exactly what's supposed to have happened to Bill and Ted in the *Bill & Ted* universe. When we see the adult Bill and Ted for the first time they're trying everybody's patience at a wedding—Bill's younger brother, Deacon, is marrying Missy, who was married to Bill's dad in the first movie and to Ted's dad in the second one—by debuting their latest attempt at a planet-aligning banger. It's called "That Which Binds Us Through Time—The Chemical, Physical and Biological Nature of Love; An Exploration of the Meaning of Meaning, Part 1," a title that makes clear to us how Bill and Ted have spent three decades pursuing complexity and significance to the detriment of their actual art even before they play the song itself, a turgid and directionless prog-rock instrumental that features Ted noodling on trumpet, bagpipes, and theremin.

The joke in the scene is Keanu pretending to be very seriously playing the trumpet, the bagpipes, and the theremin, an early synthesizer heard on pop songs such as the Beach Boys' "Good Vibrations" and the soundtracks to sci-fi movies such as the original *The Day the Earth Stood Still*. But it's hard to focus on what he's doing because of the way Keanu looks. He's clean-shaven and his face looks jarringly naked without John Wick's beard to cover it up. Keanu's face is the most effective special effect in the movie; he has rarely looked this much like an older version of his younger self. For years, the joke has been that Keanu doesn't age, but of course that isn't true, and never was. He is no more ageless than any of us are, and *Bill & Ted Face the Music* wants us to see that, because another thing the movie is about that the other two films weren't is the slow, linear, irreversible passage of real time, and what time takes from us, and the anxiety and fear it leaves us with. All of that is not exactly written on the bare skin under Keanu's beard, but, look, if you're a man who's ever grown a beard and kept it a while and then shaved it and had to reckon with the face underneath, you understand the exact way in which Keanu's face is a billboard for mortality.

Bill and Ted are now married to the former medieval princesses Joanna and Elizabeth, who despite being time travelers born during the Middle Ages seem to have adapted to contemporary adulthood more readily than Bill and Ted have. Also, Joanna and Elizabeth are getting tired of being married to two guys whose deepest loyalty is to each other, two guys who are willing to go to couples therapy with their wives to talk about this exact issue as long as they—Bill and Ted—can attend the sessions together. The only people who still really believe in Bill and Ted's potential for greatness are their young-adult daughters, Thea and Billie, who've inherited their fathers' obsession with music; everyone else thinks their story about traveling through time in a phone booth is crazy. Ted is just another rocker dad who knows he should probably sell his Les Paul but can't quite come to terms with everything that decision would signify, hopes-and-dreams-wise. Then time itself begins to unravel, and Bill and Ted are summoned to the utopian post–Wyld Stallyns–uniting–the–planet future-world from the first two films and informed that they have only a few hours left to write the ultimate Wyld Stallyns song and save reality from collapsing.

In the second *Bill & Ted's* there is a perfect line of dialogue that tells you everything about the spirit of the *Bill & Ted* movies and their unassuming, almost sneaky profundity. The robot imposters Evil Bill and Evil Ted have kidnapped Bill and Ted and are driving them to the desert so they (Evil Bill and Evil Ted) can kill their human counterparts. It's beginning to dawn on Bill and Ted that something's not right with the other Bill and Ted. Ted observes that the new Bill is kind of a dick, and Bill—who's still operating under the assumption that Evil Ted and Evil Bill are just versions of him and Ted from a not-too-distant future—says, "Yeah—I've got to work on being more considerate to myself when I become him." In the very next scene Evil Bill and Evil Ted throw Bill and Ted off a cliff to die, and before the end of the movie Bill and Ted will have been through purgatory and Hell and Heaven, but by then the most important part of *Bogus Journey* has already happened, when Bill says the line about being more considerate when he becomes his future self and encounters his past self, because Bill talks about forgiving himself as if that's an easy thing to do.

Face the Music centers its story on that idea and then literalizes it through the magic of time travel, by pitting our Bill and Ted against multiple older Bill and Teds from alternate near futures who've grown bitter and mean in failure and serve as walking, sneering metaphors for Bill and Ted's struggle to live with their own choices. Meanwhile there's another, more classically excellent-adventure-ish time-travel story, about Billie and Thea assembling a supergroup featuring Jimi Hendrix and Louis Armstrong, and there's a killer robot, and somehow Kid Cudi ends up involved as well, caught up in events that seem far above his pay grade, which is perfect casting because it's how Kid Cudi always comes off in real life. Self-forgiveness turns out to be the key to saving the universe and Bill's and Ted's respective marriages, along with community—it turns out that the magic of Bill and Ted's world-unifying song isn't the song itself but the collective energy released when everyone in the world plays the song together. So the closing-credits montage shows us that exact thing happening, but it's depicted as if we're watching it as a YouTube montage or a collaboration-mode TikTok video—lots of real people, or real-looking extras, air-guitaring in their own houses and backyards and bathtubs, or outside in some natural setting. And while the sequence is clearly supposed to feel like a celebration of music's power to obviate the distances and differences between us all, what it actually did if you watched it in 2020 was bring the movie crashing back into the reality created by the pandemic, in which all creativity suddenly became about people working from home, all sealed off from one another in little windows, in a world even the greatest song ever could not fix.

Keanu walks through all of this like a man visiting the halls of his old high school in a semilucid dream. At first your mind—or, okay, my mind—rejects the idea of present-day Keanu's beatific melancholy folding itself back into the outline of Ted Logan, because present-day Keanu reads on-screen as a man who has known sadness that Ted Logan, stalled out in San Dimas or not, has never known. Keanu's body is different, too; it produces a different voice than it used to. When that puppyish quality starts to come back the movie finds its footing emotionally. There's a little hair-toss thing Keanu does when he and Bill have to get back in the phone booth and save the world again. And of course it comes back when they start time traveling, because that's what Bill and Ted used to do when they were kids.

Face the Music was reportedly conceptualized as early as 2008 and drafted as a script by 2011; the fact that it took nearly another ten years to actually get made seems to have been more about financing than anything else. The studios had to be talked into it—and, eventually, swayed by the box-office performance of *John Wick* and the Keanaissance—but Keanu didn't. And yet Keanu's return to the character that made him and threatened to define him still has the feeling of a reckoning, a psychic reintegration in which everything enlightened-seeming and wise about modern Keanu turns out to have been present in Ted all along. In a scene midway through the film, Bill and Ted are being chased through a house by their future selves, who have an unfair advantage—they've *been* Bill and Ted in this situation, so they know what Bill and Ted are going to do before they do it. Eventually Bill and Ted realize that the only way to outwit Future Bill and Future Ted is to do something they'd never have thought to do before, so they put plastic buckets on their heads and jump out the window. It works, for a minute, and Ted has a small epiphany that reads on-screen like Keanu looking out through Ted's eyes and articulating the closest thing Keanu's ever articulated to an artistic philosophy, like Keanu finally answering the question of why he's bad at answering questions about what he does, which turns out to be the answer to everything.

"Maybe," Ted says, "we should *always* not know what we're doing."

***

In *The SpongeBob Movie: Sponge on the Run*, SpongeBob SquarePants and his dim starfish buddy, Patrick, are dreaming, and in the dream Keanu appears to them as a talking tumbleweed named Sage. The movie is mostly animated, but Keanu's head, which appears golden and Christlike at the center of a huge vascular diaspore, is played by Keanu's actual head. Although Patrick and SpongeBob are already on a quest—to rescue SpongeBob's pet snail, Gary, who's been captured by the vain and cruel King Poseidon, ruler of a sybaritic underwater city called Atlantic City—Keanu's appearance imbues that mission with cosmic, religious import.

Like the musical number starring Snoop Dogg and a crew of dancing zombie cowboys or the running gag about a soprano-sax-tooting squid jazzbo who goes by the name Kelpy G, Keanu's presence is an Easter egg planted to mildly amuse a captive-but-paying audience of parents, like a Liberace joke in a Bugs Bunny cartoon. But Keanu does his level best to simulate meaningful eye contact with the CGI sea creatures he's pretending to be sharing a scene with, and the gag where he rolls in and out of shots head-over-chin like a soccer ball is funny every time.

And the nature of the part says a lot about how far Keanu's come, how much the idea of Keanu has changed since the mideighties. Once synonymous with blissful ignorance, he's now stunt-casting shorthand for understanding and hard-won wisdom. He's a Sage in all senses, Obi-Wan Kenobi as a burning bush, the Rufus to Patrick and SpongeBob's aquatic Bill and Ted. It's not that clever of a movie and at this point having Keanu play the koan-spouting Gandalf stand-in is almost a cliché, Twitter-bait use of Keanu. But that in itself—the fact that this is now what Keanu represents in people's minds—is crazy. Of all the conceivable fates that could have awaited Keanu in the back half of his fifties, being a little bit typecast as a Zen master is one that few people would have bet on way back when. But you never know how history will choose to use you.

When the various COVID-19 vaccines first become available a rumor makes the rounds that one of them was developed with help from Dolly Parton. Everyone gets excited about this, because Dolly Parton—not unlike Keanu, who's walked a mile in her bunny suit—is one of our last remaining secular saints, and it's fun to picture her in a sequined lab coat and safety glasses, triumphantly holding up a beaker full of fresh antibodies.

Of course the story turns out to be less amazing, less about Dolly personally helping to fix the broken world like a mother lifting a car off her pinned child. It's a story about science working the way it usually does. At the start of the pandemic Dolly gave a million bucks to Vanderbilt University to help fund vaccine research, which ultimately led to her name appearing alongside those of other sponsors in the *New England Journal of Medicine*'s preliminary report on the Moderna vaccine. Dolly didn't know she'd helped create the vaccine until she saw her name connected to it in the news, the same way we found out. But the idea of Dolly Parton, Nanoparticle Chemist, is almost too appealing to let go of. It's like a biotech version of the Simpsons gag where Bart and Lisa visit a stretch of highway that Bette Midler has "adopted" and find Bette Midler herself there, picking up trash by the side of the road and chasing down litterbugs on foot.

Sometimes a celebrity is in a position to pay a million dollars and help stop people from dying of a deadly virus. More often than not, though, the purpose they serve in our lives is more abstract, and during COVID you could see them all, the whole Famous American community, struggling with the question of how to be of actual use to a grieving, freaked-out society in a world without red carpets. Did we maybe need them to get together and sing a John Lennon song into their front-facing cameras? Would that help? (It did not, it turns out.)

More than anything, what people seemed to want was distraction, the feeling of being obsessed with something other than the death tolls on the news. So we watched TV and talked about it on the Internet.

In a world where everyone suddenly had literally nothing better to do, old consumption patterns reasserted themselves, and we watched the same things at more or less the same time—there was *Tiger King* week, and later there was *Queen's Gambit* week, and then there was that week we just looked at Steve Kornacki's butt day after day after day while waiting to find out whether we'd still be ruled by medieval dickweeds come January.

And around the thirty-ninth or fortieth week of March, there began to be new TV shows that attempted to meet us where we were—i.e., on the couch, bored and exhausted and trembling with nervous energy all at once, in need of serenity, now. On Hulu's *Vacation in Place*, you could tour the Sequoia National Forest and Carmel-by-the-Sea and the shores of Lake Tahoe through the magic of HD and Steadicam. Disney+ had *Zenimation*, which stripped plot, music, and dialogue from classic Disney films and stitched their establishing shots together into mixtapes of pastoral, trippy animated nature scenes—a true fairy-godmother gift to the nation's weed-waiting areas. And on HBO Max there was *World of Calm*, a series of soothing short documentaries about nature, animals, and occasionally human beings doing slow, mindful craft projects.

World of Calm is a TV spin-off of a mobile app called Calm, which started out as a meditation app and later added the option to listen to celebrities reading bedtime stories. You can still use the app to learn to meditate, but it now features hours and hours of quasi-meditative audio and video content featuring everyone from Laura Dern to Scottie Pippen to the deceased public-television painting instructor and beyond-the-grave kitsch icon Bob Ross. Calm's user base began to swell in 2017, the first hypertriggering year of the Trump administration, but it didn't really take off until COVID happened. During April 2020, the first full month most Americans spent in lockdown, Calm acquired 1.6 million new users, many of them presumably people who'd read about "mindfulness" here and there and suddenly found themselves upset enough to try anything.

World of Calm premiered on HBO Max in October 2020, just as the Western Hemisphere prepared to face its first quarantine winter.

It builds on Calm's winning formula of celebrity-driven moments of pseudo-Zen. Nicole Kidman narrates an episode about migratory birds. Oscar Isaac explains how noodles are made—comfort television about comfort food. And in the show's fifth episode, "Living Among Trees," a Latvian man fashions a canoe from a single tree trunk using only traditional wood-carving methods, and the voice that tells us his story is Keanu Reeves.

Of course this was the next logical step for Keanu, avatar of wholesomeness. Calm App Keanu builds on his status as a zone of respite from unpleasant realities; Calm App Keanu is a Keanu you can literally incorporate into your daily self-care routine. The next step may be up to science, not the entertainment industry—Keanu as a skin-care product, or maybe an antidepressant that makes you feel like Keanu is standing in front of you, telling you everything is going to be okay. We have known him as a boy and a man and as multiple CGI characters and as a tumbleweed; he is our most adaptable movie star, in the sense that someone is always finding a new thing for him to be.

There is something deeply cynical about *World of Calm* and shows like it. It's TV aimed at people who are tired but can't make themselves go to bed, for people who can't bear another bite of news and are too mentally drained to parse a plot, but remain habituated to nightly intimacy with a flat glowing screen. It's television providing respite from the anxiety that other kinds of television help produce in us, as long as we promise to not stop watching TV—and here's where I should note that during the protracted final act of the 2020 election, every time CNN broke in with a fresh pulse-spiking news alert on vote tallies from a contested state, those updates were brought to you by Calm, which was a brilliant and dystopian stroke of marketing genius.

And yet "Living Among Trees" is both beautiful and genuinely calming. Time and cigarettes have blessed Keanu with a perfect fine-grain-sandpaper documentary-narrator voice. But he also seems to approach each narration like it's a performance, and to be making idiosyncratic, Keanuesque choices within those performances. As the voice of Steven Okazaki's 2015 documentary *Mifune: The Last Samurai*, he reads each fact about the screen legend Toshiro Mifune like it's a piece of terrible news he's just been handed. In "Living Among Trees," his voice is full of the same gravitas, but it's leavened with awe and reverence. Over shots of fog-wreathed timber and foraging animals he tells us how trees have their own sense of time, and how a forest is really one single organism that communicates and cooperates. The oaks of ald now lie in peat yet elms leap where ashes lay, as James Joyce wrote, and this blows Keanu's mind. The Calm app repackages Bob Ross as a modern-day purveyor of chill; in "Living Among Trees" Keanu gives us John Wick channeling Bob Ross, moved almost beyond the ability to express himself by these happy ancient trees.

"Living Among Trees" is also about a man, the woodworker Rihards Vidzickis, and his enviably pastoral, slow-paced, unmediated lifestyle. He hollows out a tree trunk with a chisel. ("No machines," Keanu says with wonder. "Just a skilled pair of hands, conversing with the tree.") He submerges it in icy water to soften the wood, then uses the heat from a fire—a technique called steam-bending—to mold the trunk into something recognizably boat-shaped. Then he waterproofs the wood with tar—and not just any tar, but tar made from the resin that accumulates in the roots of old pine trees as those trees prepare to die.

On headphones, it's an ASMR experience—the rhythm of the chisel biting into wood, the swish of the tar brush, Keanu saying things like "Tar is the essence of the forest, with its rich aroma and protective power" in a voice that itself feels like the rich and protective essence of the forest. He doesn't read this copy like he's reading some tree facts a producer typed up. He sounds like he's obsessed with trees, and haunted by their tendency to outlive us, and the thought that they experience time in ways we will never understand. It's a performance defined like so much of Keanu's work by an unarticulated but unmistakable sadness. Chances are we will never lead a life like the one Vidzickis lives, in which we do a single thing well and think of nothing else until we're finished. It's more than we can ask of the world. It's more than even Keanu can ask of the world—a canoe-bending life is probably not in the cards for him either, and he knows this, and it's like an arrow right in his armorless heart.

"Trees naturally call on us to slow down," he says. "To stop and listen, to be in the moment."

There is just the slightest trace of a catch in his voice as he says it, like he knows from experience just how hard it is to live that way, and how important it is to try and try and try.

QUOD DEBITUM SANGUINE

Thanks to Will Welch and Chris Gayomali at *GQ* for first offering me Keanu as a subject and to Daniel Jackson for the photos; Quinn Heraty at Heraty Law; Shannon Kelly, Diane Shaw, Garrett McGrath, Meredith A. Clark, and all at Abrams Books; Victor Quinaz, Patrick Jensen, and Martha Astorga; Chris Heath; Jessica Hopper and Joan LeMay for their patience; the Western Sound team, for same; Cafe Tropical and the Sunset Marquis; Holly Anderson, Chuck Klosterman, Molly Lambert, Wesley Morris, and Amy Nicholson; Jim and Ellen Pappademas, Mary Flaherty, and Liz Pappademas.

I am also indebted to the Los Angeles Public Library and its staff, and to Davian Aw, Monica Luca, and all contributors to the Keanu articles archive at the invaluable Keanu fab site Whoa is (Not) Me.

Written 3/16/20–1/4/21 in California

For Jenn, who took the wheel of the bus
And for Charlotte, born free in the real world

ENDNOTES

Prologue: RADIO FREE ALBEMUTH

ix. **"My boy protesting in Baltimore today":** McKenna [@singlemomsays]. "My boy protesting in Baltimore today—an in-car protest is a good idea" Twitter, May 30, 2020 https://twitter.com/singlemomsays/status/1266850598650966016
x. **"I cannot imagine his inner life at all":** Author conversation with Molly Lambert, sometime in 2020
x. Alex Pappademas, "The Legend of Keanu Reeves," GQ, April 15, 2019
xi. *John Wick: Chapter 3— Parabellum.* Directed by Chad Stahelski. Lionsgate Films, 2019
xii. **the Chateau is basically a castle:** Shawn Levy, *The Castle on Sunset: Life, Death, Love, Art and Scandal at Hollywood's Chateau Marmont* (Penguin Random House, 2020)
xiv. **"a more serious, more reflective Reeves":** Jamie Portman, "Hollywood Wants an Affair With Reeves But He's Non-Committal," *Vancouver Sun*, June 4, 1994
xiv. **"Reeves—who has answered a lot of questions about acting":** Chris Willman, "The Radical Reality of Keanu Reeves," *Los Angeles Times*, July 17, 1991
xiv. **A few years later, in another magazine interview, he starts talking about how spontaneous human combustion is real:** Rebecca Arrowsmith, "Hello, Hello— Is Anyone Home?," Juice Magazine, October 1995
xvi. **"No":** Keanu Reeves, author interview, 2019
xvii. **"The thing that matters":** Robert Bresson & Jonathan Griffin, *Notes on the Cinematograph* (New York Review Books, 2016)
xviii. **"He's always trying to reach out to truth":** John Coltrane, quoted in *But Beautiful: A Book About Jazz*, by Geoff Dyer (North Point Press, June 24, 2014)
xviii. Philip K. Dick, *Radio Free Albemuth* (Arbor House, 1985)

Chapter 1: KEANU REEVES CREATES, THROUGH HIS MERE PRESENCE ON-SCREEN, THE SENSE THAT SOMETHING CINEMATIC IS HAPPENING, EVEN WHEN THAT'S NOT ACTUALLY THE CASE

3. *Generation Um*, directed by Mark L. Mann. Company Films/Voltage Films, 2012
6. **Keanu actually shot this footage himself:** Jack Giroux, "Interview: 'Generation Um . . .' Director Mark L. Mann and Star Keanu Reeves Externalize With a Camera," FilmSchoolRejects, May 6, 2013 https://filmschoolrejects.com/interview-generation-um-director-mark-l-mann-and-star-keanu-reeves-externalize-with-a-camera-966ab8577474/

Chapter 2: KEANU REEVES FIRES A SHOTGUN INTO THE FRESHLY DUG GRAVE OF HIS FATHER, ANDY GRIFFITH

7. Keanu Russian Club, "1983 Keanu Reeves Coca-Cola Commercial," Youtube, Jun 23, 2012, https://www.youtube.com/watch?v=f9ZSPC3J6hA&
9. **the seething communication hub of the Middle East:** "Beirut is Travel Hub of the Middle East," *The New York Herald Tribune*, April 30, 1964.
9. **a hard time to be married:** "MEMORIES OF KEANU: Samuel Reeves has not seen or heard from his famous son in decades," *Honolulu Star-Bulletin*, April 22, 2001
10. **"Something," Keanu says, "about how the world is a box:** Rebecca Arrowsmith, "Hello, Hello— Is Anyone Home?," Juice Magazine, October 1995
10. *Under the Influence*, directed by Thomas Carter. CBS Entertainment Productions, 1986
11. *River's Edge*, directed by Tim Hunter, Island Pictures, 1987

11. *The Prince of Pennsylvania*, directed by Ron Nyswaner, New Line Cinema, 1988
11. *Bill & Ted's Excellent Adventure*, directed by Stephen Herek, Orion Pictures, 1989 *Bill & Ted's Bogus Journey*, directed by Pete Hewitt, Orion Pictures, 1991
11. *My Own Private Idaho*, directed by Gus Van Sant, Fine Line Features, 1991
11. *Parenthood*, directed by Ron Howard, Universal Pictures, 1989
12. *Tune in Tomorrow*, directed by Jon Amiel, Cinecom Pictures, 1990
12. *Speed*, directed by Jan De Bont, 20th Century Fox, 1994
12. *The Devil's Advocate*, directed by Curtis Hanson. Warner Bros. Pictures, 1999
12. *The Lake House*, directed by Alejandro Agresti, Warner Bros. Pictures, 2006
12. *Sweet November*, directed by Pat O'Connor, Warner Bros. Pictures, 2001
12. *A Walk in the Clouds*, directed by Alfonso Arau, 20th Century Fox, 1995
14. **large quantities of cocaine and heroin:** "Speed Hunk Keanu's Long-Lost Dad Jailed on Drug Rap," *Star Magazine*, July 12, 1994
15. **"Occasionally, the spray would wash over the shelf":** "MEMORIES OF KEANU: Samuel Reeves has not seen or heard from his famous son in decades," *Honolulu Star-Bulletin*, April 22, 2001
15. **"Sam's other children will not be attending":** Facebook page of the Victor 'Ohana, via https://angelofberlin2000.tumblr.com/post/171138505348the-victor-ohana-february-15-at-609am-there

Chapter 3: KEANU REEVES, AS A CHILD, PLAYS ON THE LOT THAT WILL ONE DAY BE A FOUR SEASONS HOTEL, IN WHAT WILL BECOME THE FIFTH- MOST-EXPENSIVE RETAIL CORRIDOR IN NORTH AMERICA

17. **Neil Young or Rick James or Joni Mitchell:** Tess Kalinowski, "Joni Mitchell, Neil Young and Gordon Lightfoot all once played in Yorkville. Would a museum of its musical past still strike a chord?," *Toronto Star*, February 28, 2021
17. **home to Gandalf's, Canada's first head shop:** Adam Bunch, "William Gibson & the Summer of Love," The Toronto Dreams Project: Historical Ephemera Blog, April 5, 2012 http://torontodreamsproject.blogspot.com/2012/04/william-gibson-summer-of-love.html
18. **"a 'professional hippie'":** CBC Digital Archives, *Toronto's Yorkville: Hippie haven in 1967* https://www.cbc.ca/archives/entry/yorkville-hippie-haven
18. William Gibson, *Neuromancer* (Ace Books, 1984)
18. **Later Gibson will write about "the truly remarkable ferocity . . .":** William Gibson, "Yorkville; X-Files Episodes . . . My City Was Gone," http://williamgibsonblog.blogspot.com/2003/05/#200231135
18. *River's Edge*, directed by Tim Hunter, Island Pictures, 1987
18. **"We didn't even do graffiti, you know . . .":** Dennis Cooper, "Keanu Reeves," *Interview*, September 1990
19. **One tabloid describes Patricia wearing her hair in a peach-colored buzz cut:** Sharon Churcher & Mike McDonough, "Keanu's Bitter Secret," The Sunday Mail (Aus), January 8, 1995
19. **"He tied us up like a human knot . . .":** Karen S. Schneider, Natasha Stoynoff, Kristina Johnson, William Plummer and F.X. Feeney, "Much Ado About Keanu," People, June 5, 1995
19. **In 2013, he lists some of the films:** "Keanu Reeves: The Movies that Shaped My Childhood," *Moviefone*, October 30, 2013 https://www.moviefone.com/2013/10/30/keanu-reeves-movies-that-shaped-my-childhood/
19. **In a Reddit AMA he will add to this list *Apocalypse Now*:** u/_Keanureeves, "Ask me, if you want, almost anything," Reddit, October 20, 2013 https://www.reddit.com/r/IAmA/comments/1ouqge/keanu_reeves_ask_me_if_you_want_almost_anything/
19. *Stroszek*, directed by Werner Herzog. Werner Herzog Filmproduktion, 1977
19. **"His performances were riveting":** Michael Kimmelman, "From Berlin's Hole of Forgottenness, a Spell of Songs," *New York Times*, December 24, 2008

20. **"the legacy of *Wolfboy*"**: Karen S. Schneider, Natasha Stoynoff, Kristina Johnson, William Plummer and F.X. Feeney, "Much Ado About Keanu," People, June 5, 1995 Karen Hardy Bystedt and Kevin J. Koffler, *The New Breed: Actors Coming of Age* (Henry Holt & Company, 1988)
20. *Hangin' In*, "Happiness is a Warm Grover." Canadian Broadcasting Corporation, 1984
20. *Night Heat*, "Necessary Force," directed by Mario Azzopardi. Alliance Entertainment, 1985
20. *Night Heat*, "Crossfire," directed by Gerald Mayer. Alliance Entertainment, 1985
21. *Letting Go*, directed by Jack Bender. ITC Entertainment, 1985
21. *One Step Away*, directed by Robert Fortier. National Film Board of Canada, 1985
22. **"I read for a Disney Movie of the Week called *Young Again*":** *The Magical World of Disney*, "Young Again," directed by Steven Hilliard Stern. Walt Disney Television, 1986

Chapter 4: THE ASSASSINATION OF CHARLES BRONSON BY A SAVAGE YOUNG KEANU REEVES

27. *Act of Vengeance* (1986, dir. John MacKenzie)
30. **"It's a complete departure":** Martie Zad, "A Coal Miner's Slaughter," *The Washington Post*, April 20, 1986
30. **"I cast him as soon as I saw him":** Sheila Johnston, *Keanu* (Pan McMillan, 1996)
30. **"He's whittling on a piece of wood":** *Once Upon a Time in the West* (1968, dir. Sergio Leone)

Chapter 5: "YOU RUN THIS ROTTEN, EVIL FOREST, AND YOU STOLE THOSE COOKIES TO DISCREDIT ME"

33. Drew Barrymore and Todd Gold, *Little Girl Lost* (Pocket Books, 1990)
34. Drew Barrymore, Wildflower (Dutton, 2015)
33. *Babes in Toyland*, directed by Clive Donner (ABC Television, 1986)
37. **"From one side, he's very childlike and innocent like Cary Grant . . .":** Carrie Rickey, "The Importance of Being Keanu," *Chicago Tribune*, June 26, 1994
37. **"The missing ingredient is charm":** John J. O'Connor, "TV Weekend; Drew Barrymore Stars in 'Babes in Toyland'," *The New York Times*, December 19, 1986
37. **on the set in Munich, he meets a woman:** Jan Janssen, "Keanu Reeves on His Love of Motorcycles and the 'Sad Keanu' Meme," Square Mile (UK), February 13, 2017

Chapter 6. YOUTH OF AMERICA

39. **"My agents tell me this movie is going to do wonderful things for me"**: Tom Green, "Psst- This Snitch is Going Places in 'River,'" USA Today, May 20, 1987
39. *River's Edge*, directed by Tim Hunter, Island Pictures, 1987
40. Various Artists, *River's Edge: The Soundtrack Album To The Most Controversial Film Of The Year*, Enigma Records, 1987
41. The Wipers, *Youth of America*, Park Avenue Records, 1981
41. **Some Milpitas adults, the *Times* wrote:** Wayne King, "Youths' Silence on Murder Victim Leaves a California Town Baffled," *The New York Times*, December 14, 1981
42. **"They were young people afraid of the police":** Jay Matthews, "California Suburb Sorts Out Fear and Confusion in Teen Slaying," *The Washington Post*, December 6, 1981
42. **"Most of the characters were based on people I had gone to high school with":** Matt Gilligan, "An Oral History of 'River's Edge,' 1987's Most Polarizing Teen Film," *Vice.com*, May 9, 2017
42. **Island Pictures president Russell Schwartz suggests to the *New York Times*:** Aljean Harmetz, "'River's Edge' Defies Experts' Expectations," The New York Times, June 6, 1987
42. **"God, that's not what it's about, man,"** John Griffiths, "Reeves' Edge," *T&B*, January 1, 1989
43. *Easy Rider*, directed by Dennis Hopper, Columbia Pictures, 1968
46. *Flying*, directed by Paul Lynch, Golden Harvest Entertainment, 1986
47. *Feeling Minnesota*, directed by Steven Baigelman, Fine Line Features, 1996
47. *Action*, "Pilot," directed by Ted Demme. Sony Pictures Television, 1999

47. *Bram Stoker's Dracula*, directed by Francis Ford Coppola, Columbia Pictures, 1992
47. *Generation Um*, directed by Mark L. Mann. Company Films/Voltage Films, 2012
47. *Knock Knock*, directed by Eli Roth. Lionsgate Premiere, 2015
47. *The Matrix Reloaded*, directed by Lana Wachowski and Lilly Wachowski (Warner Bros. Pictures, 2003)

Chapter 7. CRASH DUMMY

53. **"The seminal roles for him were *Dangerous Liaisons* and *Parenthood*":** Brooke Hauser, "Finding Neo," *Premiere*, February 2005
53. *Parenthood*, directed by Ron Howard, Universal Pictures, 1989
53. *Dangerous Liasons*, directed by Steven Frears. Warner Bros. Pictures, 1988
53. *The Night Before*, directed by Thom Eberhardt, Kings Road Entertainment, 1988
54. *Permanent Record*, directed by Marisa Silver, Paramount Pictures, 1988
54. Lou Reed, *New York*, Sire Records, 1989
55. *The Prince of Pennsylvania*, directed by Ron Nyswaner, New Line Cinema, 1988
55. **the "sissy-boy-from-coal-mining-Pennsylvania shame":** Ron Nyswaner, *Blue Days, Black Nights: A Memoir* (Advocate Books, 2004)
56. *American Playhouse*, "Life Under Water," directed by Jay Holman. American Playhouse, 1989
57. **after a long pause he'll say, "Yeah, well—on *Dangerous Liaisons* . . .":** Stephen Rebello, "Doin' Time on Planet Keanu," *Movieline*, November 1992
58. *Bill & Ted's Excellent Adventure*, directed by Stephen Herek, Orion Pictures, 1989
58. **Decades later, the Daily Mail:** Isla Harvey, "Keanu Reeves' never-before-seen audition tapes from Bill & Ted's Excellent Adventure show the young actor goofing around with his co-star in the classic comedy—as the duo now prepare to 'Face the Music'," *The Daily Mail*, August 7, 2020
59. **"The thing we'd discussed with each other going in . . .":** Alex Winter, author interview, 2019
60. **"a painfully inept comedy":** Vincent Canby, "Reviews/Film; Teen-Agers On a Tour Of History," *The New York Times*, February 17, 1989
60. **"More than anything, the picture looks paltry and undernourished . . .":** Hal Hinson, **"Bill & Ted's Excellent Adventure,"** *The Washington Post*, February 17, 1989
60. **In the *Los Angeles Times*, future Keanu interview-meltdown witness Chris Willman:** Chris Willman, "Movie Reviews : Adventure, Thy Name Is Not 'Bill & Ted'," *The Los Angeles Times*, February 17, 1989
61. **"Some of it is okay, but I found Joan of Arc doing aerobics excruciating to watch":** Steve Biodrowski, "Bill and Ted's Excellent Adventure: Writers Chris Matheson and Ed Solomon on the birth of a phenomenon," *Cinefantastique*, August 1991

Chapter 8. NONTHREATENING BOYS

65. Paula Abdul, "Rush Rush" music video, directed by Steven Wurnitzer, 1991
65. **"Another regurgitation of icons and culture by the American media":** Chris Heath, "The Pursuit of Excellence," *Details*, August 1991
66. **"People love to recognize, not venture":** William Fifield, "Jean Cocteau: The Art of Fiction No. 34," *The Paris Review*, Summer-Fall 1964
66. *Rebel Without a Cause*, directed by Nicholas Ray (Warner Bros., 1955)
66. David Dalton, *James Dean: The Mutant King* (Chicago Review Press, 2001)
67. *Beverly Hills 90210*, "Spring Dance," directed by Darren Star. Fox, 1991
67. *Beverly Hills 90210*, "Beach Blanket Brandon," directed by Charles Braverman. Fox, 1991
68. Lawrence Frascella and Al Weisel, *Live Fast Die Young: The Wild Ride of Making Rebel Without a Cause* (Touchstone, 2005)
69. **Of course when an interviewer asked him about Dean in 1991:** Steven Rea, "An Eye on the Private River Phoenix," *Philadelphia Inquirer*, October 1991

Chapter 9. DICK AND RONNIE KNOW THEIR JOBS (THE BOY LOOKED AT JOHNNY)

71. *Struggle In New York*, directed by Zoran Popovic, 1976, https://www.youtube.com/watch?v=v6cnevh5bPc&
72. "I did the drywall": Carrie Rickey, "A director explores men who dare death," *The Philadelphia Inquirer*, July 7, 2009
72. **"And the piece ends," Bigelow later recalled:** Gavin Smith, "Momentum and Design: Kathryn Bigelow Interviewed," *Film Comment*, September 1995
72. *Point Break*, directed by Kathryn Bigelow. 20th Century Fox, 1991
72. *The Loveless*, directed by Kathryn Bigelow and Monty Montgomery. Atlantic Releasing, 1984
73. *Near Dark*, directed by Kathryn Bigelow. Delaurentis Entertainment Group, 1987
73. *Blue Steel*, directed by Kathryn Bigelow. Metro-Goldwyn Mayer, 1990
73. **"My interest . . . was to sexualize the gun":** Peter Keough (ed), *Kathryn Bigelow: Interviews (Conversations with Filmmakers Series)* (University Press of Mississippi, 2013)
73. **"We had this meeting," James Cameron will tell *Premiere* in 2002:** Joanna Schellner, "Action Figure," Premiere, August 2002
74. **"This method," the program reads:** http://www.theatermania.com/content/show.cfm/section/synopsis/show/128881
75. *Point Break: Pure Adrenaline Edition* (Blu-Ray), directed by Kathryn Bigelow. 20th Century Fox, 2008
77. **Somehow everybody read the script, from Tony Scott to Tom Cruise to the Department of Defense:** Jacob V. Lamar, Jr., "The Pentagon Goes Hollywood: Filmmakers and the military enjoy a profitable partnership," *Time*, November 24, 1986
77. *Sleep With Me*, directed by Rory Kelly, United Artists, 1994
77. *Top Gun*, directed by Tony Scott. Paramount Pictures, 1988
78. **Jamie Lee Curtis said that when she and Kathryn Bigelow were working on *Blue Steel* together:** Phoebe Hoban, "Happiness is a Warm Gun," *Premiere*, April 1990
82. *Die Hard*, directed by John McTiernan, 20th Century Fox, 1988
82. *The Fast & the Furious*, directed by Rob Cohen. Universal Pictures, 2001

Chapter 10. THE BOY WHO CAME DOWN FROM THE HILL

85. **"I think Keanu and I are the nicest guys on the planet":** Paige Powell and Gini Sikes, "My Own Private Idaho," Interview, September 28, 2011
85. *My Own Private Idaho*, directed by Gus Van Sant. New Line Cinema, 1991
85. *Mala Noche*, directed by Gus Van Sant, 1988
85. *Drugstore Cowboy*, directed by Gus Van Sant, Avenue Pictures, 1989
86. **"the camera following white guys to their doom":** Roger Ebert, author interview, 2006
86. *Endless Idaho*, directed by James Franco, 2011
86. *My Own Private River*, directed by James Franco, 2011
88. **"He's like my older brother, but shorter":** Paige Powell and Gini Sikes, "My Own Private Idaho," Interview, September 28, 2011
88. **"I really would like to do Shakespeare with River"**: Ibid.
88. *I Love You to Death*, directed by Lawrence Kasdan, TriStar Pictures, 1990
89. "Now the hashish eater's demands on time and space come into force": Walter Benjamin, *On Hashish*, Belknap Press/Harvard University Press, 2006
90. *Chimes at Midnight*, directed by Orson Welles, Peppercorn-Wormser Film Enterprises, 1965
90. **Mike Parker, who's described in a 1991 *Rolling Stone* profile of Van Sant:** David Handelman, "Gus Van Sant's Northwest Passage," Rolling Stone, October 31, 1991
91. **"I don't know, man, Gus Van Sant gave me a call":** Dario Scardapane, "Lost Boys," *US Magazine*, November 1991

91. **"Well, he's probably me," Van Sant told Graham Fuller:** Graham Fuller, "Gus Van Sant: Swimming Against the Current" in *Gus Van Sant: Even Cowgirls Get the Blues & My Own Private Idaho* (Faber & Faber, 1993)
92. **the director Todd Haynes tells Van Sant:** Todd Haynes and Gus Van Sant, audio commentary track, *My Own Private Idaho* Criterion Collection DVD
92. **"We were driving in a car on Santa Monica Boulevard":** Paige Powell and Gini Sikes, "My Own Private Idaho," Interview, September 28, 2011
92. **In 1990, in *Interview*, Dennis Cooper:** Dennis Cooper, "Keanu Reeves," *Interview*, September 1990
92. **Keanu "recoils when asked how he prepared for his hustler role":** Lance Loud, "Shakespeare in Black Leather," *American Film*, September/November 1991
93. **"I took River and Keanu down to where boys prostitute themselves":** John Glatt, *Lost in Hollywood: The Fast Times and Short Life of River Phoenix* (Plume, 1995)
94. **"shacking up with drug-using streetfolk":** David Handelman, "Gus Van Sant's Northwest Passage," *Rolling Stone*, October 31, 1991
94. **"He would come up to visit me and we would do drugs together":** Gavin Edwards, *Last Night at the Viper Room* (It Books, 2013)
95. **A friend talks to *Premiere* about Harvey's time on the *Idaho* shoot:** Holly Millea, "Shooting Star," *Premiere*, December 1998
96. **In the published version of the screenplay:** *Gus Van Sant: Even Cowgirls Get the Blues & My Own Private Idaho* (Faber & Faber, 1993)
97. **"He had decided":** Ibid.
100. **"River was an exceptional person, incredible":** Michael Rebichon, "Keanu Reeves, State of Grace," *Studio*, December 1993

Chapter 11. KEANU IS AN EVIL ROBOT DOPPELGANGER AND A BREAKFAST CEREAL AND A MAN WITH A DOG'S FACE

101. **The studio isn't sure they want to release a movie called "Bill & Ted Go to Hell.":** Karen Schoemer, "Hey, Dudes, What's the Scoop This Time?," *The New York Times*, July 14, 1991
101. **"Keanu Reeves and Alex Winter sit in directors' chairs in their Bill and Ted outfits and talk to MTV's movie-news show *The Big Picture*":** Wyldstallyns4ever, "Bill & Ted interview—MTV Big Picture 1991," Youtube, November 4, 2007 https://www.youtube.com/watch?v=yQZiMCSHq4Y&ab_channel=wyldstallyns4ever
103. **Many years later in an interview, the director and licensed-breakfast-food connoisseur Quentin Tarantino:** The Tarantino Archives, "QT Talks to Yesterdayland," May 29, 2007, https://wiki.tarantino.info/index.php/QT_Talks_to_Yesterdayland
103. **Winter and Keanu took to calling the movie "Bill and Ted's Omitted Adventure":** Alex Winter, author interview, 2019
103. **"We were really excited about doing it":** Ibid.
105. *The Seventh Seal*, directed by Ingmar Bergman. AB Svensk Filmindustri, 1957
105. Melvyn Bragg, *BFI Film Classics Series: The Seventh Seal* (*Desjunde Inseglet*) (British Film Institute, 2019)
106. **As scripted, the movie's finale:** "The Movies— Bill & Ted's Bogus Journey— Early Draft Variations," Bill & Ted's Excellent Online Adventure, http://www.billandted.org/moviesbjearlydraft01.htm
107. **the "bad acid trip aspect to having your face on a cereal box":** Cory Everett, "Alex Winter Discusses His 1993 Cult Hit 'Freaked,' Says 'Bill & Ted 3' A Long Way Off From Happening," IndieWire, January 22, 2012 https://www.indiewire.com/2012/01/alex-winter-discusses-his-1993-cult-hit-freaked-says-bill-ted-3-a-long-way-off-from-happening-113756/ 107. *Bar-B-Que Movie*, directed by Alex Winter. 1988, https://www.youtube.com/watch?v=oLKJCd3u-jsc&ab_channel hejeffferrier

107. **In the early nineties:** Rosie Knight, "How Freaked Became an Unexpected Cult Hit," *Nerdist*, February 28, 2020
108. **"Che Guevara, Fidel Castro, and Tom Jones"**: Stephen Rebello, "Doin' Time on Planet Keanu," *Movieline*, November 1992

Chapter 12. OPERA ENVY

111. "I had to pick up a friend around 12:30 that night and the air was electrified": Stephen Rebello, "Doin' Time on Planet Keanu," *Movieline*, November 1992
112. *Bram Stoker's Dracula*, directed by Francis Ford Coppola, Columbia Pictures, 1992
112. **"I wasn't so sophisticated about what that [persona] was"**: Steven Rea, "Coppola Finds Keanu Reeves a Strange But Beautiful Kid," *The Charlotte Observer*, December 10, 1992
112. "with Dracula's long fingers and the shadows and all that interplay": "Rebel Yell!," *Smash Hits*, February 17-March 2, 1993
113. Sadie Frost, *Crazy Days* (2011, John Blake)
113. **"It was great to be in that environment"**: Brooke Hauser, "Finding Neo," *Premiere*, February 2005
113. *Les Enfants du Paradis*, directed by Marcel Carne. 1945
113. **"We had a place to eat, a place to sleep, and a place to play as humans"**: Jeff Dawson, "Healthy, Wealthy and Wise?," *Empire*, September 1993
113. **The profile of Coppola that Janet Maslin files for the *New York Times* on the eve of *Dracula*'s release:** Janet Maslin, "Film; Neither Dracula Nor Rumor Frightens Coppola," *The New York Times*, Nov. 15 1992
114. **"a complicated decadelong series of financial and legal problems":** "Coppola Files For Bankruptcy," The New York Times, July 2, 1992
114. **"I was bad in [*Dracula*]"**: David Ritz, "Cool or Not?," *Sunday Times Magazine*, May 1994
115. **"He tried so hard"**: Joe McGovern, "Francis Ford Coppola remembers Dracula, firing his VFX crew, and Keanu Reeves' accent," *Entertainment Weekly*, October 6, 2015
Jeff Dawson, "Little Miss Perfect," *Empire*, March 1995
115. **"I had for breakfast more paprika"**:Bram Stoker, *Dracula* (Archibald Constable & Co., 1897)
115. **"the first yuppie"**: "Cruisin' With Keanu," *Girlfriend*, February 1993

Chapter 13. TRANSUBSTANTIATION WEDDING

119. *A Scanner Darkly*, directed by Richard Linklater (Warner Independent Pictures, 2006)
119. **In 2018, Winona Ryder drops a historical bombshell in *Entertainment Weekly*:** Maureen Lee Lenker, "Winona Ryder might have married Keanu Reeves for real on the set of *Dracula*," *Entertainment Weekly*, August 18, 2018
120. **Coppola reshot the scene just south of Koreatown:** Catherine Shoard, "Francis Ford Coppola agrees Winona Ryder and Keanu Reeves might be married," *The Guardian*, August 20, 2018
121. **Her first *Los Angeles Times* profile:** Patrick Goldstein, "A Controversial, Satiric Look at Teen Angst : Winona Ryder on the Road to a Hot Career?," *Los Angeles Times*, March 23, 1989
121. ***Vogue* packs the descriptors:** Stephanie Mansfield, "Winona Ryder likes men's suits, Batman, and good thick steaks," *Vogue*, June 1989
121. **She shows *Premiere* her dog-eared copy of J. D. Salinger's *Catcher in the Rye*:** Phoebe Hoban, "Wise Child," *Premiere*, June 1989
121. **and swears to *The Face* that if anyone ever tries to make a film of Salinger's book:** Steven Daly, "Pale Ryder," *The Face*, November 1989
121. **"my favorite role to date"**: Mojo Nixon, YouTube description for "Debbie Gibson is Pregnant With My Two-Headed Love Child," https://www.youtube.com/watch?v=cXLuSHx-1fRo&ab_channel ojoNixon
122. **"may have lacked some of the technique required for period"**: David Thomson, *The New Biographical Dictionary of Film: Fifth Edition* (Abacus, 2010)

122. **"Ryder was employed not to play a range of characters well"**: Masha Tupitsyn, "Famous Tombs: Love in the 90s," The White Review, February 2013
123. **"accused in a 2002 report by the California State Medical Board"**: Kristina Sauerwein and Joe Mathews, "Doctor Gave Stars Drugs, Report Says," Los Angeles Times, December 10, 2002

Chapter 14. PLASTIC ROOTS OF THE BODHI TREE

125. **"looked either like mini-Rambos or mafiosi"**: Michael Rebichon, "Keanu Reeves, State of Grace," *Studio*, December 1993
125. **"Indian illustrations and Indian epic movies":** Martha Sherrill, "'Little Buddha,' Big Ego," The Washington Post, May 22, 1994
127. **"the wackiest bit of casting since George Burns played God":** Desson Howe, "'Little Buddha' (PG)," *The Washington Post*, May 25, 1994
127. *Much Ado About Nothing*, directed by Kenneth Branagh. The Samuel Goldwyn Company, 1993
127. **"as big as a valley"**: Lesley O'Toole, "Keanu Reeves—Life in the Fast Lane," *Shake!*, August 1994
127. **when Gus Van Sant told him and River Phoenix to read John Rechy's *City of Night***: Gus Van Sant, author interview, 2019
128. **"The parents were placing wood on a funeral pyre":** Michael Rebichon, "Keanu Reeves, State of Grace," *Studio*, December 1993
128. **Reporting for the *Los Angeles Times*, the travel writer Pico Iyer notes:** Pico Iyer, "Movie Days in Kathmandu: Bernardo Bertolucci entwines the dazzle of a $35-million production with the paradoxes of Nepal's ancient—and evolving—culture," *The Washington Post*, May 9, 1993
128. **At night he has dreams . . . He calls it the "white zone":** Kristine McKenna, "Keanu's Eccentric Adventure," *The Los Angeles Times*, June 5, 1994

Chapter 15. THE SPACE OF FREE ACTION

David Aldridge, "Peachy Keanu," *Film Review*, March 1989
133. **"I saw a lot of plays with my stepfather when I was younger":** "Keanu Reeves—I'm Gnarly!," TV Hits, July 1992
133. **"one of the breakthrough moments of my life"**: Andrew Purcell, "Keanu Reeves, John Wick's Zen Master With a Gift For Violence," *The Sydney Morning Herald*, November 2, 2014
134. **"at the right age to play Hamlet"**: Vit Wagner, "Director says Hamlet promise will drive Keanu to Winnipeg," *The Toronto Star*, October 22, 1994
134. **"a Richard Chamberlain 'I have arrived' kind of number"**: Chris Beard, "To Thine Ownself Be *Excellent*," *Canadian Adaptations of Shakespeare Project*, University of Guelph. 2004 http://www.canadianshakespeares.ca/essays/reeves.cfm
135. **"playing a SWAT operative in an action story"**: "He's a Star, But is He an Actor?," *The Independent*, August 22, 1993
135. ***Entertainment Weekly* puts him on the cover**: Melina Gerosa, "The Next Action Hero?," *Entertainment Weekly*, June 10, 1994
137. **"[B]y cutting himself loose from the precious object":** Slavoj Zizek, "Revolutionary Terror from Robespierre to Mao," *In Defense of Lost Causes*, Verso Books, 2008
138. **A few years later, when he's prompted by the journalist Chris Heath:** Chris Heath, "The Quiet Man: The Riddle of Keanu Reeves," *Rolling Stone*, August 2000

Chapter 16. THE LAZIEST BOY IN SCHOOL

141. **"When Keanu performs, it's as if he has a foot of Robert Bressonian space around him":** Kristine McKenna, "Keanu's Eccentric Adventure," *The Los Angeles Times*, June 5, 1994
141. Robert Bresson & Jonathan Griffin, *Notes on the Cinematograph* (New York Review Books, 2016)
142. **jeered at by both the *National Enquirer***: "Kids make the grade studying 'Speed' star Keanu Reeves," *The National Enquirer*, June 28, 1994
142. **a Talk of the Town piece by Susan Orlean:** Susan Orlean, "Keanu Reeves (In Theory)," The New Yorker, March 13, 1994

142. ***People* magazine quotes one of Prina's students**: "What next— Keanu U?," *People*, May 2, 1994
142. **As Chuck Stephens puts it in the San Francisco *Bay Guardian* in July:** Chuck Stephens, "Our Keanu: A public meditation," *The San Francisco Bay Guardian*, July 6, 1994
143. **The *Star* screams:** "Speed Hunk Keanu's Long-Lost Dad Jailed on Drug Rap" *Star Magazine*, July 12, 1994
143. **The *National Enquirer*'s story about the sentencing:** "'Speed' star's nightmare as dad is jailed in cocaine bust," *The National Enquirer*, July 12, 1994
143. **In August a British tabloid, the *Daily Mirror*, publishes a story:** Gerard Evans, "I'm hooked on 'Speed'," *The Mirror*, August 30, 1994
143. **"the first gay marriage in the history of show business"**: Louis de la Hamaide, "Keanu Reeves— what is he trying to prove?," *Voici*, December 11–17, 1995
144. **"In Europe, they reported the rumor as fact"**: "Careless Whispers," *Details Magazine*, February 1996
144. **"I guess I have to say I've never met the guy"**: Tim Allis, "Keanu sets the record straight," *OUT Magazine*, July/August 1995
144. **"Was it as good for you as it was for me?"**: George Wayne, "The princess diaries: Carrie Fisher on drugs, a failed marriage, and how she really got to wear those buns," *Vanity Fair*, October 10, 2006
144. **"I mean, there's nothing wrong with being gay"**: Michael Shnayerson, "The wild one: Keanu Reeves on sex, Hollywood and life on the run," *Vanity Fair*, August 1995
145. **"a bad Cole Porter–like musical"**: Keith Mayerson, *Pinnochio the Big Fag*, 2019
145. **"a new, erogenous identity"**: Holland Cotter, "Review/Art; The Joys of Childhood Re-examined," *The New York Times*, March 25, 1994

Chapter 17. THEY SAVED KEANU'S BRAIN

149. *Johnny Mnemonic*, directed by Robert Longo. TriStar Pictures, 1995
150. **"Muscle-boys scattered through the crowd were flexing stock parts at one another and trying on thin, cold grins, some of them so lost under superstructures of muscle graft that their outlines weren't really human"**: William Gibson, *Burning Chrome*, Ace Books, 1987
150. *Arena Brains*, directed by Robert Longo. Pressure Pictures, 1987
150. "We went in and asked for a million and a half": Rogier van Bakel and Eric La Brecque, "Remembering Johnny: William Gibson on the making of Johnny Mnemonic," *Wired*, June 1995
151. **"Batman directed by Fellini"**: *Jane Stevenson, "Enigmatic Actor Saves Best Lines For The Screen,"* **Calgary Herald, May 26, 1994**
151. **"not the film that I made"**: Paul Fischer, "From walking in the clouds to cyberspace," *Burst! Films*, August 1995
152. **"the version of *Feeling Minnesota* that isn't in the movie"**: Chris Heath, "The Quiet Man: The Riddle of Keanu Reeves," *Rolling Stone*, August 2000
152. **"The way that power most manifests itself is this"**: William Goldman, *Adventures in the Screen Trade*, Warner Books, 1983
152. **Longo has mused**: Robert Longo, author interview, 2019
153. **"started off with one key thought, which was: Keanu *is* Hamlet"**: Chris Beard, "To Thine Ownself Be *Excellent*," *Canadian Adaptations of Shakespeare Project*, University of Guelph. 2004, http://www.canadianshakespeares.ca/essays/reeves.cfm
154. **The *Vancouver Sun* praises his "emotional sensitivity":** Jamie Portman, "Reeves as Hamlet: Not a bad night, sweet prince," *Vancouver Sun*, January 14. 1995
154. **the "sheer virility of Larry Olivier's melancholy Dane":** Roger Lewis, "Most excellent prince," The Sunday Times, January 22, 1995
154. **"The audience was quiet throughout"**: Riva Harrison, "Sweet prince: Reeves excellent in MTC's Hamlet," Winnipeg Sun, January 13, 1995

155. **Keanu's request for "something more projective" to say:** William Gibson, "SMALL WORLD? (SALAM PAX)," williamgibsonblog.com, May 9, 2003, http://williamgibsonblog.blogspot.com/2003/05/#200269244

Chapter 18. QUATTRO FORMAGGI

158. **"We're terrible":** "Rebel yell!," *Smash Hits*, February 17-March 2, 1993
159. Dogstar, *Quattro Formaggi* EP (Zoo Entertainment, 1996)
159. *Feeling Minnesota*, directed by Steven Baigelman, Fine Line Features, 1996
160. **One of the people who stays behind that night:** "Historic event: 03/19/1992," *Weezerpedia*, https://www.weezerpedia.com/w/index.php?title=Historic_event:_03/19/1992&oldid=51736.
160. **"We talked on the phone several times"**: Bobby Hecksher, "This was the first real 'band' I was in . . . ," Bandcamp bio for *Days Of Our Drive/Sweet Piece of Ass*, 2014, https://thewarlocks.bandcamp.com/album/days-of-our-drive-sweet-piece-of-ass?fbclid=IwAR2bvPDt7PaQlkxHMvm-ZoK-A5RyUB9JWshceCbpsThB1XbJztw2JM5XaXM
161. **"I took it to drink the backwash":** *Cindy Pearlman*, "Keanu Reeves grows up— a little bit," *Chicago Sun-Times*, August 6, 1995
161. **"When you can feel it, your blood thrills, it's physical, your heart is open"**: Lesley O'Toole, "Mad Axe Attack! Keanu Reeves runs off with rock band," *The Face*, July 1995
162. Dogstar, *Our Little Visionary* (Zoo Entertainment, 1996)
162. **In 1997, *Spin* sends the writer Benjamin Weissman to follow the band:** Benjamin Weissman, "Stalking Keanu," *Spin*, December 1997
163. Dogstar, *Happy Ending* (Ultimatum Music, 2000)
163. Becky, *Take It On the Chin* (n/a, 2006)
163. **Years later, when the Dogstar thing is all over, the guys in the band who weren't Keanu will give interviews:** Lucas Fothergill, "I was in a band with Keanu Reeves," *Vice*, July 14, 2015

Chapter 19. THAT FLORIDA STUD THING

165. *Chain Reaction*, directed by Andrew Davis. 20th Century Fox, 1996
165. **"Next time, if I go do a play, I'm going to have a fax machine"**: James Kaplan, "Why Keanu Reeves won't sell his soul," *Premiere*, September 1997
166. **"They wanted me to get on the boat"**: Peter Howell, "Keanu fires up," *The Toronto Star*, November 7, 1997
167. *The Devil's Advocate*, directed by Curtis Hanson. Warner Bros. Pictures, 1999

Chapter 20. JEAN BAUDRILLARD'S DRAGULA

172. **"It's cool to get on the computer"**: Serdar Balcı, "Prince The Artist giving advice about Internet," YouTube, June 7, 2014, https://www.youtube.com/watch?v=Iy7i9ru7HB8&ab_channel=SerdarBalc%C4%B1
172. **"In 2019, on his YouTube channel, Will Smith":** *Will Smith,* "Why I Turned Down The Matrix | STORYTIME," YouTube, Feb 13, 2019 https://www.youtube.com/watch?v=hm2szuXKgL8
173. **"His gun booms as we enter the liquid space of—bullet-time":** *The Matrix*, shooting script, March 29, 1998 draft, via https://www.dailyscript.com/scripts/the_matrix.pdf
174. *Star Wars: Episode I– The Phantom Menace*, directed by George Lucas. 20th Century Fox, 1999
177. **"Against this hegemony of the system, one can exalt the ruses of desire"**: Jean Baudrillard, *Simulacra and Simulation* (Semiotext(e), 1983)
178. *Fight Club*, directed by David Fincher. 20th Century Fox, 1999
180. **"the corporate world wasn't ready for it":** Netflix, "Why The Matrix Is a Trans Story According to Lilly Wachowski," YouTube. Aug 4, 2020 https://www.youtube.com/watch?v=adXm2sDzGkQ
183. **"It's so odd to look in a mirror and to feel the same on the inside yet all semblance of your physical outward self is removed"**: Lesley O'Toole, "Cyberspace 1999," *Time Out London*, June 2–6, 1999

Chapter 21. SAFE HOUSE

189. **"Also in July, the E! Online gossip columnist Ted Casablanca reports"**: Ted Casablanca, "Speed Bump," E! Online (US), July 21, 1999
190. *The Replacements*, directed by Howard Deutch. Warner Bros. Pictures, 2000
192. *The Watcher*, directed by Joe Charbanic. Universal Pictures, 2000
193. **Weirdly, this is not the most ignominious extracinematic fact about *The Watcher*:** Ian Markham-Smith and Tom Sykes, "Angry Keanu cheated by a friend," *London Evening Standard*, September 11, 2000
193. **After *The Watcher*, Charbanic becomes best known:** "Keanu Reeves, reticent 'Watcher'," *E! Online*, September 9, 2000 http://www.eonline.com/News/Items/0,1,7048,00.html
193. "I never found the script interesting": "Keanu: I was tricked into making film," *The Guardian*, September 11, 2001
193. **"I was hanging out with them, helping them with their gear, just to go to parties and meet girls"**: Carolyn Horowitz, "Zoo banking on enhanced CD for Dogstar," *Billboard*, August 3, 1996
193. **the weekend of September 15, 2000, also happens to be a record low point for domestic box-office revenue in the 2000s**: Braeden Burge, "20 Years Ago, the Domestic Box Office Hit a Major Low—Here's Why," CBR.com, March 20, 2020 https://www.cbr.com/domestic-box-office-low-2000-heres-why/
193. **That record will stand until mid-March of 2020: Brooks Barnes,** "Movie Ticket Sales Fall to Historic Low," The New York Times, March 15, 2020

Chapter 22. WOLF AT THE DOOR

195. *The Gift*, directed by Sam Raimi. Paramount Classics, 2000
198. James Davis and Gabriel Milland, "Star Provokes Outrage As He Speaks of his New Movie as a Wife Beater: Women Will Get a Sexual Buzz if They're Beaten Up, Says Keanu," *The Daily Express*, February 24, 2001
198. **"There's a kind of submission that goes on in the female and dominance in the male":** "Married to the Job: The Star of the Matrix says the sequels to that film are 'my life and my wife'," *Now*, March 21, 2001
199. **"various quantities of an illegal controlled substance":** https://www.mtv.com/news/1453249/marilyn-manson-accused-of-contributing-to-friends-death/
199. **"A woman identified as Syme's roommate tells a tabloid"**: Dawna Kaufmann, "Keanu galpal's fatal crash triggered by pills & cocaine," *The Globe*, August 14, 2001
199. Trey Taylor, "Hollyweird: The Strange, Tragic Death of Jennifer Syme," *Paper Magazine*, September 20, 2018
200. *Mulholland Drive*, directed by David Lynch. Universal Pictures, 2001

Chapter 23. KEANU REEVES SINGS CHET BAKER

201. *Hardball*, directed by Brian Robbins. Paramount Pictures, 2001
202. *Sweet November*, directed by Pat O'Connor, Warner Bros. Pictures, 2001
205. Chet Baker, *Chet Baker Sings* (Pacific Jazz, 1954)

Chapter 24. IN EVERY IMMACULATE NANCY MEYERS DREAM KITCHEN A CARDIAC EPISODE

207. *Something's Gotta Give*, directed by Nancy Meyers. Sony Pictures, 2003
209. **"I had met other actors for the part"**: Brooke Hauser, "Finding Neo," *Premiere*, February 2005
209. *The Private Lives of Pippa Lee*, directed by Rebecca Miller. Screen Media Films, 2009
209. *The Prince of Pennsylvania*, directed by Ron Nyswaner, New Line Cinema, 1988
209. *Tune in Tomorrow*, directed by Jon Amiel, Cinecom Pictures, 1990

209. *The Tracey Ullman Show*, ""Kay's Gift / Merry Catnip / Two Lost Souls / Simpson Xmas," directed by Sam Simon. 20th Century Fox Television, December 17, 1989

Chapter 25. GIVING THE ARCHITECT THE FINGER

211. *The Matrix Reloaded*, directed by Lana Wachowski and Lilly Wachowski (Warner Bros. Pictures, 2003)
211. *The Matrix Revolutions*, directed by Lana Wachowski and Lilly Wachowski (Warner Bros. Pictures, 2003)
211. Rage Against the Machine, *Rage Against the Machine* (Epic Records, 1992)
211. **"the proverbial painting of God that seems always to stare directly at you"**: Slavoj Zizek, "Ideology Reloaded," *In These Times*, June 6, 2003

Chapter 26. A BIBLE WRITTEN IN HELL

217. *Constantine*, directed by Francis Lawrence. Warner Bros. Pictures, 2005
217. **Unlike most smokers, he picked up the habit late**: "I started smoking at 30 and now I can't stop: Keanu Reeves reveals the bad habits picked up on film sets," *The Daily Mail*, December 7, 2008
219. Alan Moore and Stephen Bissette, *Swamp Thing: The Curse* (DC Comics, 1985)
219. Garth Ennis and Will Simpson, *Hellblazer: Dangerous Habits* (DC Comics, 1994)
220. **"I will leave the issue of blasphemy to the experts"**: David Denby, "Devilment," *The New Yorker*, March 7, 2005

Chapter 27. PHILIP K. DICK ENERGY

223. *A Scanner Darkly*, directed by Richard Linklater (Warner Independent Pictures, 2006)
223. *Side By Side*, directed by Chris Kenneally (Tribeca Film/Axiom Films, 2012)
223. Philip K. Dick, *A Scanner Darkly* (Doubleday, 1977)
226. **"I had to be with people"**: Paul Williams, "The most brilliant sci-fi mind on any planet: Philip K. Dick," Rolling Stone, November 6, 1975
226. Lawrence Sutin, *Divine Invasions: A Life of Philip K. Dick* (Da Capo Press, 2005)
226. Emmanuel Carrère, *I Am Alive and You Are Dead: A Journey Into the Mind of Philip K. Dick* (Macmillan Publishers, 2005)
227. Arthur Byron Cover, "Vertex Interview with Philip K. Dick," *Vertex*, February 1974
227. Uwe Anton and Werner Fuchs, "So I Don't Write About Heroes: An Interview with Philip K. Dick," *SF EYE*, Spring 1996
227. **"I think he would've loved it"**: Riz Virk, "Philip K. Dick, the Matrix, Aliens and Alternate History: My Conversation with Tessa B. Dick," Hacker Noon, December 28, 2019, https://medium.com/hackernoon/philip-k-dick-the-matrix-aliens-and-aternate-history-my-conversation-with-tessa-b-dick-c20d1626d0da

Chapter 28. KEANU REEVES IS AN ARCHITECT WHO SAYS "COME TO PAPA" TO A BOWL OF SOUP AND SANDRA BULLOCK Doesn't KNOW HOW TO PRONOUNCE "DOSTOEVSKY" AND WITHOUT EVEN TOUCHING THEY FALL IN LOVE

231. *The Lake House*, directed by Alejandro Agresti. Warner Bros. Pictures, 2006

Chapter 29. TRANSLUCENT PLACENTAL BLUBBER

235. *The Day the Earth Stood Still*, directed by Scott Derrickson. Warner Bros. Pictures, 2008
236. **"Per a Fox press release"**: Natalie Johnson, "20th Century Fox stops the world to beam *The Day the Earth Stood Still* into deep space," MarketWatch, December 9, 2008
237. *Henry's Crime*, directed by Malcolm Venville. Moving Pictures Film and Television/Maitland Primrose Group, 2011
238. **"That's what I'm for"**: Thomas Pynchon, *The Crying of Lot 49* (J.B. Lippincott & Co, 1965)

Chapter 30. AND FEATURING KEANU REEVES AS 'KEANU REEVES'

241. **A 1974 article in the Hawaiian Journal of History draws a line**: Peggy Kai, "Chinese Settlers in the Village of Hilo before 1852," *Hawaiian Journal of History*, volume 8, 1974
241. **According to a 2019 Reddit post summarizing this study's Keanu-relevant content**: u/Annakinmcfly, "Stories about Keanu's distant ancestors in Hawaii," *Reddit*, May 27, 2019, https://www.reddit.com/r/KeanuBeingAwesome/comments/btvezm/stories_about_keanus_distant_ancestors_in_hawaii/
242. **Even when he tells Jimmy Fallon**: The Tonight Show Starring Jimmy Fallon, *Keanu Reeves Almost Changed His Name to Chuck Spadina*. YouTube, June 24, 2017 https://www.youtube.com/watch?v=BkUVRGCidjE
242. *Even Cowgirls Get the Blues*, directed by Gus Van Sant. Fine Line Features, 1993
242. **who in Tom Robbins's novel says**: Tom Robbins, *Even Cowgirls Get the Blues* (Houghton Mifflin, 1976)
242. *John Wick: Chapter 3— Parabellum*. Directed by Chad Stahelski. Lionsgate Films, 2019
243. *Street Kings*, directed by David Ayer. Fox Searchlight Pictures, 2008
244. *47 Ronin*, directed by Carl Rinsch. Universal Pictures, 2013
244. *Always Be My Maybe*, directed by Nahnatchka Khan. Netflix, 2019
244. **reportedly led to Keanu parting ways with longtime manager Erwin Stoff:** Nikki Finke, "Keanu Reeves And Longtime Manager Erwin Stoff Hit Bumpy Road: Actor Almost Left 3 Arts But Instead Others There Repping Him," *Deadline Hollywood*, October 25, 2012
245. **According to producer Brian Grazer:** Wolf Schneider, "American Cinematheque Award: Steve Martin," November 11, 2004
245. **Ben Stiller wrote *Tropic Thunder* thinking Keanu**: Bradford Evans, "The Lost Roles of Tropic Thunder," *Vulture*, March 24, 2011
245. **"It was very important to me that it be someone who was Asian-American"**: E. Alex Jung, "Keanu Reeves Walks Into the Chateau Marmont: An Always Be My Maybe Casting Story," *Vulture*, June 3, 2019
246. **"Since I first watched *Speed*, I was very aware that Keanu was Asian American"**: Ibid.

Chapter 31. GOOD CLEAN FUN

247. **In the spring of 2010, a celebrity photographer named Ron Asadorian:** "Know Your Meme: Sad Keanu" https://knowyourmeme.com/memes/sad-keanu
249. **On May 23, 2010, someone notices the Asadorian photo**: Green-Ovale.Net, "Keanu Reeves on a Bench" (https://archived.moe/tv/thread/9442160/)
250. **A Sad Keanu meme with an out-of-context Keanu quote attached:** u/Rockon4Life45, "Keanu. More sadness in comments," https://www.reddit.com/r/pics/comments/cb8uo/keanu_more_sadness_in_comments/
251. **Keanu is asked about it in 2011**: TeamMeme (2011, Jan 18) *Sad Keanu BBC Interview*. YouTube https://www.youtube.com watch?v=UtuWviofkb4&ab_channel eamMeme
251. *Ode to Happiness,* Keanu Reeves & Alexandra Grant, Steidl (April 21, 2011)
252. *To the Bone*, directed by Marti Noxon. Netflix, 2017
253. **imagines Paul Newman playing the role:** Zachary Leeman, "An interview with Derek Kolstad, screenwriter of John Wick," Flickering Myth, October 24, 2014, https://www.flickeringmyth.com/2014/10/interview-derek-kolstad-screenwriter-john-wick/
255. **"The one thing that I was really moved by was the protocol of it"**: Robert Longo, author interview, 2019
255. "With John Wick": Ibid.

Chapter 32. ROOM 214

257. *Man of Tai Chi*, directed by Keanu Reeves. RADiUS-TWC, 2013
259. *Knock Knock*, directed by Eli Roth. Lionsgate Premiere, 2015
262. **A viral tweet from 2019 consisted of four images of Keanu:** Lisa Respers France, "Keanu Reeves not touching women is a thing," CNN.com, June 12, 2019
265. *The Neon Demon*, directed by Nicholas Winding Refn. Amazon Studios, 2016
266. *Too Old to Die Young*, directed by Nicholas Winding Refn. Amazon Studios, 2019
269. *The Bad Batch*, directed by Ana Lily Amirpour. Amazon Studios/Vice Films, 2019

Chapter 33. FLAWLESSLY TAILORED KEVLAR HAIRSHIRT

271. *John Wick: Chapter 2*. Directed by Chad Stahelski. Lionsgate Films, 2017
276. *John Wick: Chapter 3— Parabellum*. Directed by Chad Stahelski. Lionsgate Films, 2019

Chapter 34. DIGITAL GHOST

279. *Replicas* (2019, dir. Jeffrey Nachmanoff)
279. **the lowest wide-release opening of Keanu's career:** Jeremy Fuster, "Whoa! Keanu Reeves Suffers Career-Worst Box Office Opening With 'Replicas', The Wrap, January 13, 2019, https://www.thewrap.com/replicas-keanu-reeves-career-worst-box-office-opening/
282. **"Which is interesting," Key told *ET Canada*:** ET Canada (Youtube) *Key And Peele React To Keanu Reeves' Thoughts On 'Keanu'* https://www.youtube.com/watch?v=RJHjbu3P3vs&ab_channel=ETCanada
282. **"I'm here with BuzzFeed to play with some puppies and answer some questions":** BuzzFeed Celeb (Youtube) *Keanu Reeves Plays With Puppies While Answering Fan Questions*, May 17, 2019, https://www.youtube.com/watch?v=rOqUiXhECos&ab_channel=BuzzFeedCeleb
283. **Keanu makes a surprise appearance at the video-game trade show E3:** Game Clips and Tips (Youtube) *Cyberpunk 2077 Keanu Reeves at E3 2019 Xbox Conference*, June 9, 2019, https://www.youtube.com/watch?v=VWGUCoBpyLk&t=10s&ab_channel=GameClipsAndTips
285. **by January, fans have figured out that the game's customization options can be tweaked:** Megan Farokhmanesh, "Cyberpunk 2077 bans unauthorized Keanu Reeves sex," January 27, 2021 https://www.theverge.com/2021/1/27/22253112/cyberpunk-2077-keanu-reeves-sex-mod-ban
285. **Cheezburger.com runs a blog post:** "12 'Breathtaking' Memes That Celebrate Keanu Reeves, Our New Wholesome God," Cheezburger.com, 2019, https://cheezburger.com/8572165/12-breathtaking-memes-that-celebrate-keanu-reeves-our-new-wholesome-god
285. **In a 2019 essay for *Vox*, Constance Grady:** Constance Grady, "The past 20 years of culture wars, explained by the word 'wholesome'," Vox, April 11, 2019, https://www.vox.com/the-highlight/2019/4/4/18282247wholesome-memes-culture-aesthetics-aspirational-explained
286. **Just hours after it happens:** KnowYourMeme: Mini Keanu Reeves, June 17, 2019 https://knowyourmeme.com/memes/mini-keanu-reeves
288. **"the extreme hype for dogs, particularly surrounding":** https://bitscreener.com/coins/keanu-inu

Conclusion: The Essence of the Forest

291. **"I think each movie is a part of your life":** Vittorio Storaro and Ric Gentry, "Writing with Light: An Interview with Vittorio Storaro," Film Quarterly, January 1994–1995
291. *Bill & Ted Face the Music*, directed by Dean Parisot. United Artists Releasing, 2020
296. *The SpongeBob Movie: Sponge on the Run*, directed by Tim Hill. Paramount Pictures, 2020
298. *A World of Calm*, "Living Among Trees," directed by Emma Webster (HBO, 2020)
299. **Calm acquired 1.6 million new users:** Sarah Todd, "Meditation app Calm is booming in anxious times," *Quartz*, November 18, 2020
300. *Mifune: The Last Samurai*, directed by Steven Okazaki (Strand Releasing, 2015)